THROWING THE LASSO.

THE
FRONTIER SERIES
Illustrated
A
THOUSAND
MILES
WALK.
BOSTON
LEE & SHEPARD.

THE PAMPAS AND ANDES.

A

THOUSAND MILES' WALK

ACROSS

SOUTH AMERICA.

BY

NATHANIEL H. BISHOP.

WITH AN INTRODUCTION

BY

EDWARD A. SAMUELS, Esq.,

AUTHOR OF "ORNITHOLOGY AND OÖLOGY OF NEW ENGLAND,"
ETC., ETC.

THIRD EDITION, ILLUSTRATED.

BOSTON:
LEE AND SHEPARD.
1870.

STEREOTYPED AT THE
BOSTON STEREOTYPE FOUNDRY,
No. 19 Spring Lane.

TO

PROFESSOR SPENCER F. BAIRD,

ASSISTANT SEC'Y OF THE SMITHSONIAN INSTITUTION,

This Work is Dedicated,

AS A TOKEN OF SINCERE REGARD,

BY HIS FRIEND,

THE AUTHOR.

PREFACE

TO THE SECOND EDITION.

When, a few weeks since, I saw my little book of South American travels issued from the press, I supposed that my connection with it had ended. My publishers now ask for a preface to a second edition. I take this occasion to express my thanks for the very kind manner in which my boyish descriptions of a boy's travels have been received by the public and the press. I can only wish that my book had been more worthy of the liberal patronage and the generous praise which have been bestowed upon it.

If I had followed my own inclinations, I should have given my narrative a thorough revision, and thus have corrected some of the crudeness of my first literary effort. To this revision, however, my publishers objected, on the ground that it would raise the suspicion of genuineness as to these being the travelling observations of a lad seventeen years of age, and impair also the freshness of the narrative. My book has therefore been given to the public with but slight alterations from the original draft.

I should have been glad to have made the story of my travels more fruitful in scientific results. But I had no instruments for making accurate observations, and had not the opportunity to preserve and transport many objects of natural history for comparison and verification. Such observations as I have made on topics relating to natural history, during my wandering on the inhospitable Pampas of South America, if they are superficial, I have sought to make them at least truthful.

NATHANIEL H. BISHOP.

OXYCOCCUS PLANTATION,
MANNAHAWKIN, N. J.

INTRODUCTION.

In placing this little volume before the public, a few words, regarding the manner in which the incidents and material composing it were acquired, may be of interest to the reader.

The young gentleman who made the pedestrian trip, of which this forms the narrative, was a native of Massachusetts. I had missed him from his accustomed place for some time, but was ignorant of his contemplated journey, or even that he had gone away, until my attention was called to the following paragraph in the columns of the Boston Daily Advertiser of January 12, 1856, from its Chilian correspondent:—

> "Valparaiso, November 27, 1855.
>
> "There arrived here, a few days since, a young man belonging to Medford, Mass., who has walked across the Pampas and Cordilleras, more than a thousand miles, unable to speak the language, and with an astonishingly small amount of money.
>
> "So much for a Yankee."

My friend was but seventeen years of age when he entered upon his difficult undertaking; but by dint of perseverance, backed by an enthusiastic love for nature, he accomplished a task that would have seemed insurmountable to many older and more experienced than himself. To use the language of Dr. Brewer, the able author of the Oölogy of North America, he was "a young and enthusiastic naturalist, whose zeal in the study of Natural History prompted him, alone, unaided, and at the risk of his life, to explore the arid plains of South America, while yet a mere lad in years and stature, though his observations there exhibit the close and careful study of maturer years."

The young traveller started on his journey of upwards of twelve thousand miles, by sea and land, with a cash capital of forty-five dollars, and returned home with fifty; thus proving to those who wish to see the world that energy, industry, and economy are as potent to assist them in their efforts as unlimited wealth.

On his return, I requested him to furnish me with an account of his journey; this he has been unable to do, from press of business, until recently, when he gave me a copy of his journal, which, in a slightly revised form, is now published.

EDWARD A. SAMUELS.

CONTENTS.

CHAPTER I.

PASSAGE OF THE RIVER PLATA.

CHAPTER II.

IN THE RIVER PLATA.

CHAPTER III.

BUENOS AYRES — THE PROVINCE AND CITY.

CHAPTER IV.

VISIT TO THE TIGRE AND BANDA ORIENTAL.

CHAPTER V

ASCENDING THE PLATA AND PARANÁ.

CHAPTER VI.

A VISIT TO THE PAMPA COUNTRY.

CHAPTER VII.

LIFE ON THE PAMPAS.

CHAPTER VIII.

LIFE ON THE PAMPAS — CONTINUED.

CHAPTER IX.

FROM RIO QUARTO TO CERRO MORO.

CHAPTER X.

FROM RIO QUARTO TO CERRO MORO — CONTINUED.

CHAPTER XI.

SAN LUIS AND THE SALINE DESERT.

CHAPTER XII.

ON THE TRAVESIA.

CHAPTER XIII.

MENDOZA.

CHAPTER XIV.

A WINTER IN SAN JUAN.

CHAPTER XV.

A WINTER IN SAN JUAN—CONTINUED.

CHAPTER XVI.

VIENTE DE ZONDA.

CHAPTER XVII.

ADVENTURES OF DON GUILLERMO BUENAPARTE.

CHAPTER XVIII.

CROSSING THE ANDES.

CHAPTER XIX.

CROSSING THE ANDES — CONTINUED.

CHAPTER XX.

FROM THE ANDES TO THE PACIFIC.

A THOUSAND MILES' WALK.

CHAPTER I.

PASSAGE TO THE RIVER PLATA.

ONE cold November morning, in compliance with previous orders, I reported myself ready for duty at the shipping office of Messrs. S. and K., Commercial Street, Boston, and having received, as is customary, one month's wages in advance, proceeded with my baggage to Battery Wharf, at the foot of which lay the bark M., destined to be my future home for many weeks. As but one of the crew had already gone on board, I had ample leisure for examining the vessel, on board of which I was to receive my first lessons in practical seamanship, and to endure privations hitherto happily unknown to me. The M. was not prepossessing in appearance, and I confess that her model did not give a favorable idea of her sailing qualities: vessels, like horses, have peculiar external points by which their virtues may be judged, and their speed determined. As I gazed upon her long, straight sides, square bows, and box-like hull, it seemed to me that her builders must have mistaken her ends; for, *certes*, had her spars been reversed, she would have made better progress by sailing stern foremost. Some knowing ones, who have since examined this specimen of marine architecture of twenty years ago, have sustained my suspicion that the M. belonged to that enduring fleet of cruisers, now scattered over the great deep, which were originally built in the State of Maine, of which report is made that "these vessels are built by the *mile*, and sawed off according to the length ordered by the buyer."

The mate, who was occupied in receiving live stock, — i. e., two young pigs, — ordered me to stow my things "for'ard;" an order somewhat difficult to comply with, as the forecastle was well filled with firewood, ropes, blocks, swabs, and the various other articles used on shipboard.

I crawled down the dark passage, and was feeling about to discover the dimensions of a sailor's home, doubting, meanwhile, whether, in reality, this narrow hole could be the abode intended for human beings, when suddenly a gruff voice called down to me, "Come, youngster, bear a hand! Make yourself lively! We must clean out this shop before the crew come down; stir yourself, and pass me up the pieces." Obeying these peremptory commands, I applied myself to work, and in an hour's time my companion declared the place "ship-shape, and fit for sailors." I would remark, *en passant*, that this declaration was made in the face of the fact that mould and dust covered the timbers and boards, and cockroaches filled the many crevices. "But," said my companion, with a philosophical air, "if the place were carpeted, and lighted with a fine lamp, the fellows would be the more dissatisfied; the better treated they are, the worse they growl." At the time I inwardly dissented from the truth of this remark; but subsequent experiences taught me the old salt was right.

As I had been of service in removing all the lumber, I thought to repay myself by securing a good bunk, and therefore chose an upper one. After I had given it a thorough cleaning, and had carefully stowed away my mattress and blanket, one of the new crew entered the forecastle, and, on noticing my labors, at once removed my bed, and placed his own in its place, remarking, at the same time, that it was a highly impolite and lubberly action for an understrapper to "bunk down where he didn't belong; upper bunks were *men's* bunks; lower ones, boys'." Although I pleaded ignorance of the etiquette of the forecastle, and selected another resting place, my shipmate continued his lecture on the rules of the sea, and hinted at the future "rope's-endings from the little man aft," as he called the mate, in store for me.

During his harangue two or three of my old schoolfellows came aboard, and, on visiting my quarters, remarked upon the poor accommodations and filthiness to which I was to be doomed; upon which remark the old tar broke out with, "And so this is a young gentleman going to sea for the first time? O, ho! All right. I'll be his guardian, and keep an eye on him when he's aloft, and, to start fair, if my opinion was asked, I'd say we'd better go up the wharf, and splice the matter over a social glass." At this hint, so delicately conveyed, we gave the fellow a sum sufficient to allay his thirst, had it been never so great, and he at once took leave of us, only to return, however, in a few minutes, declaring that he had lost every cent, at the same time reiterating his offer to become my friend for a consideration.

The noise of the tow-boat now called us on deck, where we found a perfect Babel of confusion, caused by the throng of porters, boarding-house runners, idlers, and sailors' friends, who were giving and receiving advice in quantities to last until the vessel returned to her port. About this time I was touched on the shoulder by a rough-looking personage in a sailor's dress, who took me aside, and inquired if I really intended going to sea. "Because," said he, "if you are, let me give you a bit of advice. I'm an old *shell*, and can steer my trick as well as the next one; and as we're to be shipmates, and you're young, all you've got to do is to stick close to me, and I'll larn yer all the moves." After showing so kind an interest in my affairs, he hinted, like the other man, that there was "still time enough to step up to the house, and splice the main brace." As I was ignorant of this point in seamanship, I handed him some money, that he might perform it alone, when he disappeared. I saw nothing more of him for the next half hour; and it was only when the vessel was about moving off that he staggered over the rail, to all appearances well braced; and as he expressed a desire to handle all on board, from the "old man" (the captain) "in the cabin to the doctor" (cook) "in the galley," I concluded that his splicing had received especial attention, and that his strands would not unravel for several hours to come.

These scenes on board of the M., while getting

under way, were comparatively tame to others that I have since witnessed on other vessels. I have known men to be carried on board ship by boarding-house keepers, who had enticed them into their dens of infamy, and who had drugged them so powerfully that they did not recover their senses until the vessel had left the port. In this manner, fathers of families, mechanics, tradesmen, and other persons wholly unfitted for a sea life have been carried off, unknown by their friends. When full consciousness returned to the unhappy victims, they sought the officers for an explanation, when I have seen them so beaten and kicked, that in apprehension for their lives, they bowed in submission to a tyranny worse than that of slavery itself.

After lying for more than twenty-four hours, windbound, in the outer harbor, all hands were called before daylight, and though the mercury stood but a few degrees above the freezing point, the decks were washed down; after which operation the anchor was weighed, and we set sail out upon the bosom of the broad Atlantic. When we were fairly under way, we were set to work stowing away chains and ropes, securing the water casks upon deck, lashing the anchors upon the rail; then a short breathing spell was allowed us. While looking to windward, an old sailor, with whom I had commenced a friendship, which I was determined to strengthen, said, "Here, boy: do you see that land, there? It is the last you will see until we drop anchor in the River Plata." I gazed long upon it. It was Cape Cod. Its white sand-hills looked cold and drear, as the sea beat against their bases, some of which were smooth and sloping, others steep and gullied by the rains. An hour after this the breeze freshened, the light sails were taken in, and the topsails double-reefed; and as the sea ran higher, and our little vessel grew proportionably uneasy, I began to experience the uncomfortable nausea and dizziness of seasickness, which, added to the repulsive smell and closeness of the forecastle, completely overcame my fortitude, when retiring to my bunk I tried to make myself comfortable.

About five o'clock in the afternoon all hands were mustered upon the quarter-deck, and the watches chosen. To my satisfaction I was selected by the mate, and had the further gratification of finding that old Manuel, my friend, had also been chosen for our watch — a result which evidently delighted him as much as myself. Ours was the larboard watch, and remained upon deck, while the captain's, or starboard watch, went below. The duties of sea life had now fairly commenced.

The two hours that followed, from six to eight, were passed in a pleasant conversation with the old Frenchman, Manuel. He informed me that he had his eye on the moves of the crew, and he concluded that there was but one sailor on board: it was left to my sagacity to infer that he meant himself.

Two of the crew, who had shipped as ordinary seamen, were ignorant of the duties for which they had contracted, and each man in the forecastle had shipped as an American-born citizen, with protection papers received from the Custom House, which legally asserted him as such. These papers they had obtained from their boarding-house masters, who had purchased them at twenty-five cents each, and had retailed them to their foreign customers at seventy-five cents apiece. Of this *American* crew, two were Germans, or Dutchmen (an appellation given by sailors to all persons from the north of Europe), one of unknown parentage, who could only speak a few words of English, two Irishmen, one Englishman, another who swore point blank to being a native-born citizen of the States, an old mariner from Bordeaux, and myself. The law that makes it the duty of a captain to take with his crew a certain proportion of native-born Americans, had surely not been complied with here. To one of our crew I cannot do otherwise than devote a few lines.

The "doctor," or cook, had already introduced himself, and informed us in a short and patriotic speech, delivered at the galley door, that he would confess that his father was a distinguished Irish barrister, and that he himself possessed no little share of notoriety in the old country. He had once been taken by a celebrated duchess, as she rode past in her carriage, for a son of the Marquis of B. His amusing vanity drew many expressions of contempt from the tars, who pronounced him to be "an idle Irish thief," which only served to make him wax more warm in his assumptions of gentility. He was interrupted in the midst of a high-flown harangue by the loud squealing of the pigs, which squealing reminded him that his duties must not be neglected for the purpose of edifying a crowd of ignorant tars.

Our watch lasted until eight bells, when I went below, but had very little appetite for supper — a meal consisting of salt beef, biscuits, and a fluid which the cook called tea, although, on trial, I was sadly puzzled to know how it could merit such an appellation.

Of the three weeks which followed this first experience of nautical life and its miseries, I can say but little, as I labored during this period under the exhausting effects of seasickness, which reduced me to such a degree of weakness that I once fainted on the flying jib-boom, from which position of peril I was rescued and brought in by my friend Manuel. But this distressing malady wore away, and at last became altogether a memory of the past. Despite hard fare and labor, I not only recovered my lost flesh, but grew rugged and hearty, and, moreover, became tolerably familiar with the duties of a life at sea.

I have alluded to our cook, and to his ineffable conceit, mock sentimentality, and Hibernian fertility of invention.

It was his opinion that the "low-lived fellows" on board ought to feel highly honored by the presence in their midst of at least one gentleman — a title which he continually arrogated to himself. I am sorry to say, that as a cook he was not "a success." He cared very little about the quality of the food he served to us; and its preparation was usually a subordinate consideration, with him, to the indulgence of his master passion, — the perusal of highly-colored novels, — to which he devoted every possible moment.

In the hope of improving my wretched diet, I applied myself to the study of this man's character, and, having soon discovered his assailable point, supplied him with some works of fiction more entrancing than any he had hitherto possessed. I bought them just before our leaving home, thinking that perhaps some such an opportunity might offer for making a friendship with some of my messmates. His delight at receiving them was extreme; and I received in exchange for my favors many a dish that added a zest to my food, which it had hitherto altogether lacked.

Whenever I wished to be entertained with some marvellous account of "life in the highest circles of Great Britain," I had only to request from the sympathetic cook a passage or two from his eventful life. It was his constant lament that he had never kept a dialogue (diary) of his travels, which, according to his account, must have surpassed those of most mortals in adventure and interesting incidents.

Of our crew, his countryman, the "boy Jim," was his favorite. This Jim was the red-shirted sailor who had promised to instruct me in all the "moves" of an experienced salt, before we had left the wharf at Boston. A very few days of our voyage, however, served to prove, that he not only had no claim to the title of "old salt," but also that he had never learned to "steer a trick at the wheel." The first order that he received from one of the mates was, "Boy Jim, lay aloft there, and slush down the foretop-gallant and royal masts!" Seizing a tar bucket, and pointing aloft, he exclaimed, "Shure, sir, and which of them sticks is it that ye mane?" thus laying bare his ignorance of all nautical matters, and bringing on himself the ridicule of the whole ship's crew.

As with head winds we slowly drew near the variables, or horse latitudes, rainy weather, accompanied by squalls of wind, commenced, and for twenty-one days and nights we were wet to the skin: clothes, bedding, all were saturated from the effects of a leaky deck; and it was a common occurrence to find, on awakening from slumber, a respectable stream of water descending into the close and crowded forecastle. When on deck our oil clothes did not protect us, for from our having worked in them constantly, the oil coating had worn off: so, at the end of a watch, we wrung out our under garments, and turned into our narrow bunks, where we quickly fell asleep, and forgot our miseries and troubles, until we were aroused to them by the gruff voice of some sailor of the other watch, shouting down the companion-way, "Ay — you — Lar-bowlines — ahoy — there; eight — bells! Lay up here, bullies, and get your duff." Or, perhaps, "Do those fellows down there ever intend to relieve the watch!" exclaimed in no pleasant tones by the captain of the other watch.

The rainy season was succeeded by as delightful weather as we could have desired. A fair wind sprang up a few days before crossing the line, and with straining canvas we sped on towards Buenos Ayres. The days passed pleasantly, and our duties became light and agreeable. Enjoyable as were these tranquil days, the nights were still lovelier in those latitudes. The moon seemed to shine with an unwontedly pure and spiritual light, and with a brightness known only to the clear atmosphere of the tropics.

As we glided along, night after night, under a firmament studded with countless lights, and over a broad expanse ruffled with short, dark waves curling crisply into foam, I could hardly conceive a scene of more quiet beauty. Standing upon the forecastle deck, a glorious vision frequently met our gaze: a phosphorescent light gleamed beneath the bows, and streamed along the sides and in the vessel's wake, looking like a train of liquid gems to the imaginative observer. If we looked aloft to the white canvas of our wide-spread sails, we seemed borne along by some gigantic bird, of which the sails were the powerful wings, to the distant horizon, in which were the Southern Cross and other larger constellations, burning, like beacon lamps, leading us on to our destined port.

During these days and nights our attention was not unfrequently attracted to the dwellers in the deep, which were constantly sporting around us. Schools of black-fish and porpoises continually crossed our track; and large numbers of flying-fish often shot across our bows, sometimes leaving at our mercy a few stragglers upon the decks.

Upon such nights as I have described, when acting as lookout by the windlass bits, old Manuel frequently came to my side, and conversed upon the various topics connected with his past life, which had been an eventful one. He was born in Bordeaux. His mother died when he was an infant, leaving him to the care of his father, who owned and commanded a small vessel engaged in the coasting trade.

While very young, Manuel preferred playing about the streets of his native city, and hiding, with other boys, among the vines which covered his father's dwelling, to following any plan of education proposed by his father. Under the direction of an uncle, however, he attended school when nine years old, and learned to read and write during the two succeeding years. So rapid was his progress, that the uncle, who was wealthy, offered to defray his expenses if he would fit himself for the university; but Manuel preferred following the fortunes of his father for a season, and accordingly sailed with him along the coasts of France and Spain. But the voyage was not destined to be a pleasant one. The boy was continually offending his father, who was a cold and unlovable man; and one afternoon, while performing certain antics upon the main-topsail-yard-arm, the old gentleman called him down, and rewarded his exertions with a lusty application of the end of the main sheet, which rope's-ending was not to Manuel's taste. He availed himself of the first opportunity, deserted the vessel, and joined a fine ship sailing to Havana. Before reaching Cuba he had become acquainted with the ropes, and not wishing to return to his parent until time had soothed his outraged feelings, he left the ship, and became a destitute wanderer in a foreign land. He was at that time twelve years of age. Being led into bad company, he joined a slaver, bound for the west coast of Africa. The *galota* in which he sailed reached the Rio Congo, and received on board nine hundred negroes, nearly all of whom were landed safely in Cuba. His wages, as boy, amounted to fifty dollars per month; but, though engaged in so profitable an undertaking, his sense of right caused him to leave his unprincipled associates, and to seek employment elsewhere. Since that time he had served beneath the flag of nearly every maritime nation, and had also fought in the China wars.

For thirteen years he had sailed from Boston and New York, choosing the American republic as his adopted country, for which he was willing, as he declared, to shed his best blood, should necessity require.

While conversing with Manuel, one morning before sunrise, I was surprised by his suddenly jumping to his feet and scanning the horizon. At length he exclaimed, "There is a sight you may never see again. I have crossed the line many times in this longitude, but never beheld that before to-day!" At this moment the mate, who had been keeping a long lookout, disappeared below, returning in a moment with the captain. Looking in the direction pointed out by the old sailor, I discerned far away to the south-south-east, broken water; and, as the daylight advanced, we were soon able to distinguish two detached and rugged rocks, rising out of the sea, together with many smaller peaks rising out of the water around them. One of these bore a striking resemblance to a sugar-loaf. This group was the St. Paul's Rocks. When first seen they appeared dark and drear; but, as our vessel approached them, we discovered that the excrements of myriads of seafowl, with which they were covered, had made them of a glistening white, presenting a strange appearance, not wholly devoid of the picturesque. Here, at no less a distance than five hundred and forty miles from the continent of South America, these peaks, the summits of mountains whose bases are planted in unfathomed depths, arise.

The rocks lie in longitude twenty-nine degrees fif teen minutes west, and are only fifty-eight miles north of the equator. The highest peak rises but fifty feet above the sea, and is not more than three quarters of a mile in circumference.

These isolated rocks have been visited by a few persons only. Darwin, the naturalist, made a thorough investigation into their natural history. Among birds, the booby gannet and noddy tern were found; both species being very tame, depositing their eggs and rearing their young in great numbers. Darwin, in his account of the tenants of these rocky islets, observes, "It was amusing to watch how quickly a large and active crab (*Grapsus*), which inhabits the crevices of the rocks, stole the fish from the side of the nest, as soon as we had disturbed the parent birds. Sir W. Symonds, one of the few persons who have landed here, informs me that he saw these crabs dragging even the young birds out of the nests, and devouring them. Not a single plant, nor even lichen, grows on this islet; yet it is inhabited by several insects and spiders. The following list completes, I believe, the terrestrial fauna: A fly (*Olfersia*), living on the booby, and a tick, which must have come here as a parasite on the birds; a small brown moth, belonging to a genus that feeds on feathers; a beetle (*Quedius*), and a wood-louse from beneath the dung; and, lastly, numerous spiders, which, I suppose, prey on these small attendants and scavengers of the water-fowl."

I afterwards met, among the many roving characters with whom the traveller becomes acquainted, a person, who, in his younger days, had been engaged not only in privateering, but also in the lucrative, though inhuman, slave traffic. He knew of many instances when slavers and freebooters had been obliged to visit St.

Paul's from necessity, not only for the purpose of securing the rain-water that is caught in the cavities and depressions in the rock, but also to procure a supply of the fish which play about the islets in large schools, or, more properly, perhaps, shoals, or schules.

Although our vessel was built before the age of clippers, and consequently made slow progress through the water, St. Paul's was far astern by ten o'clock. A fresh breeze sprang up, and, as it continued fair, we were wafted along smoothly day after day towards our destined port.

At length the sudden changes of the atmosphere, and careful consultations of the officers, and admonitions "to keep a bright lookout ahead," warned the forecastle hands that we were nearing the Rio Plata, the great *River of Silver*, whose broad mouth we were soon to enter, there to gaze upon the shores of another continent.

The nights seemed cooler, and the beautiful appearance of the heavens, as the sun, with a broader disk, sank beneath the western horizon, particularly attracted our attention. As it slowly disappeared, clouds of many varied hues gathered above it like heavy drapery, as if to conceal its flight; while others, taking the form of long ranges of mountains, with here and there a tall peak towering up into the clearer firmament, presented a panorama of exquisite beauty and grandeur. But all evenings were not of this description. Sometimes the heavens darkened, and for two or three hours not a breath of air moved the murky atmosphere. Long, dark swells came rolling towards us from the south-east, sure indicators of the distant *pampero*, the hurricane of La Plata. When these swells were visible, the crew at once became active: every light sail was snugly furled, and the topsails double reefed, for our captain was a prudent man, who had sailed long enough in these latitudes to know the fearful devastation that is often occasioned by the *pampero.* Before our voyage terminated we had an opportunity to appreciate this trait in his seamanship.

One afternoon, when within four or five days' sail of the mouth of the Plata, the sky became overcast with murky clouds, while the distant thunder and lightning in the south-west warned us of the proximity of the hurricane. "All hands" were called, and we hurried to our stations; but before everything could be made snug aloft, a fierce shower of hail descended, pelting us mercilessly; and glad enough we were to get below, at four bells, to supper. The wind increased, and blew very hard for an hour or more, when it became calmer; but still the heavy sea came rolling towards us, making our stout bark toss and pitch about as if old Neptune were irritated at her sluggish ways. We congratulated ourselves at our easy escape from the *pampero*, but we should have remembered the old saying, "Never shout until you are out of the wood."

As we were below, discussing various subjects, we were joined by the cook, who descended the ladder, requesting the loan of a novel, declaring that he was dying by inches of the "onwy." "Get out of this, you and your trash!" shouted an old tar: "this is no place for distinguished characters."

But the "doctor" did not appear to be disconcerted

in the least at this rude salutation and reference to his pretensions.

"Ah, boys!" he exclaimed, with a touch of sentimentality, "how can ye be so boistherous? Here we are, every hour dhrawing nearer and nearer to that mighty river which runs past Buenos Ayres; and does not the thought of it inspire ye with romantic feelings? As for meeself, I can scarce slape at night for the ecstatic thoughts that crowd me brain. Ye may all laugh," he continued, as some of the sailors interrupted him with a boisterous laugh, "but it does not alter the case in the laste, for it is thrue. To-night, when I was standing in the galley, the thought came to me, that perhaps the boy here," pointing to myself, "would like a few stanzas of poetry for his dialogue (diary), which he is keeping; so I, in my mind, composed a few lines, which, if he wants, I will recite to him.

At this, some of the sailors exclaimed, "Get out of this, for a dirty sea-cook as you are, and don't attempt to spoil sensible people."

I, however, said that I would be pleased to receive his stanzas, and, preparing my pencil and paper, wrote down the following lines as he recited them, together with the interpolations and remarks of the sailors. Striking a beatific attitude, the poet began: —

"I saw her; yes, I saw her."

Old Salt (gruffly). "What if you did? If she saw you, she sickened, I dare swear!"

The Doctor (continuing).

"Tripping along so gayly,
With mantilla fluttering in the wind."

Old Salt 2d. "Shaking in the wind's eye, in a squall."

The Doctor.

> "Eyes like a dove's in mildness,
> Or an eagle's in its wildness."

Old Salt 1st. "More like a hen's with one chicken."

Old Salt 3d. "Or a sick rooster with one tail-feather."

The Doctor.

> "Smiles they were sweet,
> Lips together did meet."

Old Salt 1st (dubiously). "Lips together did meet? I wonder, mateys, if she wasn't smacking them after a glass of grog?"

The Doctor.

> "Clamors of war and terrible drums,
> Noise of trumpets and the hum of tongues,
> Can frighten the timid, but not her;
> For brave as a lion, dauntless as fire,
> She's ruled by love, and not by ire."

Here some of the sailors pretended to faint; others reeled off to their bunks, saying that the doctor's poetry was "worse than his duff, and that wasn't fit to give a measly hog;" while one old fellow ascended to the deck, declaring that he "couldn't sleep after hearing such blasted nonsense, until he had taken a salt junk emetic."

The doctor would have continued his poetry, notwithstanding the ridicule of the "low, ignorant fellows," as he called them; but he was interrupted by the voice of the mate, calling down to the cook to "doctor the binnacle lamp," when the poet hurried up the companion-way, leaving me to turn in, and dream of

> "Lips that together did meet,
> Clamors of wars, and terrible drums,"

until the man at the wheel struck eight bells.

CHAPTER II.

IN THE RIVER PLATA.

AT length the day for making preparations for nearing land arrived. One fine afternoon the order was given to have everything ready for entering the river. All hands were kept on deck, and every one manifested an unusual readiness to work. The lashings were cut adrift from the anchors; the chain drawn out of the locker, and overhauled upon the deck; and the other matters attended to, which are not to be neglected on a ship about coming to an anchorage. Towards night, the changing color of the water, which in the deep ocean is of a dark blue, but which had now become of a greenish tinge, told us of the proximity of land.

At sunrise of the next morning, the cry of, "Land on the starboard bow!" awoke me from a sound slumber. Hurrying on deck, I was able to discover a faint streak of red in the distant horizon, which a sailor declared to be "the loom of the land;" and by eight o'clock the low shores of the Uruguayan republic were distinctly visible from our deck, and the monotony of our sea life was at an end.

As it was necessary to take a pilot on board, we were obliged to first make Montevideo, the great seaport of the Banda Oriental, or Uruguayan republic, which country, as most of my readers are doubtless aware, was formerly a constant bone of contention between Buenos Ayres and Brazil, but is now independent of both, and according to all accounts promises to become the greatest producer of wool of the South American republics.

A light breeze wafted us past the rocky isle of Flores to Montevideo, where, about dusk, we dropped anchor at a distance of three miles from the shore.

While aloft, I had time to observe that a conical mountain, with smooth sides, and crowned by an old fort, was connected with the main land by a peninsula, in such a manner that a fine bay was formed, where a large fleet of vessels were lying at anchor. The fort on the mount showed a light, four hundred and seventy-five feet above the level of the sea. The town lies on the opposite side of the bay, to the eastward of the mountain, from which fact it derives its name.

By the time the sails were furled, and several additional ranges of chain overhauled, night came on, and the anchor watch was set, with orders to call the mate if it lightened in the south-west, the region of *pamperos*.

My watch was from nine to ten: when I was relieved, I went below with a light heart, and "turned in" to my bunk, with the prospect of unbroken rest. It was perhaps an hour later that I was awakened by the confused sounds on deck, caused by the "letting go" the second anchor, and the loud calling down the companion-way for "all hands on deck." Hurrying above, we found that a *pampero* had struck the vessel, which was moving through the water at the rate of at least four miles an hour before the force of the hurricane. When the second anchor became fast, however, the vessel's course was checked, she swung around, broadside to the wind, and held her ground. The force of the wind striking our backs was so great that we were obliged to take shelter beneath the bulwarks to recover our breath.

The darkness was intense, save when flashes of lightning illumined every headland along the coast, and threw out in bold relief the mountain and its castle. But duty called us from the protection of the bulwarks to the chain lockers. Vainly, however, did the officers vociferate their commands; not a word could we understand; but we instinctively laid hold of the chain, and, guided by flashes of lightning, paid out many fathoms. Hardly had we accomplished our object in giving scope to the cable, when a noise like thunder announced that one of the sails, the main spencer, had broken adrift, and in an instant it beat and clattered across the quarter-deck. From side to side it tore, cutting the rigging to pieces, with the block at its clew. Half an hour's labor was ineffectual in securing the sail, though ends of braces were strongly passed around it; it continually broke loose, tumbling upon the deck all the men who were clinging to it, and we might have labored much longer, had not Manuel crawled aloft, and cut the sail adrift, by coming down the jack-stay, knife in hand.

The spencer had not been securely fastened before from between the harness-casks, the mizzen staysail, which had been carefully furled, seemed endowed with life, for in an instant it ran up its stay like a bird, and was at once torn to shreds.

At this point the prospect was fair for a wreck. The captain brought an axe on deck to prepare for the last resort. But such a fierce wind fortunately could not last long; its own force must prove exhaustive: it soon came only in gusts, and two hours later it had greatly subsided.

The scene now around us challenged our attention; and, until morning, I leaned across the rail, completely engrossed with the many curious phenomena before me.

The air was filled with electrical flashes, which at times rendered the tall mount plainly visible, and brought out the spars of the fleet in the bay in weird-like prominence against the gloomy background.

The fort on the height seemed clothed with flame, while the short, quick waves around the vessel gleamed with phosphorescent light. The *pampero* had struck the vessel during the watch succeeding mine, and the man on duty became so frightened that he did not call the mate. Luckily, that officer discovered the true state of affairs in time to prevent a serious disaster.

The dawn of the following morning revealed a sight such as might be expected after so violent a hurricane. In one part of the harbor were two vessels, whose crews were hard at work in clearing them from the entanglement of their rigging, which was completely wrecked.

Close by lay two others, with their topmasts gone, and in the distance were many others in a similar condition; while from the town came floating logs, boxes, barrels, and other lumber in great quantities, telling of the havoc of the *pampero*.

The effect of the wind was even felt to a greater extent farther up the river, where some fifteen or twenty small vessels were capsized, and many of the crews drowned.

A new and beautiful English bark, that had left her anchorage for Buenos Ayres the night before, we saw two days afterwards; but she was nothing but a dismantled hulk, with only the stump of her mizzenmast left: every spar had been blown away, and one of her men killed by a falling mast.

Though the *pampero* season generally lasts from March to September, this wind is likely to blow at any time; and a careful captain will always be prepared for it. The state of the mercury in his barometer, together with the appearance of the heavens in the south-west, must be carefully watched. These winds, coming from the cold summits of the Andes, sweep first across an undulating, then a flat country; and, meeting no obstacle to break their force, do great damage to the settlements about Buenos Ayres, as well as to the shipping in the River Plata, and are felt many miles out to sea.

The River Plata, at its entrance, between Cape St. Mary on the north coast, and Cape St. Antonio on the south, is one hundred and seventy miles; and we can see that the *pampero*, in traversing this broad channel, has a most unobstructed course.

At noon a pilot came aboard, bearing a letter from the owner's agent; and at about eleven o'clock the following night we hove up both anchors, and, with a fine breeze, sailed up the river. Thirty-six hours later, we dropped anchor in the outer roads of Buenos Ayres, seven or eight miles from the city, whose plastered dwellings and lofty cathedral were plainly seen from the decks of our vessel.

CHAPTER III.

BUENOS AYRES. — THE PROVINCE AND CITY.

FOR a whole month I was obliged to remain by the vessel, awaiting the arrival of the orders that were to set me free. During this period, to prepare the vessel for a long stay, the lighter spars were sent down, the flying jib-boom sent in, sails unbent, &c. The tides in the River Plata are governed by the wind, and have no regularity in rising; the current of the river is at the rate of three miles per hour. Vessels drawing above eleven feet of water remain in the outer roads, while smaller craft can approach within two or three miles of the city; all of these discharge and receive their cargoes by the assistance of lighters, generally schooner-rigged, and principally manned by foreigners, — chiefly French, Italian, Spanish, and Portuguese.

At last, about the 20th of February, a Boston vessel entered the river, bringing letters from home, and I was gratified by the information from the captain, that, after seeing the American consul, who had received orders to discharge me from duty, I should be at liberty to depart on my long pedestrian journey. I went ashore at the earliest opportunity, and at once called upon Colonel Joseph Graham, the American consul, who received me with great kindness, but condemned my intention of crossing, alone, so wild a country, with the people and language of which I had no acquaintance; he, however, furnished me with the necessary papers of protection, together with letters of introduction to various persons in the interior. During my stay in the consul's office Dr. Henry Kennedy, a young North American physician, came in, and although a stranger to me, presented me, after a few minutes' conversation, with a letter of introduction to Mr. G—n, a resident of Rosario. This act of kindness towards a stranger proved the generous character of Dr. Kennedy, and it is with a feeling of gratitude that I recall his name here. I was now my own master, and at once went about the city in search of information relative to crossing the country.

The consul and one or two other parties had given me the names of persons to whom I was to apply for the necessary information to guide me in my journey. I was surprised, however, to find that the foreign merchants knew so little of the interior; for, after several days' inquiry, the principal fact that I learned was, that to cross the pampas on foot it would be necessary to accompany one of the troops of carts that carried merchandise to the other provinces, as otherwise I would find it impossible to obtain food or to follow the right trail. One of my informants was a stout little Irish gentleman, who quoted a message sent to Sir Woodbine Parish, by a gentleman who crossed the country several years before; and as his description is almost true of the Buenos Ayrean, or southern road across the pampas, I will present it here. He said,

"The country is more uninteresting than any I ever travelled over, in any quarter of the globe. I should divide it into five regions; first, that of thistles, inhabited by owls and biscachas; second, that of grass, where you meet with deer, ostriches, and the screaming, horned plover; third, the region of swamps and morasses, only fit for frogs; fourth, that of stones and ravines, where I expected every moment to be upset; and, last, that of ashes and thorny shrubs, the refuge of the tarantula and binchuco, or giant-bug.

"And now," continued the little Irishman, "I ask leave to put you a question. How many days can you conveniently go without water?

"Two or three, perhaps," I replied.

"Well, then, you will never last to cross the plains," was his encouraging answer; "for, mark you, a merchant of this city crossed last summer, and went without water for *twenty-one days.* I think you had better return to America, and give up travelling for information."

Such were the stories — some true, and many, like that of the Irishman, utterly fabulous — that were told me by the different individuals upon whom I called during my short stay in Buenos Ayres. In the course of my inquiries I learned that a train of wagons would shortly leave Rosario, a small town upon the River Parana, about two hundred miles north of Buenos Ayres, for Mendoza, a town situated at the base of the Andes, and I resolved to visit the place in time to catch the caravan. A steamboat plied between the city of Buenos Ayres and Rosario, but as it was not to sail for a fortnight, I had ample time for surveying the adjacent country, and even for making a flying visit across the Plata to the Banda Oriental.

The State of Buenos Ayres usually monopolizes the attention of visitors to the region which is known as the Argentine Confederation, on account of her favorable situation on the seaboard, her possession of the only maritime port in the vast confederacy, and the predominating influence which these advantages have secured to her in peace as well as in war. The state contains an area of fifty-two thousand square miles, and is, consequently, but little larger than the State of New York. Her population, according to an estimate formed some ten years since, amounted to some three hundred and twenty thousand souls; of whom one hundred and twenty thousand are inhabitants of the city, while the remainder are sparsely distributed over the extensive plains that commence a few miles from the coast, and, running inland, stretch across and far beyond the limits of the state. The population of the city itself is composed of a great variety of types and colors, among which, however, the whites are rapidly predominating; as every year introduces new blood from Europe and North America, while parties interested are doing their best, in connection with the government, to divert a portion of the Irish immigration from the United States towards their own province. The government furnishes immigrants with land free of charge, but an extortionate price is not unfrequently paid, in the end, for a farm.

The study of the mixed races which inhabit, not only this province, but also the entire region between the Paraná and the Cordillera, has as yet received but little attention from the student of ethnology. The lines of demarcation, however, between race and race, are clear and distinct; and the future ethnographer of this region will have no difficulty in tracing the population, through its intermediate stages of gauchos, zambas, mestizos, etc., to its origin with the immigration from Old Spain and other European countries, and to the aboriginal and negro stocks.

Throughout the state the soil is richly alluvial to a depth of two or more feet, beneath which lies a stratum of clay, differing in kind and quality according to its location. Thus strata of white, yellow, and red clays have been discovered in different regions of the same province, furnishing the population with abundant material for the manufacture of tiles, bricks, and innumerable articles of pottery.

For nearly two hundred miles west of the La Plata, the soil produces a luxuriant growth of herbage, which is choked, however, in many places, by extensive *forests* of gigantic thistles, which grow to such a height that men, passing through them on horseback, are hidden by the lofty stems. So heavy is this growth that, at times, the thistle fields are impassable to man, and serve to the wild animals of the pampas as an undisturbed lair. These thistles are fired, from time to time, by the gauchos; after the ground that they covered has been burnt over, a fine sweet crop of grass starts up, upon which the cattle feed luxuriantly.

A native author, of eminent accuracy, who has carefully studied the statistics and resources of the province of Buenos Ayres, has published the following estimate of the value of real estate and other property in the country, in 1855:—

State of Buenos Ayres, its Extent, Value, &c.

Fifty-two thousand miles of uncultivated lands, at $1000 per square mile, . . .	$52,000,000
Six million head of cattle, at $6 per head,	36,000,000
Three million mares, at $1 per head, . .	3,000,000
Five million sheep, at $1 per head, . . .	5,000,000
Half a million swine, at $1 per head, . .	500,000
Houses, &c., in the country, ...	10,000,000
Total value, ...	$106,500,000

The following statement, derived from the Buenos Ayres Custom House, for the first six months of 1854, may serve as a means of estimating the number of horned cattle in the state: —

Hides exported in six months, 1854, . . .	759,968
Deduct quantity received from the provinces,	121,166
Total exports of Buenos Ayres hides, in six months, ...	638,802
Add a corresponding six months' exports for balance of the year, ...	638,802
Estimated export for 1854, ...	1,277,604

The following were some of the agricultural productions of Buenos Ayres in 1854, as computed by Señor Maezo: —

Wheat, ...	200,000	fanezas.
Maize and barley, . . .	70,000	"
Potatoes, ...	60,000	"

The *faneza* is nearly equal to four English imperial bushels, or to 2218.192 cubic inches.

Of late years the value of provisions, hides, tallow, and horns has been greatly enhanced.

I am informed that under the government of General Rosas, the price of beef was fixed by law at fifteen cents per arroba (twenty-five pounds), and that the severest punishment was inflicted for any attempt to evade or infringe upon the regulation. The price of beef during my stay in the province was never less than sixty cents per arroba.

Frequent revolutions have naturally hindered, in a very great degree, the development of the resources of this province. Since 1810–11 it has been subjected to continual and sudden changes of government: at one moment, as it were, attempting to form the corner-stone of a vast confederation, in a short time the scene of the wildest anarchy, and soon prostrate under one of the most grinding despotisms that the nineteenth century has beheld.

Buenos Ayres, the richest and most powerful of the provinces of La Plata, holds herself aloof from the remainder, preferring a state of isolation, through dislike for President Urquiza, to joining with her sister states in laying the foundation of a strong and permanent confederacy. Her import and export duties, together with port charges, stamps, direct taxes, &c., constitute a considerable revenue; and these resources would, undoubtedly, give her a powerful influence over the other states should she finally become a part of the Argentine Confederation. Though a coolness, almost amounting to ill-will, is manifested by the people of Buenos Ayres towards those of the neighborhood provinces, a treaty has been lately signed by the two governments, in which each promises aid and assistance to the other in case of attack from a neighboring or foreign power. It is evident, from their careful movements, that all the La Plata states stand in dread of their grasping and powerful neighbor — the empire of Brazil.

The city of Buenos Ayres is laid out in the usual Spanish-American manner — in squares, measuring one hundred and fifty yards upon a side; the streets, of course, cross each other at right angles, and run due north and south, east and west. They are regular throughout, but are very roughly paved. With some exceptions the dwellings are of but one story in height, and are built of brick, overlaid with a white plaster, which gives them a very neat appearance; but the heavy iron gratings with which every window is protected detract not a little from the beauty of the dwellings; and a stranger unaccustomed to Spanish architecture may readily, at the first sight of these forbidding gratings, believe himself among the prisons of the city. The roofs are covered with oval or square tiles.

Buenos Ayres is rich in public institutions. Her theatres and places of public resort are eight in number, besides the governor's mansion, the House of Representatives, and the Casa de Justicia, or Hall of Justice. Besides these may be enumerated the Tribunal of Commerce, the Inspection of Arms, the Artillery Arsenal, the Ecclesiastical Seminary, the Museum of Natural History, Public Library, Custom House, Mint, Bank, and Jail.

The treatment of the inmates of the latter institution

secures for them a degree of comfort far less than that which is reached in our own reformatory institutions.

In addition to the public buildings enumerated above, there are also suites of rooms occupied by the Ecclesiastical Court, the General Archives, Topographical Department, Statistical Department, Medical Academy, Historical Institute, etc.

The citizens of Buenos Ayres have well provided for the unfortunate. Besides granting licenses to mendicants, and allowing them to go from door to door *on horseback*, the municipality has established an asylum for orphans and a foundling hospital.

Besides the cathedral, there are thirteen Catholic churches, two monasteries, and three convents. There are two hospitals, one for males, the other for females; but these institutions have neither the conveniences nor skilful physicians which those of more enlightened or longer established countries possess. There are also three foreign hospitals, supported by the English, French, and Italian governments.

The *plazas*, or public squares, are nine or ten in number; one of them is overlooked by the lofty cathedral and by the Casa de Justicia, and contains a monument, erected in commemoration of past events of national importance, and especially of the Declaration of Independence from the mother country.

Many improvements have been made in the city in late years, chief among which is the new brick sea-wall, of considerable height, protecting the town from damage by high tides of the river.

From this wall, projecting into the stream, there was in process of construction at the time of my arrival a mole or wharf, of great length, which has since been completed, enabling small vessels and lighters to discharge their cargoes unassisted by the clumsy carts that formerly were the sole means of communication with the shore. The piles that support this wharf are pointed with iron, a precaution rendered necessary by the peculiarly hard formation of the river bed at this locality.

As the soil is impregnated with nitrate of potash, the well and other water is rendered unfit for table use. The wealthier citizens have deep cisterns at their residences, in which rain water is preserved; but the poorer classes have no other beverage than the river water, which is carried around the city in barrels, upon horses and mules, and retailed at a moderate price.

Slavery, which existed in these regions in a mild form until 1813, was, during that year, abolished by law. The system never assumed, in point of fact, that form which existed in our own republic, but was so lenient that the slaves were treated rather as children, or favorite servants, than as merely so much property.

Its gradual extinction set in many years before the period of legislation upon the subject. During the struggle for independence, the slave frequently fought side by side with his master, and manifested an equal anxiety with him to be liberated from the dominion of Spain. In consideration of services rendered during these patriotic struggles, and from a conviction that the system was far from beneficial to a newly-organized republic, the slaves were emancipated, and their descendants now form a valuable and active class, retaining little of the indolence usually ascribed to the unfortunate races from which they sprung.

During the ascendency of Rosas, the negro population was devotedly attached to Doña Mañuelita, his celebrated daughter, and their influence with her was almost boundless. It is related that in 1840, while an attack by Lavalle was momentarily expected, a young man from the town of San Juan was in Buenos Ayres, and was forbidden, under pain of death, to leave the city. An aged negress, who had, in former years, been in the service of his family, happened to recognize him, and learned his anxiety to depart. "All right, my friend!" she said; "I will go at once, and get you a passport." "Impossible!" exclaimed the young man. "Not at all," replied the negress. "La Señorita Mañuelita will not deny it to me."

In a quarter of an hour she brought a passport, signed by Rosas, enjoining his mercenaries to oppose no hinderance to the bearer's departure.

Thus gained over by petty favors from the all-powerful dictator, the negroes formed a corps of zealous spies and adherents of Rosas, whose secret observations were carried on in the very midst of the families whom he suspected. They also formed a brigade of excellent troops, on whose fidelity he was able to rely at all times.

Don Domingo F. Sarmiento, from one of whose works the above anecdote is derived, is one of the most enlightened patriots and philosophers of South America. He is a native of San Juan, a town in the interior of the Confederation, but has travelled extensively in Europe and the United States, and was for many years a resident of Chili, whither he was banished by Rosas in 1840. He has done much by his writings to advance a practical knowledge both of the principles of agriculture and of education in his native country, and is earnestly endeavoring to secure the coöperation of the government and legislature of Buenos Ayres in the advancement of those sciences. He desires to see some portion of the European emigration diverted from the United States to Buenos Ayres, the government of which province, indeed, offers land freely to all who will settle in the interior; and he has recently published, among other valuable works, a treatise on agriculture and education, entitled "*Plan combinado de Educacion comun, Silvicultura e Industria Pastoril*," especially designed for the province of Buenos Ayres. He is also translating into Spanish the writings of Adams, Jefferson, and others of our early statesmen, which we may hope will enlighten the Spanish republics of South America on a subject that they seem at best to very imperfectly understand.

A word concerning the currency of this province, and I will dismiss it from the reader's attention. Rosas, before he was driven from power, established a paper currency, which, being of small nominal value, was intended to supply the place of coin. These bills were struck off with the value of from one to several hundred *pesos* stamped upon them. But their value fluctuated to such an extent, that while at one time one Spanish dollar could purchase twenty *pesos*, a few weeks later not eight could be obtained with the same sum. At the present time a *peso* is valued at four or five cents of our money.

It is said that the president, having put this currency into circulation, realized thousands of dollars from it by monopolizing the money market, and causing the paper to rise or depreciate at his pleasure. I have seen a four-*real* piece coined by him, or by order of his goverment (which amounted to the same thing), with these words stamped upon it: "Eterno Rosas" (Eternal Rosas). This man was, in every sense of the word, a tyrant — cool, calculating, and selfish; possessed of a degree of cunning and penetration, that aided him in discovering his most secret enemies. Ruthless in the execution of his designs, he spared neither age nor sex; even the venerable mayor, his earliest friend, his more than father, was murdered in cold blood by a party of *masorgueros* (men of the Masorca, or club, a band of butchers and assassins, on whom Rosas relied for the perpetuation of his reign of terror), at the bidding of their atrocious chief.

In a work published at Montevideo, in 1845, by Don José Rivera Indarte, a native of Buenos Ayres, he gives the following estimate of the numbers who died through the hatred or caprice of Rosas: Poisoned, 4; executed with the sword, 3765; shot, 1393; assassinated, 722, — total, 5884. Add this to the numbers slain in battle, and those executed by military orders, at a moderate computation 16,520, we have 22,404 victims. If we deduct from this — allowing some latitude for the prejudices of Señor Indarte — one third for exaggeration, we still have 14,936, — a fearful aggregate of victims to the ambition of a Gaucho chief.

But his career has ended; the exiled patriots have returned from Brazil and Chili, and in place of his there exists another, and, it is to be hoped, a better, government. He was at one time the absolute ruler of his country; and his long and cruel reign has left an effect upon its inhabitants which many years of wise legislation alone can eradicate.

CHAPTER IV.

VISIT TO THE TIGRE AND BANDA ORIENTAL.

THE steamer in which I expected to embark for Rosario, on the Paraná River, would not sail from Buenos Ayres for ten days or a fortnight, and I began to look around me for some occupation, by means of which I might become more acquainted with the localities about the city. I was eager to visit the gaucho in his home upon the pampas; and when a young man, who had just arrived from New York, invited me to accompany him across the Plata to the Republic of Uruguay, I did not wait for a second invitation, but accepted his offer upon the spot.

I knew nothing more of this young man than that he had come to Buenos Ayres recommended to the first merchant of the place; but that his purpose for the visit was a secret one, I did not at the time suspect. He prepared himself for the journey by simply providing himself with a large blanket, a revolver pistol, and a *sounding-rod.* The first two articles seemed rational enough; but the rod, which he carried as a cane, required an explanation.

We received from a countryman a letter of introduction to Edward Hopkins, Esq., who was about to sail in the "Asuncion" for the north side of the river. This gentleman was at the River Tigre, twenty-one miles from Buenos Ayres, and acted as agent for the United States and Paraguay Navigation Company. As there was no other way for crossing the Plata to the particular part of the coast where my friend wished to land, he decided to visit the Tigre, and embark in the Asuncion.

Having bargained for seats with the driver of the diligence that ran between Buenos Ayres and the village of San Fernando, near the Tigre, we set out one fine morning, accompanied by a native gentleman, who spoke English imperfectly.

Our *cochero* was a conceited fellow, and felt the dignity of office to an unnecessary degree. We had no little amusement during our journey with him in watching the phases of his character: once, when the cart of a milkman became entangled in the harness of our horses, he became so laughable in his wounded pride and impotent rage, that we had difficulty in restraining our faces to a decently sober appearance. As we became disentangled, and drove on, he, in the midst of a volley of *carrambas*, denounced all cartmen who had the impudence to cross the track of the mail-coach. And such, in fact, his vehicle was; but, as we noticed that the contents of the mail, instead of being confined in a mail-bag, or other suitable receptacle, were scattered here and there in various corners of the coach, some tucked beneath the cushions, and others lying under our feet, the opinion that we formed of the native postal arrangements was not of the highest.

For nearly a league we passed over a Macadamized road, shaded here and there by willows that ran along the river. We soon passed the deserted *quinta* of General Rosas. The house was built upon arches, the materials being brick and plaster. Around it were artificial groves, and little lakes and canals of water.

To the right of the house, on the side nearest the city, were numerous little brick buildings, where the tyrant quartered his troops. The situation was very beautiful, and the surroundings altogether were interesting.

Farther on were *casas* (houses) of country gentlemen, with orchards of peach, olive, and quince, which, with the foliage of many varieties of shrubs, made the prospect on all sides most beautiful.

If a well-regulated estate particularly attracted our attention, we universally found, on inquiry, that its owner was a foreigner, whom the *cochero* dignified by the low word *gringo*, which is equivalent to "paddy" in our own language; and in this estimation, I afterwards found, our countrymen and all strangers are held by the indolent and treacherous country people.

Wheat, potatoes, onions, beans, tomatoes, &c., thrive wonderfully upon the farms; and, if the whole agricultural department were in foreign hands, the country, with its fine climate, and rich and easily-worked lands, could produce almost every kind of vegetable. With the exception of a few English and Scotch, the French from the Basque provinces are the most energetic and thrifty farmers. In a few instances the Yankee plough has been used with great success, in place of the miserable wooden one of the natives.

We met large covered wagons carrying produce to the city, and troops of mules and donkeys freighted with thistles, in bundles, to heat the ovens of the bakers; also others with peach and willow trees, which had been raised for firewood, an article bringing a good price, on account of its scarcity.

As we approached the Tigre and Las Conchas, we found that the country is undulating; but beyond the line of the latter, it stretches out into the pampas as far as the vision can reach.

The diligence entered San Fernando about noon; we found it a little town, surrounded with fruit trees left to the care of nature, the people being satisfied with her products without wasting time in laboring to improve them.

Two miles distant was the River Tigre, which empties its waters into the wide Plata; towards the river we directed our steps, and we arrived in time to dine with Edward Hopkins, Esq., the gentleman whom we had come to visit.

Mr. Hopkins, who has acted as our consul in Paraguay, and as agent for the United States and Paraguay Navigation Company, invited us aboard the little steamer Asuncion, which had been put together at this place a short time before.

This company had been formed in the United States for the purpose of opening commercial intercourse with Paraguay, a country that had, under the dictator Francia, excluded foreigners. Lopez, its present ruler, had been on very intimate terms with our countryman, Mr. H.; and, taking advantage of this intimacy, and the president's friendly feeling towards the United States, the above company was formed; and it soon sent out from Providence, R. I., a clipper schooner of beautiful mould, containing, in pieces, a small steamer and "hoop boat," with their appropriate crews, carpenters, millwrights, &c.

The schooner was damaged in the Tigre; but her cargo was landed, and the Asuncion put together, and sent up the Paraná to Paraguay. A cigar manufactory, employing three hundred native girls, was set on foot, a colony formed, and the steamer was to run between that country and Buenos Ayres, when an event occurred that blasted the prospects of the North Americans. A brother of Mr. Hopkins was stopped in the street for some trivial cause (probably galloping his horse) by a *vigilante*, whose language was insulting, whereupon difficulty ensued. As representative of his government, Mr. Hopkins interfered; and then followed the expulsion of our countrymen from the unexplored and little-known Paraguay. The United States steamer Water Witch, then lying in the Plata, ascended the river, and was fired upon from a fortification; several balls lodged in her hull, and one man was killed. The Water Witch destroyed the structure, and retired down the river to Montevideo, while the company's men settled at the Tigre until matters could be adjusted. The Asuncion was then engaged in carrying sheep across to the Banda Oriental, the country on the north shores of the Plata, which is known on some maps as Uruguay.

San Fernando, in conjunction with the Tigre, is the watering-place of the *ton* of Buenos Ayres, many of whom pass the summer in the village. The next day after our arrival was passed in pleasant conversation with our countryman, and during the evening a large party of ladies and gentlemen sailed down the river to two islands covered with groves of peach trees, where they took *maté* (tea), and danced La Samba Cueca, to the music of the guitar. I did not accompany them; for, having met a young man whose desire for travel had caused him to leave home, we passed the night wandering among the willows on the banks of the stream, and at an early hour on the following morning retired to rest as the piano frog was chanting his reveillé.

This was a spot where the naturalist would love to dwell. Above our heads sang many curious birds, and around us were still more curious insects.

On the neighboring church of Las Conchas, the *carpentero* built its oven-like nest, and parrots filled the air with their cries, while the mocking-bird rattled out his medley as in our own country.

As strangers, we were cordially received by the natives who occupied the houses close at hand, and many were the *matés* (cups of Paraguay tea) we took, because the pretty señoritas informed us that their language and *maté* were inseparable, and not until the foreigner became addicted to its use could he ride a horse, throw the lasso, learn the language, or win a fair maid.

I have already alluded to the *yerba*, sometimes called *yerba maté*, from which the Paraguay tea is made.

It is to South America what the tea of China is to Europe and the United States; nor are its qualities very greatly different from those of the Asiatic herb.

The *yerba* trees grow in forests, called *yerbales*, on the rivers of Paraguay, and attain a considerable size.

At the time of gathering, a party of peons are sent into the forest, who collect the branches, sprigs, and leaves in vast piles, which are afterwards thoroughly scorched. This being accomplished, the leaves and twigs are packed in a raw hide, which contracts as it dries, compressing the *yerba* into an almost solid mass. In this condition it is sent to market.

The *maté* is a small gourd, which forms the general drinking-cup in all the regions which I visited. An infusion of the *yerba* having been made, with accessories, as in our own country, it is sucked from the *maté* through a tin or silver tube, called the *bombilla*, which is provided at its lower extremity with a strainer, which prevents the fine particles of the *yerba* from rising to the mouth. The name of the gourd or cup is not unfrequently coupled with that of the tea itself in mentioning the article.

At last everything was ready for our departure; and at eleven o'clock one starlight night we sailed slowly along the little Tigre, and, passing the peach islands at its mouth, in an hour after, were fairly on our passage across the Plata, which at this point is nearly thirty miles wide. Upon arriving off the San Juan River, early the next morning, the tide was out, and the bar at the mouth of the stream impassable, which obliged us to remain stationary until afternoon, when the rising tide permitted us to wind up the stream, and through luxuriant foliage, the home of the tiger-cat, and once the lair of the fierce jaguar, which is now, however, rarely met with, having been driven from his ancient hunting-grounds by parties of natives who had been exasperated by his continual depredations. Now the little tiger-cat and wild dogs are their tormentors, and annually a tiger hunt comes off at the mouth of the river.

We arrived at our destination in due time, and the cargo of sheep was safely landed. Preparations for the night had hardly been completed, when from a certain quarter were heard loud and prolonged sounds, so wild and fearful that our attention was directed towards it.

"It is the voices of wild animals scenting the sheep-fold," said one of our party. The shepherd dogs on the borders of the stream pricked up their ears, and the hair stood up stiffly upon their backs as they walked around the sleeping flock, growling savagely.

While we listened, the sounds grew more and more distinct, and shortly we were upon our feet to repel an attack from a pack of wild dogs. Perceiving that we were too strong to be molested with impunity, they withdrew, snapping and growling, for a short distance, where they continued their music for two or three hours, and then drew off to another *estancia.*

These animals hunt in packs, and though of a cowardly nature, will, when fierce with hunger, attack man The following incident, which occurred a few days prior to our arrival, proves this often-contested fact.

A *capataz* (foreman) of an *estancia* (farm), while returning from a distant village to his home, met a pack of these dogs. The instinct of the brutes told them that the tired horse could not outstrip them in the long run. They gave chase, and soon brought the horse and rider to the ground The *capataz* had no other weapon than his knife, which proved ineffectual for his defence, and both man and horse were torn to pieces and devoured.

On the day after our arrival we saw at the *estancia* house three of these dogs, which had been taken from caves near the River San Juan. The largest was about a year old; although he associated with the house dogs, he would not suffer any person to approach him, and exhibited all the traits of his wild brethren that serenaded him almost every night. The two others were only a few weeks old, and were as playful as kittens.

These wild dogs are of a slight frame, and are generally of a brown and yellow color; the mouths are of a dusky-brown, or black. Without doubt they descended from the domestic dogs brought into the country by the Spanish or Portuguese Jesuits during the period of the early settlement of the La Plata provinces.

Early upon the following morning, the gauchos pointed out the path that led to the *estancia* house, and my friend Ned and myself set out to visit it. Larks, partridges, and many other birds started from the grass as we pursued our way on foot. All these birds were exceedingly tame; and had we been in possession of a gun, we should have arrived at the house with a bag of game.

The farm was owned by a German, who gave us a cordial welcome, and insisted upon our remaining to breakfast.

The estate was a small one for that country, embracing but ten or twelve square miles. The owner purchased it of the last tenant, who sold for a fair price, but, when he received the money, declared that the German must pay him extra for the buildings. The new owner, having, as he supposed, paid for "top and bottom," refused to give an additional sum; but the native was inexorable, and the buyer, knowing that a foreigner receives no justice from South American tribunals, wisely settled the affair, after much loss of time and money, by paying the full demand. Almost every bargain that is consummated between a foreigner and a native results largely in favor of the latter party. By bribery, falsehood, or perjury, — he cares but little which, — the native will outwit the "gringo," and then, in a most barefaced manner, tell him that it is by superior wit and talent that the end is thus brought in favor of a *Christian;* for so all true Catholics of both republics, the Banda Oriental and Argentine, are called, or call themselves, with no little egotism.

After partaking of a nourishing meal, — farina, soup, and meat, — Ned strapped his bundle to his back, carefully loaded his revolver, and, after several studied inquiries as to certain locations along the coast of the Plata, bade me to prepare to follow him. Our new friends offered us horses, saddles, &c.; but Ned had a particular reason for travelling on foot, and so, bidding our German friends adieu, we posted off in a westerly direction. Our landmark was the mud hut of an *estancia*, about seven miles distant, situated on a swell of the prairie. About the *estancia* we were leaving were several high hills, which sloped off into the rolling plain. A portion of these hills were barren, and broken rocks cropped out at their bases; but the plains or rolling ground about them, upon which the cattle fed, was covered with fine grass, occasionally intermixed with flowers. Just beyond the house, at the base of one of the hills, we descried a shepherd sitting upon the rocks, apparently watching his flock, that fed upon the plain; but a closer scrutiny proved that he was fast in the delights of a *siesta*. Puffs of wind that came around the hills flaunted his *chiropá* and *poncho* in a wild manner, which, together with his long beard, gave him the appearance of an old gypsy.

"Now we are clear of all eaves-droppers," said my friend, "and as we go along, I will tell you what strange circumstances brought me here, and why I left a good home and profitable business to wander mysteriously on this side of the Plata. I am sometimes visionary. My friends say so, and I believe it to be so; but the cause that tempted me to leave a wife and child was not so visionary as some of my friends have declared, and I mean to prove to them their error by returning to New York, in one year's time, a rich man. I can prove by history that a small vessel, sailed by Spanish pirates, went ashore upon this coast, not twenty, or at the most fifty, miles from the spot that we are now upon. She had a large amount of money on board, which was taken ashore, and buried not far from the wreck: two or three trees mark the spot; they are old now, but are probably still standing. If they are not standing, I have still another landmark to tell me where the treasure lies.

"The first fact which I stated is supported by history; that portion regarding the treasure is known only to me. The man who imparted the secret was an invalid for many years past, and, therefore, unable to come for the treasure himself. He confided it to me upon his death-bed, in New York city, about a year since. We had been intimate for years, and could rely on each other. Why he kept the secret from me for such a length of time, I cannot surmise, unless it was because he hoped to recover, and come for it himself. He died poor, and his words to me were of this import: 'Go to the Plata, and after coming into possession of this hidden wealth, return with it to New York, give to my widow three quarters, and keep the other fourth for yourself.'

"I have now only to seek out certain localities; when these are found I shall know just where to sink my rod, and I am certain of success. The reason that I have imparted a portion of this secret to you is, that I must have some person to assist me in taking the treasure to some vessel in the outer roads of Buenos Ayres. As soon as we have ascertained that all is right, I shall despatch you to the Tigre to purchase a boat, and as you have been long enough on board ship to 'know the ropes,' you will not deem it too great a risk to watch for a fair wind, and navigate the craft across the river. We will then load up, and steer some fine night, with the tide in our favor, for the Mary H., that lies off the city. The captain will not be there; but the mate is a confidential friend, and we will get our things on board without any trouble from the Custom House officers.

"When I tell you that I have sold out a profitable business, and expect to spend at least fifteen hundred dollars in this enterprise, you will credit me with sanguine hopes, and conclude that I must have strong and good reasons for risking myself and the support of my family in such a romantic undertaking."

I had before this heard of the Rio Plata gold hunters; but what could I do? Advise my friend to go home to his wife, of whom he often spoke in terms of strong affection, or assist him in his labors, and follow after the *ignis fatuus* that had lured him from friends and domestic pleasures? I answered him after this wise. "Ned," said I, "I shall offer no opinion regarding this gold hunt, nor discourage you from an undertaking for the success of which you confess you have embarrassed yourself and purse; but I also have a mission to perform. I came to this country with the intention of crossing the pampas to Mendoza, from which town I mean to cross the Andes to Valparaiso, Chili. From the latest and best authority I have learned that the mountains will be impassable after the first week in May, and as it is now late in the season to insure a safe journey to Valparaiso, it will be necessary for me to leave Buenos Ayres in the next steamer, which will be ready to sail in a few days. Until the sailing day I will devote my time to your plans, but no longer."

Though Ned spoke with enthusiasm, and promised the reward of one thousand dollars in case of success, I remained obstinate, and debate was dropped.

As we trudged on our journey, various birds and animals were at times seen by us. Once two small deer approached us, and acted as if influenced by great curiosity, and again, a tall ostrich started out of the grass, and, raising her plumed wings, ran off at the top of her speed.

Having reached the *estancia* house, — our landmark already referred to, — we halted to ask for water. The little that the family had was in an old barrel; by the side of it was a cow's dirty horn, out of which we drank. We continued our journey to the next stopping-place, five miles beyond. This was a small hut surrounded by corrals, the whole serving as an outpost to a large *estancia*. The occupants were a lazy gaucho and his negress wife, who invited us in, and offered *maté;* but as our object was to find some suitable shelter for the night, we did not remain long, but pushed on towards the River Las Vacas. Darkness coming on, we hurried to several mud huts that loomed up in the distance. Upon arriving at them, we found a young gaucho, who led us into a room where a powerful-built, supercilious-looking personage was sitting. Glancing at us carelessly, he asked us several questions; but being ignorant of the language, we could only make use of the "Spanish Teacher" that my friend had brought with him: we could not discover whether he understood our requests or desires. He treated us in a very distant manner, calling a gaucho, and ordering us off to a low, mud hut, where a woman was cooking a strip of meat by a small fire.

The interior of the hut was filthy in the extreme, the broken walls covered with vermin, and the whole dwelling filled with blinding smoke. Shortly after our entrance, several gauchos came in, and conversed together in low tones.

After a few minutes they approached us, who were seated upon a log, and addressed numerous inquiries to my companion. Ned, with the utmost simplicity, opened his "Teacher," and pointed out several sentences. The fellows at first looked at the book, and turned over several leaves with a puzzled air, then, breaking out in a loud laugh, threw it back into his lap. Soon one dark-visaged gaucho drew his knife, and commenced slashing it above the head of my companion, seeming undecided, however, to strike him.

At this manifestation of mischief, our hands grasped our Colt's revolvers; and if the knife had touched either of our bodies, we should have drawn our weapons and shot down our assailants. "If they strike us, shoot all except the old hag, who can do nothing more than give the alarm, and take to your heels," muttered my companion.

We sat thus for half an hour, during which time the gauchos made several attempts to strike at our legs, but did not succeed. They were at length called away by the old woman, who offered them their supper. We at last asked them by signs for a bed; they pointed to a pile of dried skins that lay heaped up in one corner of the hut. At this the indignation of my friend could hardly be kept within bounds. Having been accustomed to all the comforts that the great metropolis of our country could furnish, he determined no longer to suffer the inhospitable treatment of gauchos. Telling me to follow him, he moved towards the door of the shanty, which was nothing more than a large hide, swinging to and fro in the entrance.

But the gauchos would not allow us to leave; and after a vain attempt at arguing the matter, we were at last obliged to stretch ourselves upon the hides, and lying side by side, kept watch in turn, with pistols in hand, through the long and uncomfortable night. When I say uncomfortable, I mean the whole strength of the word, for the hides were alive with vermin, and their passage over our bodies and its attendant irritation, half crazed us both. But the longest night has an end. An hour before daylight the gauchos arose from the ground, which had been their bed, and lassoing their horses in the corral, galloped off to different parts of the *estancia.*

As soon as we saw that the disagreeable fellows were certainly gone, we arose and hurried away from the hut. The woman followed, and begged us to come back and eat meat; but we were only too willing to leave without a breakfast. We learned, some days later, from an Englishman, that the owner of this *estancia,* whose name was Moreno, belonged to a family of the most villanous character.

During the revolutions, and while the country was in the midst of civil war, an elder brother of this Moreno became a general, and perpetrated the most horrid deeds of cruelty. With a band of *soldiers* he traversed that portion of the country, cutting out the tongues of hundreds of cattle, and leaving the animals to become the prey of the wild beasts and birds. He visited a great number of *estancias,* and slaughtering the owners, male and female, placed in their stead his own submissive tools.

At the close of the war, justice cried out against him, and the villain fled the country, leaving a part of his ill-gotten possessions in the hands of his brother.

Four or five miles beyond Moreno's, we passed a white-washed *casa* (house) belonging to another man equally bad with our late host.

We now entered a thinly-wooded country, with thorn trees and cacti, in which large flocks of *palomas*

— a species of turtle dove resembling our own species — were abundant. Just before reaching the River Las Vacas we came upon a hut of cornstalks, out of which, to our surprise, walked an unmistakable son of Erin. He commenced at once with, "Sure, and is it yerselves that's afoot? Where be your hosses? Walk into the house and be seated."

Hurrying into the house, he commenced an onslaught upon a lot of fowls and two or three dogs, driving them out: we entered with him. He was a perfect specimen of the "Irish-born citizen." He had originally come to the country as cook to an English bark. He had much to say about the travels and dangers that he had gone through. Speaking of the conduct of Great Britain in meddling with the affairs of the Banda Oriental, he expressed his dissatisfaction in the most forcible language.

"The English and Frinch intervinshun," said he, "kilt me, as it did all the furriners. Before it I owned two thousand head of cattle and hosses, and had plinty of land, and was comfortable. I had a wife, though I didn't have time to get married to the crathur; and lucky was I that I hadn't, for she run off wid me money and half of me property. I hears that the Turks are fighting the queen, and are like to succeed. God bless them if they do. I hope she may be taken."

We left him as soon as possible, and pushed on to the River Las Vacas, which we soon reached, and crossed in a boat. We remained two days in the little town on its banks, during which time Ned made many inquiries for certain localities, but without success. Finding that nothing could be learned here, we hired horses, and set out on our return to the San Juan River, following along the coast of the Plata. Every few minutes would Ned halt and repeat the three Spanish words that he had studied for many weeks, and could now pronounce correctly. Turning to our guide, an old lame gaucho, he would say, half inquiringly, "*Los Tres Hermanos?*" but at each time the old man shook his head.

At last we came upon a high bluff, and the gaucho, halting, pointed with his finger to two small islands, green with heavy foliage that fringed their shores, and exclaimed, "*Los Dos Hermanos!*" But those were not the islands that Ned was seeking. "*Los Dos Hermanos*," or "The Two Brothers," were islands of greater size than those which my friend sought.

"*Los Tres Hermanos*," or "The *Three* Brothers," had been described to him by the dying man as "three small pointed rocks;" but Ned could not find these. He had consulted every chart that he could procure, but not one had the three rocks upon it. Could it be that "The Two Brothers" had been confounded with some other islets?

But I will not dwell upon our unsuccessful search. Suffice it to say that we both returned to the Tigre in the same steamer that had brought us across the Plata. I left Ned busily at work upon a small boat, in which, when finished, he intended to cross the river, and, disguised as a roving naturalist, to skirt along the river coast in search of "*Los Tres Hermanos*." When I parted from him, he said, gayly, "Good by, my friend. You have yet to travel a long road before you reach North America. I shall be there some months before you."

After returning to the United States, I wrote to New York, as he had requested; but some time elapsed before an answer came, and then my worst fears were realized. Disappointed in his search for gold, he had accepted the first offer for employment that presented itself, and had become the mate of the little steamer that carried us across the river when he first embarked in his romantic speculation.

During the passage of the steamer to the upper Paraná, he fell overboard one night, and was carried into the rapids of the river and drowned.

CHAPTER V.

ASCENDING THE PLATA AND PARANÁ.

FROM the River Tigre I proceeded on foot to Buenos Ayres. When within a league or two of the city, I passed a fine *quinta* inhabited by a Scotchman, who had resided several years in the republic. Two Irishmen, mounted high upon a cart, were driving through the gate, and one of them, after scrutinizing my appearance, shouted to me, "Sure you're an Irishman — are ye not?"

I answered that I was a North American, and belonged in Boston; when the other man inquired if I happened to be acquainted with a family by the name of Kelley, adding that the head of said family was a half brother to his wife.

I tried to show my questioner that Boston was a large place, with inhabitants so numerous that I had not yet had the pleasure of the acquaintance of his relatives; and, after giving the latest news of the great metropolis, and what was transpiring when I left it, I parted from the cartmen and pursued my journey, philosophizing on the wonderful race of the Irish, and the fact that, no matter what corner of the globe we may be in, we are certain to find this people represented, sometimes by a great many individuals.

When I reached the city of Buenos Ayres, I learned that the boat was to leave on the next morning; and, to prevent detention, the consul gave me a note addressed to the captain of the port, who at once furnished me with a passport. Persons about leaving the province are required to advertise their intended departure during three successive days in one of the three or four daily papers that are published in its principal city. This regulation is designed to prevent the departure of debtors for other "parts unknown," without settling their accounts; but the law is no less ineffectual than inconvenient, as it has been found utterly impotent to accomplish the object for which it was designed. Before sailing, I visited the bark, to bid adieu to the rough but honest hearts that had been my associates during our long passage from Boston. I was received with joyful demonstrations. I divided the contents of my trunk among the sailors, and, after a pleasant chat with the mate, was about to leave the vessel, when the "distinguished Irish barrister's son," our cook, hinted that he had a word for my private ear. I followed him to the galley; closing the doors, to keep out intruders, he offered me a seat, and began the following conversation: "My dear friend, do you ever partake of that which makes men's sinews as strong as iron bands? If so, here is the bottle just smuggled aboard by the 'patron' who brought you from the city. No! you won't dhrink? I'm less bashful. Here's to a short parting, and may you not yield your heart, as I once did mine, to any señorita on your journey." Here he took a good pull at the bottle, and continued: "What shall I do without you? I'm puzzled to know, with no kindred intellect on board to cheer me on the homeward passage. However, I have long intended to prepare a work on the 'Irish Karák-ter in America,' that will occupy my mind, and make the time pass less tediously. It will make at laste five volumes, and I'm keeping a 'dialogue' (diary) for notes every day." After he had enlarged on, and explained the character of, his embryo book, I turned the subject by remarking that it seemed strange that a man of his poetic nature had never been entangled in the bonds of love. "Ah, now! ye've said it," exclaimed the "doctor." "I have passed through that experience; but the cratur, woman, has been no blessing, as the poets say, but a perfect bane, to my poor heart. It was woman who drove me from my position in society to this galley." Here the cook was obliged to draw a pull of comfort from the bottle. "When I was only sixteen years of age," he continued, with a sigh,—whether of love or in consequence of the strength of the liquor I was uncertain,—"my father had a frind, who was also an Irish barrister; this gintleman had a daughter like an angel. I was young and beardless, she a few years older than meself. I became so deeply enamoured that I offered her me hand and me hat (heart); at which she softly replied, 'Mr. W., you are too young.' I, however, pressed me suit, for women want a deal of coaxing; but she only smiled. At last, when I grew quite urgent,—for an Irishman coorts in earnest,—she referred me for an answer to the second of Samuel, tinth chapter, and the last part of the fifth verse. I turned at once to it, for I thought that by it she meant to accept me suit, and in a bashful way told me as she did; when what was my horror and shame to read the following words: 'Tarry at Jericho until your beard be grown, and then return.'

"Would you believe it, my friend?—this little incident became known to my acquaintances, and for shame I was forced to leave the country; and for eleven years I never saw ould Ireland again." I thought that, considering his beardless condition, the Irish girl's answer was quite *Pat* to the occasion. The rum was now deeply affecting my friend's intellect; and just as he was about to recite a "stanza," I rose to leave, saying that I could protract my stay no longer. Embracing me affectionately, and repeating the lines about "tarrying in Jericho until your beard be grown," he bade me adieu; and the last I heard of him was his singing at the top of his voice, "O, whiskey! whiskey is the life of man! O, whiskey for me, Johnny!" Bidding farewell to the rest of the crew, and refusing some pieces of silver which old Manuel insisted upon forcing into my pockets as fast as I could take them out, I went over the rail, and with the "patron" pushed off from the vessel towards the city.

About noon on the following day, the Uruguay, in which I had taken passage, weighed anchor, and commenced the ascent of the river against a strong current which made the old boat tremble from stem to stern. The passengers on board were a motley crowd—merchants, soldiers, gauchos, and emigrants of every size and color. One hundred men, women, and children from the Basque provinces were on their way to Paraguay. Two hundred more were soon to follow in another party, they having already arrived at Buenos

Ayres. This immigration was the commencement of a plan of President Lopez, who was encouraging French immigrants to come, rightly believing that they would benefit his little republic. Among the Basques whom I saw was the wife of Montez, the president's interpreter, on her return from a European tour. This lady, who acted as matron for her countrywomen, spoke seven languages fluently. She was enthusiastic regarding the prospects of the new colony.

Late in the afternoon we passed the islands of *Martin Garcias* and *Los Dos Hermanos*, and entered the beautiful Paraná, whose current is more gentle than that of the Plata. The country by the river is flat, until we near Rosario, where the banks come down to the water's edge in the form of sand hills. The undergrowth was thick in a few spots, which served, a few years since, as hiding-places to the dreaded jaguar, an animal which is, however, now seldom met with south of Santa Fé.

At noon on the 30th of March we dropped anchor before the town of El Rosario (the Rosary), having been forty-eight hours in the trip. I was paddled ashore from the steamboat by a native in a log canoe, and succeeded in landing with dry feet. Luckily meeting an Englishman, I was directed by him to the house of Mr. G., to whom I had letters of introduction; and from him and his amiable wife, a native of the country, I received every attention that even a long acquaintance would have warranted.

Rosario, situated in latitude 23° 56′ south, longitude 60° 32′ west, is about three hundred feet above the level of the sea. The town contains seven or eight thousand inhabitants, the greatest portion of whom have sprung from the Spanish and Indian stock; while the amalgamation of races has introduced a great variety of shades of complexion, as well as of character, among the population. The streets, like those of Buenos Ayres, intersect each other at right angles. The sidewalks are paved with a coarse-grained brick, about fourteen inches long by six broad, and a little more than an inch in thickness.

Rosario has one church and two schools, of which one is a private seminary, and the other supported by a public fund. There is also in process of erection a small hospital, to contain two wards, one for male and one for female patients. It was nearly finished at the time of my visit, and would soon be ready to receive the poor invalids of the vicinity. This hospital was erected, without assistance from the authorities, by means of a subscription raised among the wealthy citizens. The people of Rosario, unlike the inhabitants of most Spanish-American towns, appear to take great pride in the advancement of the place, which is beginning to rival Santa Fé, a large town to the northward, which formerly monopolized the interior trade; but of late years, in consequence of the energy of its merchants and its proximity to Buenos Ayres, Rosario has diverted a large portion of the business from Santa Fé to herself, and continues to encourage it by proposing to build a bridge seventy yards in length across a river that lies between Cordova and Paraná. If this enterprise is not abandoned, it will attract to Rosario many caravans which are accustomed to trade higher up the river. The Sabbath prior to my departure had been appointed for a meeting of the citizens to act regarding this matter.

A new line of diligences had been running for three months between Rosario and Mendoza; they left monthly, while another line ran more frequently to Cordova, a town in the interior.

Rosario supports a printing-office and a semi-weekly newspaper, that promises soon to be issued daily. Sloops, schooners, and small brigs are constantly arriving and departing; and with all these facilities for business and travel, Rosario, in its present growing condition, will shortly prove the most important town of the Paraná.

The police force is organized in the usual South American manner, and consists of a few mounted *vigilantes* armed with swords, and dressed in peaked cloth caps, long red ponchos, and pantaloons, underneath which the frills of the *calconcillas* (gaucho drawers) may be seen.

Like physicians, they are allowed to gallop their horses in the streets, while all others are prohibited, under penalty of a fine of one dollar, from doing so. *Vigilantes*, when sent to arrest a person, are usually accompanied by a higher officer, as they are an ignorant body of men, and frequently not of the strictest integrity.

Although Rosario is the seaport, or commercial town, Paraná is the present capital of the Argentine Confederation. A national bank had, not long before my arrival, been established by the confederacy, of which the headquarters were fixed at Paraná, with branches in the provinces; but before it had been six months in operation, the whole affair exploded, as the confederate states, unlike Buenos Ayres, have little or no revenue. The government had also appropriated sums towards building a railroad from Cordova to Mendoza or Copiapo. Mr. Allen Campbell, a well-known North American engineer, was engaged to superintend the construction of the road; but, in view of the poverty of the country, the dangers arising from civil wars, the paucity of emigration to the interior, and the universal indolence of the natives, it is hardly possible to predict for this undertaking any remarkable success for many years to come.

CHAPTER VI.

A VISIT TO THE PAMPA COUNTRY.

WHILE awaiting the expected departure of the carts for Mendoza, I remained with my kind host and his amiable wife, the G.'s. During the interim, I occupied myself in becoming acquainted with the habits of the people. One morning, after I had been in Rosario for several days, a North American — as we from the United States are called — drove into my host's *patio*, and announced that he had "come to see the young chap from the north." I introduced myself as the person in question, when he cordially grasped both my hands, and said that he was glad to meet an old friend again; he regarded all from his own country as such. He informed me that he lived out on Don B.'s *estancia*, and, having heard that a countryman was in town, he improved the first opportunity of visiting him. Of course he had many inquiries to make concerning news from home, which I answered as well as I could, and soon we were friends.

This man's career had been somewhat remarkable. A sailor first, then variously employed, and now a "breaker in" of wild colts and mules, he possessed the faculty of adapting himself to all circumstances peculiar to the true North American. His experiences had been varied, and he well illustrated in his career the truth of the old adage, "A rolling stone gathers no moss." He was thoroughly conversant with all the peculiarities of pampa life; had observed well the habits of the birds and animals that live on the plains; was an adept in throwing the lasso, and mastering wild colts and horses.

"You are here after information, I guess?" interrogated my new friend. "If so, come with me for a few days, and I will show you how to be a gaucho. My shoulders are lame with being tossed in the saddle while breaking colts; but the job is through with for a while, and I'd just like to show you about."

"But you have only one horse," I replied. "Where can I find another?"

"Never mind," responded Don Daniel, as my friend styled himself. "Jest you mount him; I can get another: I've lots of friends around the river, and any one will find me a hoss: if it comes to the wust (worst), I can *find one* myself."

An extra blanket was furnished me from the house, and I placed myself at the disposal of Don Daniel.

The little iron-gray stallion that was to carry me into a strange land pawed and curvetted, and seemed anxious to be off. The *alforjas*, or saddle-bags, had been well filled by my lovely hostess. Don Daniel's *chifles*, or water-vessels, consisted of two cow's horns, one of which he filled with water for his new *amigo*, Don Yankee; the other he filled at a store with *aguardiente* for himself.

"Don Yankee," said he, as he busied himself about this important matter, "you have come from Boston, the home of temperance doctrines: stick to your colors, and don't mistake this horn"—pointing to the one filled with liquor—"for the one filled with water, as there will not be more than enough for myself. I take it for my lame shoulders by an internal application."

"*Ejo mio, adios*" (God be with you, my son)! exclaimed the kind-hearted señora. "Don't fall into a *biscacha* hole," warned her husband; and we were off.

Don Daniel bestrode a good-looking horse, that he had contrived *to find* somewhere. "Hurry!" said he, clapping spurs to his animal, as we turned a corner. "If that lazy *porteño* sees us, there will be no hoss for Don Daniel."

Although we were moving at quite a rapid pace, I remonstrated with my companion against his using other people's horses without their consent.

He only laughed, and said, "Poh! you are green, my boy. It is the custom here. When the *porteño* needs his hoss, he'll take a friend's animal, as I have done. We are all friends in this country; and I'll send his hoss back before a week is out. Now, *caro mio*, push yourself just a *leetle* for'ard,—so,—that's it; don't ride like a pole,—so,—so: here comes a breeze; isn't this jolly? Now I feel that pain in my shoulder: a leetle rum won't hurt it; you can try the water-cure."

And on we galloped over the smooth, grassy plains, while the sun, resembling a huge red shield, sank before us into the grass.

The next day's travel brought us to the very heart of the gaucho dominion. As far as the vision extended, and still farther beyond, a level plain, covered with grass, spread out, on which vast herds of cattle, the wealth of the herdsmen, were feeding. On we rode, our horses devouring space with almost untiring speed.

Thus far during our day's ride we had not met with a single human being. Nothing possessing life, except cattle and horses, had we seen. But at length we fell in with a large herd; and attending them were two gauchos, sitting on the ground, engrossed in a game of cards, their horses standing beside them. As we approached, they respectfully touched their hats, and wished us a "*buenas dias*" (good day). We inquired of them the name of the owner of the neighboring herds, when they replied that we were upon the *estancia* of Don Carlos B., in whose service they were employed as *peons*. We again put our horses to the gallop, and sped on over the smooth turf. All day the same speed was kept up; for our animals were true pampa steeds, and scorned a trot. Having traversed many miles, we met with another herd of cattle, which, instead of moving from us, as did the droves which we passed in the morning, seemed differently minded. Two or three old bulls left their several companies, and approached the spot where we drew up our horses. The old fellows seemed very courageous, lowering their heads, and shaking their long, shaggy locks, as if determined to contest our passage, or protect their weaker companions, who were closely huddled behind those pampa kings. We dismounted, and, leaving our horses, advanced towards the bulls. But the moment we touched the ground the animals assumed another character: as we advanced on foot towards them, they bellowed loudly, and, turning, with their heads down and tails up, scampered off as fast as fear could impel them, the ground trembling under the tread of hundreds of heavy hoofs.

Daniel laughingly explained, while we were mounting our horses, that, in those distant parts, cattle know man only when he is mounted upon horseback, and that a gaucho on foot is so rarely beheld that he is always mistaken for some unknown beast of prey.

As night came on, we dismounted, and, taking off the *recardo*, or country saddle, spread it upon the grass for a bed; we then hobbled our horses, and, after making a meal off a strip of roasted beef, lay down to a night's welcome sleep.

At dawn we were again in motion, and, after galloping a mile or two, met a solitary gaucho, who was chasing a herd of cattle. On our calling to him, he instantly wheeled his horse, and, on inquiry, informed us — for your gaucho is a polite fellow — that we were upon the *estancia* of Don Carlos B.

"Don Carlos!" we exclaimed. "Why, we were upon his estate yesterday, and have galloped many miles since then. Can it be that his *estancia* is so large?"

"Yes," answered the gaucho. "Don Carlos is the largest *estanciero* within two hundred miles."

"How large is his farm, then?" I asked.

The gaucho confessed that he was ignorant, and neither did his master know; for many years before a *pampero*, or hurricane, carried away the boundary stakes.* And even his estate is small beside that of Candioti, the once great pampa lord, who possessed upwards of two hundred square leagues of territory, and was owner of nearly a million head of cattle, besides

* General Rosas, late president of the Argentine Republic, owned an *estancia*, south of Buenos Ayres, that contained seventy-four square leagues. — Darwin's *Voyage*.

hundreds of thousands of horses and mules. Candioti lived in Santa Fé, and once had not a *real* of his own; but before he died he sent annually to Peru many thousands of mules, and a hundred heavily-laden wagons of merchandise. Since his death, his estate has been divided among his large family of illegitimate children.

As we continued to draw the gaucho out, he warmed up with his subject, and enthusiastically praised his master, Don Carlos. He dwelt with especial pride upon his great prowess; told us how he twice inflicted deep wounds upon the body of Don Vicente Moreno, the famous fighter, on the last feast day. He informed us that his great man, "Don Carlos, can catch a shaven and greased pig by the tail, and shoulder it; can ride the wildest bull upon the pampas, until, worn down by fatigue, it allows the don to lead it to the corral." In fine, so many and varied were this gentleman's accomplishments, that we wondered that we had not heard of him before.

From what we heard of Don Carlos, we imagined him to be a mighty personage; or at least I did, and Don Daniel pretended to, and believed his dwelling to be almost a palace, judging by his immense wealth, of which we had had abundant proofs in our long ride. Seeing that we were struck with the gaucho's enthusiasm, he offered to lead us to the presence of his master, which offer we accepted. Galloping across the pampa, we at last discovered a small object, like a speck in the distance, which the herdsman pronounced to be the residence of his master.

As we drew near the house, my previous fine notions received a severe shock; for, instead of an elegant mansion, with verandas and towers, we found a hut of stakes, cornstalks, and mud. Two or three holes knocked through its sides served as windows and ventilators. A few peach-trees grew behind the building; but they were not planted to supply the family with fruit, but served for fuel for the *estanciero*; few trees grow on these plains save those planted for firewood.

Don Carlos came out of his mansion; for the barking of no less than twenty dogs had heralded our approach, long before we reached the door. Dismounting from our horses, we repeated a solemn Ave Maria, to which the don made some appropriate reply, and then invited us within doors, and introduced us to a dark-complexioned woman, whom he called Doña Maria, his wife.

Maté yerba, the South American tea, was brought out, and served by the lady herself, who, in preparing it, reclined on the ground in a position far from graceful. A kettle, one or two tawdry North American chairs, and an old table, seemed to form the only furniture of the household. Our attention was attracted by several crania of oxen that lay scattered about the hut, and, thinking that they might have been kept as relics of departed favorites, I asked no questions; but I learned afterwards that the skulls were pampa chairs, and were used as such by the natives.

The don was a small, dark-complexioned man, with black, restless eyes, that were constantly scanning surrounding objects. His father was a Spaniard, his mother an Indian woman. Although he was forty years old, he had visited the capital but half a dozen times. When he was absent, he said, his mind wandered back to his *estancia*, and he was not satisfied until he was again among his herds. Though hospitable in his manner, he was a misanthrope, and placed but little confidence in mankind.

When we informed our entertainers that we had come from North America, we were beset with numerous questions. "Where is North America?" "Can a man travel there on horseback in two months?" "Is it situated in England or France?" "Is your moon like ours?" "What food do your people eat?" and such other queries were made.

We found that the don's family was composed of several sons and one or two daughters; but no two of the children were of the same complexion. I wondered at this, as I was ignorant of the fact that our host was a polygamist; and though Doña Maria acted as his present wife, and as mother to children not her own, she never murmured, for her husband was her lord and master.

All these sons were treated alike, and lived together in perfect contentment, while some of the degraded beings who bore them acted as cooks and servants to the household. A little corn was boiled and eaten with meat, without salt; and after reverently crossing themselves before the crucifix, which occupied a corner, the family betook themselves to their saddle-cloths —for it was now night—to rest.

The morning dawned beautifully upon us. As the heavy mist rolled off the pampas, we beheld the gauchos departing in various directions to their respective herds, for it was their duty to prevent the animals from straying off the *estancia;* and though thousands upon thousands of cattle bear upon their hides the brand of the proprietor, it is rarely that one is lost. Each gaucho can recognize every animal that belongs to his particular herd, let the number be hundreds.

The gauchos returned to breakfast at about eleven o'clock, and while they were eating their beef and taking *maté*, I took a walk into the vicinity of our host's dwelling. Close at hand were two or three large staked enclosures called corrals, into which the horses used by the family were driven nightly for convenience' sake. At the time of my visit, all the animals save one had been turned out to graze; this one remained, as is customary, tied to a stake throughout the day, to be in readiness for any emergency. The poor fellow stands all day without eating a mouthful of food. He could not eat grain, having learned to eat nothing but grass; and as hay was an unknown luxury on the pampa, he was obliged to wait until night came for his food.

As I wandered about the place, my attention was drawn to the little parties of animals grazing around me. The oxen were very large, and would compare most favorably with the finest in North America. The cows so resembled the oxen in roughness of form and size of limb, that I at once pronounced them inferior to our own in beauty. Out of thousands of cows upon the *estancia*, only three were milked, and these but once a day. These cows, more civilized than their relatives upon the plains, yield only five or six quarts of milk daily, and I wondered at their barrenness, but was afterwards informed by the *estanciero* that they gave him all the milk he wanted for cheese, and, therefore, he need not care to improve the stock.

The size of the horses I noticed to be, on the average, smaller than that of our own animals, though there were many noble specimens, both of size and beauty, feeding on the plains. These large horses are generally selected to sell to Chilians; for the people of Chili prefer large animals, and even *trot* their horses in some of the cities.

The pampa horses never feel the brush or comb; their coats are rough, and, instead of heavy manes and flowing tails, they can boast of little in either. In one thing they can claim superiority over our own most valuable animals: a pampa horse can gallop a whole day with a man upon its back, and can endure privations that would soon kill our stable-reared pets.

When I returned to the hut, I informed our host that in my country animals are habitually kept housed, in better buildings, in many instances, than his own residence; and, moreover, in place of allowing them to dwindle to mere skeletons, by living upon dead grass in the winter time, as many of his horses did, they are fed upon an article called hay, — prepared grass, — and grow fat and sleek on grain.

"What!" exclaimed Don Carlos, "horses in houses! Who ever heard of such a thing?" And the look he gave implied that his private opinion was that North Americans are greater fools than he took them to be.

It was useless to argue the great value of our horses in comparison with his; he could not believe that a horse ever was worth two hundred dollars; he had twenty thousand, which he valued at four dollars each, and forty thousand horned cattle, that he estimated at eight dollars per head.

I would here remark that the same kind of cattle could have been bought ten years since for half the price he estimated his worth; but now the herdsman had discovered that by slaughtering animals for their hides thousands have been wasted, and now the demand far exceeds the supply, and the price of raw hides can never be cheaper than it is at present.

Don Carlos, unlike the farmers of the Banda Oriental, did not believe in sheep grazing; therefore he never permitted his flocks to increase beyond fifteen thousand. An offer of fifty cents a head would have been immediately accepted, and when he received the money, he would have placed it in a goat-skin, with others of his treasures, and buried it in the ground.

I had noticed in one of the corrals some curious cattle, of a breed unknown to me; on inquiry I learned that they were of the *Niata* breed, which originated among the Indians of the southern pampas, and was once more numerous than the kind now common. This breed is seldom met with at present, and Don Carlos had secured these in his corral by order of a foreigner in Buenos Ayres, who intended sending them to Paris. These animals have low, heavy foreheads, the lower part being recurved. The teeth project from the mouth, the lips being short and incapable of being closed; in fact, they bear resemblance to pug-nosed dogs. This has the effect of giving them a fierce and terrible look. Our host remembered the time when a severe drought prevented the usual growth of grass, and dried it up; but while other cattle lived through the season, many of the *Niata* breed were found dead upon the plains, because, on account of the peculiar formation of their jaws and lips, they could not lay hold of the grass.

Each of the *estanciero's* daughters had a pet ostrich, the two being representatives of both of the South American species. One of these was about as tall as an average-sized man, the other of the two species about two thirds as tall. The first-mentioned one was caught when young within two miles of the house, and its species is quite common on the pampas; the smaller variety, known to the gauchos as the *Avestruz teteze*, was brought from Patagonia, south of the River Negro, by one of General Rosas's old soldiers. Neither of these varieties can compare with the great African bird, their feathers being destitute of that beauty and delicacy which has made the last-named bird famous in all countries. In fact, the South American ostriches are properly cassowaries, a three-toed species; the African has but two toes, and is, besides, nearly twice the size of the others.

As there have been many conflicting and incorrect accounts published concerning these birds, I will here give the most interesting, and I believe correct, information that I have been able to gather.

The male bird prepares the nest, and is obliged sometimes to gather the eggs into it, the female often being careless as to where she deposits them. I have been told that the male will attack man if the nest is disturbed, leaping up and attempting to strike him with his feet.

When pursued, the ostrich readily takes to the water, swimming slowly but fearlessly; it has been observed migrating from island to island, swimming apparently without great effort.

The food of these birds consists of grasses, various roots, and the sweet pod of the *algaroba* tree, with which they swallow stones, shells, and other hard substances, to assist in digestion.

In the spring months — in south latitude, September, October, and November — the male selects his wives, from three to eight in number, and assumes full control of their movements, fighting off any bachelor bird that may attempt to carry on a flirtation with any of his family. Some gauchos assert that the whole family of hens deposit their eggs in one nest or its vicinity. In such cases the eggs number from eighteen to fifty. It would seem that so large a number it would be difficult to cover; but ostrich eggs seem to suffer but little by neglect during incubation.

A gentleman who travelled as far south as the Rio Negro states that some eggs are allowed to remain outside the nest, and these are broken by the parent, when the young in the others are hatched, to attract the flies upon which the chicks feed during the first few days of their lives.

Fleet of foot, possessed of great endurance, the ostrich is captured only by the continued efforts of several horsemen, who either drive it in circles or give it direct chase, each horse when tired being relieved by a fresh animal and rider.

When the bird has become so exhausted that it can be approached within forty or fifty yards, the *boliadores* — three balls attached to cords of equal lengths, which are fastened to one thong — are whirled around above the head of the gaucho, until they have attained a proper impetus, and launched at the bird, whose legs become entangled, and he falls an easy prey.

Gaucho throwing the Boliadores.

The male bird is easily distinguished from the female by his larger head, and the darker color of his plumage. The gauchos sometimes kill them for food, eating the wings and feet only.

I had heard of the method by which wild colts are rendered submissive, and requested Don Carlos to permit me to witness the operation. The gauchos had finished their meal, and as they were about to depart for the pampas, we saddled our horses, and, mounting, were ready to accompany them. On the fellows galloped like the wind, swinging the ends of their bridles over their heads, and shouting boisterously to each other. Three miles were quickly passed over, and we drew up before a herd of several hundred animals, nearly all of which were mothers with their foals. A beautiful young mare attracted my attention, and I must confess I wished to possess her. I desired the don to select her for the one to undergo the breaking-in process. I saw at once that I had made a *faux pas*, for all the gauchos burst into a loud laugh, and declared that "North Americans must be queer people. Who ever heard of training a *mare* to the saddle?" "Why!" exclaimed another, with a contemptuous curl of his lip, "do you work mares in your country? Why, man, I would as soon think of putting a saddle upon my poor old mother's back, and forcing a bridle into her mouth, as of breaking in a *mare!* The people of North America are savages!"

Mares are respected in the country of the herdsman, and it is considered an ungrateful and indecent act to require labor of the mothers of horses.

Seeing that, through ignorance, I had lowered myself in the opinion of the pampa lord and his followers, I concluded to hold my peace in future, and await events without trying to shape them. At last Don Carlos selected a fine young horse, and pointed it out to one of his men as a fit subject for his skill.

The gaucho loosened the lasso from behind him, and made the running noose, which is held in one hand, while in the other are grasped several coils ready to run out at the proper moment. The victim was separated from the drove, and the horse bestrode by the gaucho started after it with the rapidity of the wind. The fugitive strained every nerve to distance his pursuer; but as a trained horse, if mounted by a herdsman, can generally overtake a free one, however fleet he may be, the lasso soon left the gaucho's hand, his horse wheeled, and braced his feet for a shock which in an instant occurred, the noose settling over the head of the victim, and checking him in his flight so suddenly that he fell in a somerset upon his back.

At first the colt was stunned by the fall; but, recovering, he arose to his feet, and began pulling upon the lasso until his eyes seemed as if about to start from their sockets. A second gaucho now galloped to the assistance of his friend, and, skilfully throwing his lasso around the hind legs of the victim, started away in another direction, by which movement the colt was thrown to the ground, and his hind legs stretched out to their full length. The feet were now tied together with a strip of hide, the lassoes were removed, and the poor animal was helpless on the ground, and panting with fear.

But the real work of breaking him in was yet to be

done. A saddle was placed upon his back, and a piece of lasso thrust into his mouth to serve as a bridle; the bonds on his feet were then loosened enough to permit him to rise to his feet, and two men held him by the ears, while his eyes were being covered with a poncho. The question, "Who is to ride him?" was hardly asked before each gaucho asserted his right to a seat upon his back.

The youngest son of the *estanciero* was selected to prove his horsemanship to the North Americans. He jumped into the saddle with a determination to conquer, and shouting, "Let go!" drove his sharp iron spurs into the animal's flanks. The colt did not move a muscle, but seemed overwhelmed with astonishment and fear.

Another application of the spurs seemed to recall him to his senses. He backed slowly, and then plunged forward with astonishing force, rose upon his hind legs, and then fell to the ground, turning and twisting his body in every conceivable contortion, but to no purpose; his future master was upon him, and it was useless attempting to unseat him. The beast now attempted a new course; he dashed forward in a gallop across the plains, moving with a speed that only fear and rage could give him. We followed as fast as our horses could travel; but he distanced us, until, stopping suddenly, he plunged, reared, kicked, and pranced in his efforts to unseat his rider; but at every movement, the steel spurs of the gaucho stung him in the flanks. An hour passed, but the colt was untamed, and he now attempted another plan for procuring his freedom. Bending his neck until his nose touched the ground, and throwing his legs together, he jumped into the air, throwing his rider at each jump nearly two feet above his saddle.

"Now comes the *vuelto malo*" (bad turn), shouted Don Carlos; "look, *hijo mio!*" The colt's nose again touched the ground; he then attempted to throw a summersault; he almost succeeded; if he had, he would have crushed the boy; but the rider watched the right opportunity, and adjusted the position and weight of his body, so that the horse was forced to settle upon his feet, when he again broke into a gallop; but his step was feeble, and his strength gone, and he would fain lie upon the grass if his terrible persecutor would permit.

His great exertions at length overpowered him, and, conquered, he allowed the gaucho to dismount, and place a halter over his head. What a change had come over the animal that two hours before was galloping over the plains with the freedom of the winds! He stood perfectly still, his eyes closed; his flanks were covered with sweat, which rolled off his body in large drops; blood oozed from the wounds inflicted by the spur, and trickled down his limbs; the nostrils were dilated, and blood was seen about the nose and mouth; every vein stood prominent upon his swollen body, and his whole appearance was that of intense suffering and fear.

"What a cruel system!" I involuntarily exclaimed. "How the poor animal has suffered!"

The gaucho again laughed, and answered, "Why do you pity him? he is worth but three dollars. There are plenty more better than this one."

The young conqueror of eighteen led home his prize,

and placed it in the corral, where it lay for several days, unable to stand, eat, or sleep. Such is the course of training, or breaking in, of wild colts. At the expiration of ten days after the first lesson the animal is again ridden, and a third lesson completely breaks him, when he is increased fifty cents in value, which sum is paid the gaucho for his trouble, and the pains he has to endure from the conflict.* Of course the colt's mouth is too tender to bear the hard iron bit for many days.

After we returned to the house, the gauchos, to further show their prowess and accomplishments, prepared for some of their favorite games. First came the trial of "breasting horses."

Two gauchos mounted their steeds, and, after receiving and answering the proper challenge, separated, taking stands about forty rods apart. At a given signal, they spurred their horses, and, as if bent on destroying each other, rushed with the greatest force their steeds together, breast to breast. So great was the concussion, that the riders were forced from the animals' backs, and tumbled, half stunned, to the ground. But they quickly recovered; and, as both were anxious for a second trial, they mounted again and dashed together, this time only one being unseated, but he was so lame that he declined a third trial.

Next came the trial of crowding horses.

Two mounted gauchos placed their beasts side by side, and, spurring the animals on the flanks, each strug-

* In conversation with many gauchos who break in colts for the *estancieros*, I have been informed this is the price paid them for their labor, and in hard times even a less sum is paid. This was in the far interior of the pampa provinces. — *Author.*

gled to crowd the other. The horses seemed to share their riders' spirits, and at last one little beast crowded his opponent up to the door of the cook-house, and finally through it. This was followed by another game.

A bar was placed across the corral entrance, at about the height of the horse's head. A gaucho mounted, and then retired several rods from the corral, when he turned, and galloped towards the gate, and, without checking his speed, threw himself out of the saddle, and, passing with the horse under the bar, regained his seat, without having left the animal or touched the ground. Loud applause followed the achievement, and others followed in the game, all with good success.

As I had seen, in the early part of the day, the skill with which the gaucho can throw the lasso, Don Carlos expressed the desire to show his skill with the *boliadores*. Mounting his horse, and removing the three balls which were fastened to the peak of his saddle, he gave chase to a cow, and, when within thirty or forty yards of her, whirled the balls around his head with great force, and cast them towards her. Away they flew through the air like chain-shot, and, fastening themselves about the hind legs of the fugitive, tumbled her to the ground in an instant.

The three *boliadores* are made of round stones, enclosed in hide covers; they are attached to the lasso by long sinews of animals. Wooden balls are used when it is feared that stone *boliadores* might break the legs of the animal or bird to be captured.

Estancia life has a degree of loneliness and quiet that would be unbearable to any one but those who have been reared in it, or have lived in places similar in character to the surrounding country.

On the *estancia* lives the proprietor and his family, alone in the solitude of the plains. Around them is one continual monotony, with no moving thing, as far as the eye can reach, save the herds that graze in the vicinity of the house. Day after day the same routine is followed, until, from very habit, it becomes a second nature. The young herdsman has the few characters around him to imitate; and as he sees but little of the outside world, — and then only when some *dia de fieste* attracts him to the nearest village, — he grows up an exact copy of his father; so far as character and general mental qualities go, a veritable "chip of the old block." Therefore, when we take into consideration the isolated life of the gauchos, we should willingly pardon some of their many failings.

The gauchos of the towns give no more correct idea of their pampa brethren than do the domesticated Indians of our western country of the savage tribes of the prairies and forests before the arrival of the pilgrims. It is only away upon the vast plains that the gaucho is found in the same half-civilized state that he was in fifty years ago.

A distinguished Argentine statesman and author, wishing to fairly civilize the gauchos, formed a society for the purpose, to which many of the leading *estancieros* of the province of Buenos Ayres lent their influence. It was the object of the society, first, to persuade the herdsmen to eschew all gewgaws, such as silver mountings for their horses, trinkets, the peculiar costume of the pampas, the poncho, chiropa, frilled drawers, wide belt, and colt-skin boots. After they had effected their first object, and dressed the fellows in pantaloons, coat, and boots, they intended to offer them the means of education and enlightenment, by means of teachers, books, &c. The plan has not been carried out, and, according to the last accounts from the country, it had not met with any real encouragement. The gaucho will still be a gaucho, in spite of all the efforts of philanthropists to educate him.

The character of the gaucho is a curious combination of deceit, superstition, and hospitality, the latter not real, but only assumed, with the expectation of gain or reward. Though they show aversion to manual labor, and are generally proud-spirited (particularly in the provinces of Buenos Ayres and Cordova), they are easily amused; the guitar and mazes of the dance possess strong attractions for them, and they will enter into *la zamba cueca* with a wonderful degree of interest.

The gauchos exhibit a combination of the customs of other countries. They use the lasso after the manner of the Mexican *vaquero.* Miers shows that their habit of cooking meat upon a stick or iron spit (*asador*) came from the Moors, through Spain. They have borrowed several of their customs from the aboriginal inhabitants, — the use of the yerba, sucking it through a tube from the gourd, the *maté*, also that formidable weapon, the *boliadores*, and the lariat, or lasso, which is used by the pampa tribes and Patagonians.

The *estancia* life is best fitted to develop the true gaucho character; there is a freedom of feeling experienced in coursing over the boundless plains that is peculiarly agreeable to him.

A little sketch of *estancia* life will, perhaps, not prove uninteresting to the reader.

First, regarding the right of possession and equality of standing of the members of the family relative to the property upon which they live.

The *estancia* is generally left by will to the wife and children, the wife one third, the boys and girls equal shares. Sometimes she who has been called wife, is not legally entitled to the name; but this matters little; she had the right of the property while her spouse lived, and the same rule follows after death, unless specially mentioned in the last will and testament, by her lord, to the contrary. The members of the family rarely divide the property, but live together as before the head of the family died, each member consulting the others before making any sales of stock, &c.

The peons, or laborers, that live upon the *estancia*, rise half an hour before sunrise, take a *maté* without sugar (unless the proprietor is unusually considerate), and at sunrise select the horses from the drove in the corral. A portion of the number mount, and gallop off to their respective herds, to select a new pasturage ground, and to prevent them from straying away.

The remaining peons select the half-broken colts, and, after tying them to stout stakes, entangle the animals with coils of the lasso, tripping them off their feet, and rolling them on the ground. This is to teach the young horse to be gentle under difficulties, or, in other words, not to prance and kick when anything touches the heels.

At about eight or nine o'clock the peons return, and report to the *capataz* (foreman), or to the *estanciero* himself, the condition of the animals under their respective supervisions. The daily ration is then given them, which they cook and eat. Perhaps a colt or mule is to be ridden for the first time; if so, this exercise follows their breakfast. At noon the peons return to the little shanties that surround the dwelling of their master, and, after taking a few *matés*, and perhaps another *asado*, they stretch themselves upon the ground to enjoy the siesta hour, which, however, often becomes hours in length.

The last departure to the plains occurs about three o'clock, and all the men return about dusk; they sup on the simple roast, drink a few *matés*, then roll themselves up in their ponchos, and sleep soundly, with only a skin or hide beneath them, until, from habit, they awake at the usual hour, and commence the duties of another day.

The Sabbaths and feast days are strictly kept by the gauchos in their own peculiar way. They consider it wrong to work on these days, and when they do, a fine is imposed upon the offenders. But it is perfectly allowable for men and women to dance, gamble, and fight upon a feast day. If the traveller is by any chance in one of the small mud towns in the pampa country, he will see gauchos gallop up into the place from *estancias* ten, fifteen, and even twenty leagues distant.

They pass the day in testing horsemanship, stealing, pitting fighting-cocks, confessing sins to the padres, and not unfrequently the *grand finale* is a general *mêlée*, from which few escape without a wound. On such occasions, he who can particularly distinguish himself as a *diablo* is generally treated by the crowd, who ply him with *aguardiente*, and other liquors, until he sometimes mistakes friends for foes. A fine of twenty dollars was once imposed on Sabbath and feast-day breakers, — those who were caught at work.

As the priests had many saints to distinguish by honoring them with particular days, the list received continual acquisitions. St. John's day, St. Paul's day, Saint this one, and Saint that, cheated the laboring classes of the towns out of a living; for all these days were better adapted for losing money than for acquiring it. But General Rosas cut down the long list of holidays to the number now observed, which is more than large enough for a fair share of frolic and piety.

When dressed in full regalia, the herdsman's appearance is very picturesque: in place of pantaloons he wears a *chiropá* and *calconcillas.* The former is a square piece of cloth drawn about the thighs, and fastened around the waist with a belt; it descends as far as the knees, from which downward the leg is covered with the *calconcillas*, a wide pair of linen or cotton drawers, finely worked, and ornamented with two or three frills. The feet are encased in a pair of *botas de potro*, being the skin stripped from the leg of a colt, and rubbed until it has become soft and pliable. The heels are decorated with a pair of iron or silver spurs, of huge proportions, that rattle and jingle as the gaucho moves about. A shirt, poncho, and hat complete the costume.

For ornament and use, the gaucho carries a long knife, placed crosswise in his belt behind. The hilt is very broad, and contains pockets to hold tobacco, flint and steel, and horn of tinder; the outside of the *tirador*, as the belt is called, is covered with silver and base dollars, that are the gaucho's pride.

Upon a feast day the fellow decks out his horse with silver ornaments, and rides forth to see and to be seen. Not unfrequently his wife rides behind him, seated upon a poncho laid upon the horse's croup; but she is inferior to his horse in the estimation of the rider, upon which animal is lavished almost all the wealth (if he is poor) of the owner.

We passed a most pleasant day with Don Carlos, and when we retired to our couches we felt that the visit had been well worth the time it had cost.

On the next morning, as soon as etiquette would permit, we bade adieu to our host and his family, and, mounting our horses, commenced our long ride back to Rosario.

Nothing occurred of importance, or that would interest the reader, and the next day we were welcomed cordially by the G.'s, my friends at Rosario.

CHAPTER VII.

LIFE ON THE PAMPAS.

AT sunrise on the day but one following that mentioned at the close of the preceding chapter, I left the house of my hospitable friend, after bidding farewell to my amiable hostess, and proceeded with Mr. G. to a plaza on the outskirts of the town, from whence all troops of carts or mules take their departure for the interior provinces of the country.

We entered the square in time to find Don José Leon Perera, the *patron* or owner of the caravan, who was reclining upon a skin beneath the cart that contained his personal property, enjoying his cigarito, and finishing his fifth *maté*. This gentleman received his visitors with a pompous wave of the hand, and requested us to be seated, pointing at the same time to an old wheel lying not far off upon the ground.

Some minutes having passed in exchanging compliments, after the manner of the country, Mr. G. informed the *patron* that he had with him a young man who had come from *El Norte* with the intention of crossing the pampas, and that he proposed accompanying the caravan on foot; moreover, as he was inexperienced, it would be necessary to place him beneath his (Don José's) protecting care. At mention of my crossing the plains on foot, Don José, with a stare of astonishment, declared it could not be done. To the second proposition — that of his assuming my guardianship — he acquiesced, however, and mentioned upon what terms I could accompany him. For the use of a horse (in case I should need an animal), and a place in a cart for my baggage, seventeen dollars would be required of me — a sum sufficient to have purchased two ordinary horses, at the prices which they then were sold at.

Four dollars were demanded for the supply of meat, of which I was to have an ample allowance; and besides this sum, a fee of one dollar was to be given to a native — a fellow of villanous appearance — who was to be my *compañero* (companion) and cook. It was to be his particular duty to see that his *protégé* was well attended, well fed, and guarded from all harm if the Indians should attack the caravan. Of course I was to believe that great valor would be exhibited, and much blood be spilled, by the brave individual who was to be my protector. My new guardian and the other drivers of the carts differed widely from the inhabitants of the pampa provinces. They belonged in the northern part of the republic, in the distant province of Santiago, and spoke the ancient language of their fathers, — the Quichua, — while the *patron* and two or three natives of the lower states conversed in the Spanish or common language of the country. Knowing that I should be unable to converse with Don José or his peons while upon the journey, I made a number of inquiries in relation to the manner of living, and what I might expect on the trip, all of which, with the assistance of Mr. G., were comprehended by the natives, and I was answered that luxurious living, sympathizing friends, and unalloyed enjoyment were to be the accompaniments of my journey across the pampas. The anxiety that had caused me many sleepless nights previous to the interview with the *patron* and his Indian peons now disappeared, and I looked forward to opportunities for gleaning, in a rich field, a harvest of information and valuable facts not yet familiar to my adventurous countrymen.

Matters having been settled by my paying Don José in advance the full demands he made, Mr. G. took me aside, and prayed God speed me on my way. "If you have money with you," said he, "by no means let it be seen, as these drivers do not bear a good name, and they would not scruple to rob you should opportunity offer. The *patron* I believe to be honest, and while he is with the troop you have nothing to fear." He then bade me farewell, pressed my hand cordially, and we parted.

Towards noon about one hundred oxen were driven into the plaza, when each peon, having received his allotted six, conducted them to his cart. A piece of tough wood, six or seven feet in length, five inches in width, and three in thickness, served as a yoke; it was laid on the neck, just back of the animal's horns, and lashed securely to them by a long strip of raw hide, thus causing the whole strain to come upon the head and neck, instead of upon the shoulders, as is customary with cattle that are yoked as in the United States.

The carts were most cumbrous affairs, and in appearance were not unlike a *rancho*, or native hut, set upon wheels. The body consisted of a framework of sticks, covered upon the sides and back with small reeds, and roofed with cattle hides, which rendered them secure against the heaviest rain. The carts, which probably exceeded twelve feet in length, were only four feet wide, and, being mounted upon two wheels of extraordinary diameter, were sufficiently novel and striking to my uneducated eyes. The only iron used in their construction consisted of a few scraps used to strengthen the nave of the wheel; all the other parts were fastened together by bands of hide, and wooden pins. The heavy tongue rested upon the yoke of the first pair of oxen, and from it ran long ropes of hide, which connected with the yokes of the second pair and leaders.

The method of driving the oxen practised by these people is most barbarous. There projects, a few feet from the roof, running forward of the cart, a portion of the ridge-pole, from which is suspended, by a piece of lasso, a becket that swings to and fro with the motion of the cart. This becket supports a heavy cane, nearly thirty feet in length, having at the end a sharp iron nail that serves to quicken the movements of the leaders; above the second pair is another goad, differing from the first by projecting from a wooden cone that hangs beneath the cane-pole.

This instrument is called the *picano grande*, and it requires a skilful hand in its guidance, in consequence of its weight and the constant oscillatory motion when the wagon is moving. The driver holds one end in his right hand, and, by constant thrusts, drives it into the animals without mercy. By lifting the end of the *picano*, the part outside the becket is lowered, and the perpendicular goad touches the backs of the second pair, while in his left hand the driver holds the *picano chico* (little goad), and spurs the tongue oxen, or those nearest the wagon, upon which the severest labor falls. The principle upon which the cattle are guided is also peculiar. If the driver wishes the ox to turn to the left, the goad is applied to that side, and the animal follows the direction *pricked* upon him; if to the right, the *picano* is applied to that side, with a similar result. I have seen the unfortunate beasts goaded until the blood trickled from their wounds; but still they followed the instrument, upon whichever side they felt its sharp sting. With small carts, having but one pair of oxen, the driver sits upon the yoke and tongue of the vehicle, *picano* in hand, with his legs coiled beneath him *à la Turque.*

Everything was in readiness for the journey, but the butcher had not arrived with the meat for provisions, a delay at which the *patron* gave vent to many a *carramba* of impatience. Shortly, however, a little, rickety, two-wheeled cart, lashed together with strips of hide, was driven into the plaza, and its owner distributed the expected meat among the different carts. While he was thus employed, some women, carrying a little tinsel-covered *Santa*, passed around the caravan, and each peon devoutly kissed the garments of the image, to insure, as I supposed, a prosperous journey.

At last the caravan commenced its march, and we bade farewell to Rosario and to civilization, Don José the *patron* and Don Manuel the *capataz* leading the caravan, on horseback.

First following them were, creaking loudly, fourteen clumsy carts loaded with *yerba*, sugar, iròn, and other merchandise. Next came fifteen or twenty spare oxen, as many horses, with about a dozen mules, driven by an old guide, two youngsters, and the carpenter of the troop, who also acted as assistant *capataz*. I walked in advance of the *patron*, though he advised me to enter the cart, as walking, he said, was injurious to the system.

Our course lay over a level country covered with fine grass, which, having been pastured by cattle, was very short. After journeying four miles, we came to a halt; the oxen were unlashed, and allowed to feed by the roadside, while the men kindled a fire of thistles, roasted a strip of meat, and took their gourds of Paraguay tea.

The manner of cooking meat on the pampas is worth a moment's attention. After an animal has been killed, the meat is cut into pieces, without any regard to anatomy, or to the butcher's "regular cuts," and an iron spit called the *asador* is run longitudinally through each strip. The *asador* is stuck into the ground close by the fire, and, being carefully watched, the steak is gradually cooked in a manner that would gain no discredit in a well-regulated kitchen. The result of this method of cooking is that none of the juices of the meat are lost.

When our *asados* were sufficiently roasted, the chief took them from the fire, and, driving the point of the spit into the ground, invited me, with a profound salaam, to commence my repast. Cutting a small piece from the roasted strip, and taking it upon the point of my knife, I put it, as a matter of course, into my mouth. At this the group around me broke into a boisterous laugh, and one swarthy fellow volunteered his services in teaching me how to eat *à la gaucho.* Drawing from his belt that inseparable companion which the gaucho never parts with — a long knife — the fellow cut off a strip of meat, and, holding one end with his fingers, dropped the other into his mouth; then followed a quick upward stroke with the knife, so close to his lips that I involuntarily started, severing the meat, and leaving a huge piece between his teeth. This feat was accomplished so rapidly that it astonished me; but as I found that it was the universal custom among the peons, I attempted to imitate them. But on the first trial the blade of my knife came in contact with the end of my nose, cutting it enough to draw blood. At this a loud laugh went through the group, at the expense of "Bostron the gringo," which name they insisted upon calling me, notwithstanding my efforts to show that Boston, and not Bostron, was my native city.

After the usual *siesta*, we continued our journey. Nothing of importance occurred until sunset, when, as I glanced across the plain, it seemed to at once become endowed with life. As the sun sank below the horizon, the owners of innumerable little burrows, which I had noticed through the greater part of the afternoon all over the plains, came out of the holes in such numbers as to astonish the uninitiated. As I watched one of the holes, I saw first a little round head, enlivened by a pair of black, twinkling eyes, peeping out; then followed a dusky body, and, finally, the animal, having become satisfied that our intentions were not unfriendly, sat by his doorway with the greatest nonchalance imaginable; but in a moment, after observing us curiously, he scampered off to join the hundreds, if not thousands, that were playing about in the grass around us.

Sometimes we saw an old female trotting along with four or five young ones on a visit to a neighbor; and frequently we saw some of these *reunions*, in which, while the old people were exchanging compliments, the juvenile members of the family chased each other merrily about the mounds.

These animals, which bore some resemblance to the marmots, were called by the natives *bizcacha*. The species is the *Lagostomus trichodactylus* of naturalists. Its habits are similar to those of the proper marmots; in size it exceeds the opossum of North America.

About the entrance of the burrows I noticed that a quantity of rubbish is usually collected, such as the bones of deceased relatives and of other animals, mixed with thistles, roots, &c. These *bizcachas* are found all over the pampas, as far south as the confines of Patagonia, beyond which, however, they have never been observed.

The singular habit of collecting all compact substances about their burrows seems peculiar to these animals. A traveller's watch, which had been lost, was found at the entrance to one of their domiciles, the animals having dragged it from the camp near by.

Darwin says the *bizcacha* is found as far north as 30° south latitude, and "abounds even to Mendoza, and is there replaced by an Alpine species."

It is not an inhabitant of the Banda Oriental, east of the Uruguay River.

The following accounts of North American species will be interesting to the reader, since they give a good idea of the habits of nearly allied species. Audubon and Bachman, in their Quadrupeds of North America, say of the prairie dog, "This noisy spermophile, or marmot, is found in numbers, sometimes hundreds, of families together, living in burrows on the prairies; and their galleries are so extensive as to render riding among them quite unsafe in many places. Their habitations are generally called dog towns, or villages, by the Indians and trappers, and are described as being intersected by streets (pathways) for their accommodation, and a degree of neatness and cleanliness is preserved. These villages or communities are, however, sometimes infested with rattlesnakes and other reptiles which feed upon these animals. The burrowing owl (*Surnia cunicularia*) is also found among them. Occasionally these marmots stood quite erect, and watched our movements, and then leaped into the air, all the time keeping an eye on us. Now and then, one of them, after coming out of his hole, issued a long and somewhat whistling note, perhaps a call or invitation to his neighbors, as several came out in a few moments. They are, as we think, more in the habit of feeding by night than in the daytime."

Lieutenant Abert, who observed the prairie dog in New Mexico, says it does not hibernate, "but is out all winter, as lively and as pert as on any summer day." Another observer states that it "closes accurately the mouth of its furrow, and constructs at the bottom of it a neat globular cell of fine dry grass, having an aperture at the top sufficiently large to admit a finger, and so compactly put together that it might almost be rolled along the ground, uninjured."

Perhaps different winter temperatures in different localities may govern the habit of hibernation.

The following sketch, from Kendall's narrative of the Texan expedition to Santa Fé, is so interesting that I present it to the reader: —

"We sat down upon a bank, under the shade of a mesquit, and leisurely surveyed the scene before us. Our approach had driven every one to his home in our immediate vicinity, but at the distance of some hundred yards the small mound of earth in front of each burrow was occupied by a prairie dog, sitting erect on his hinder legs, and coolly looking about for the cause of the recent commotion. Every now and then, some citizen, more adventurous than his neighbor, would leave his lodgings, on a flying visit to a friend, apparently exchange a few words, and then scamper back as fast as his legs would carry him. By and by, as we kept perfectly still, some of our near neighbors were seen cautiously poking their heads from out their holes, looking craftily, and at the same time inquisitively, about them. Gradually a citizen would emerge from the entrance of his domicile, come out upon his observatory, peek his head cunningly, and then commence yelping, somewhat after the manner of a young puppy, a quick jerk of the tail accompanying each yelp. It is this short bark alone that has given them the name of dogs, as they bear no more resemblance to that animal, either in appearance, action, or manner of living, than they do to the hyena.

"Prairie dogs are a wild, frolicsome, madcap set of fellows when undisturbed, uneasy, and ever on the move, and appear to take especial delight in chattering away the time, and visiting from hole to hole to gossip and talk over each other's affairs; at least, so their actions would indicate. When they find a good location for a village, and there is no water in the immediate vicinity, old hunters say they dig a well to supply the wants of the community. On several occasions I crept close to their villages without being observed, to watch their movements. Directly in the centre of one of them I noticed a very large dog, which, by his actions, and those of his neighbors, seemed the chief or big dog of the village. For at least an hour I watched this village; during this time the large dog received at least a dozen visits from his fellow-dogs, who would stop and chat with him a few minutes, and then run off to their holes. All this while he never left his seat at the entrance to his home, and I thought that I could perceive a gravity in his deportment not discernible in those by whom he was surrounded. Far is it from me to say that the visits he received were upon business, or had anything to do with the local government of the village, but it certainly appeared so."

The *bizcacha* does not live alone, for in each burrow I found a pair of small owls, of the species known by the name of the "Burrowing Owl of South America" (*Athene cunicularia*, Molina). As these birds are somewhat peculiar in their habits, and some few errors have crept into the writings of various authors regarding them, I will, for the information of those interested, present the following sketch of their habits, the result of observations which I made during my long journey.

I first met with this owl on the banks of the River San Juan, in the Banda Oriental, one hundred and twenty miles west of Montevideo, where a few pairs were observed devouring mice and insects during the daytime. From the river, travelling westward thirty miles, I did not meet a single individual, but after crossing the Las Vacas, and coming upon a sandy waste covered with scattered trees and low bushes, I again met with several.

Upon the pampas of the Argentine Republic they are found in great numbers, from a few miles west of Rosario, on the Paraná, latitude 32° 56′ south, to the vicinity of San Luis, where the pampas end, and a travesia or saline desert commences.

On these immense plains of grass it lives in company with the *bizcacha*. The habits of this bird are said to be the same as those of the species that inhabits the holes of the marmots upon the prairies of western North America. But this is not strictly correct, for one writer says of the northern species, "we have no evidence that the owl and marmot habitually resort to one burrow;" and Say remarks that "they were either common, though unfriendly, residents of the same habitation, or that our owl was the sole occupant of a burrow acquired by the right of conquest." In this respect they differ from their South American relatives, who live in perfect harmony with the *bizcacha*, and during the day, while the latter is sleeping, a pair of these birds stand a few inches within the main entrance of the burrow, and at the first strange sound, be it near or distant, they leave their station, and remain outside the hole, or upon the mound which forms the roof of the domicile. When man approaches, both birds mount above him in the air, and keep uttering their alarm note, with irides dilated, until he passes, when they quietly settle down in the grass, or return to their former place.

While on the pampas, I did not observe these birds taking prey during the daytime, but at sunset the *bizcachas* and owls leave their holes, and search for food, the young of the former playing about the birds as they alighted near them. They do not associate in companies, there being but one pair to each hole, and at night do not stray far from their homes.

In describing the North American burrowing owl, a writer says that the species "suddenly disappears in the early part of August," and that "the species is strictly diurnal."

The *Athene cunicularia* has not these habits. It does not disappear during any part of the year, and it is both nocturnal and diurnal, for though I did not observe it preying by day on the pampas, I noticed that it fed at all hours of the day and night on the north shore of the Plata, in the Banda Oriental.

At longitude 66° west our caravan struck the great saline desert that stretches to the Andes, and during fourteen days' travel on foot I did not see a dozen of these birds; but while residing outside tho town of San Juan, at the eastern base of the Andes, I had an opportunity to watch their habits in a locality differing materially from the pampas.

The months of September and October are the con jugal ones. During the middle of the former month I obtained a male bird with a broken wing. It lived in confinement two days, refusing to eat, and died from the effects of the wound. A few days later a boy brought me a female owl, with five eggs, that had been taken from her nest, five feet from the mouth of a burrow that wound among the roots of a tree.

She was fierce in her cage, and fought with wings and beak, uttering all the while a shrill, prolonged note, resembling the sound produced by drawing a file across the teeth of a saw. I supplied her with eleven full-grown mice, which were devoured during the first thirty-six hours of confinement.

I endeavored to ascertain if this species burrows its own habitation, but my observations of eight months failed to impress me with the belief that it does. I have conversed with intelligent persons who have been familiar with their habits, and never did I meet one that believed this bird to be its own workman. It places a small nest of feathers at the end of some occupied or deserted burrow, as necessity demands, in which are deposited from two to five white eggs, which are nearly spherical in form, and are a little larger than the eggs of the domestic pigeon.

In the Banda Oriental, where the country is as fine, and the favorite food of the owl more plentifully distributed than upon the pampas, this bird is not common in comparison with the numbers found in the latter locality. The reason is obvious. The *bizcacha* does not exist in the Banda Oriental, and consequently these birds have a poor chance for finding habitations.

On the pampas, where thousands upon thousands of *bizcachas* undermine the soil, there, in their true locality, the traveller finds thousands of owls. Again, along the bases of the Andes, where the *bizcacha* is rarely met with, we find only a few pairs. Does the hole, from which my bird was taken, appear to be the work of a bird or quadruped? The several works that I have been able to consult do not, in one instance, give personal observations relative to the burrowing propensities of this owl; from which fact, it will be inferred that it never has been caught in the act of burrowing.

We continued our journey while the sun left in the western heavens beautiful clouds of purple and gray as souvenirs of his company through the bright, warm day.

Around us on the plains were many animals in droves and herds, all preparing for the night. Troops of wild colts galloped homeward past us at the heels of their anxious mothers, who occasionally halted as if to dispute our right of passage through their territory. Darkness now set in, and soon the caravan halted for the night. I made my bed upon a raw hide, spread upon the top of the cargo in the cart, and was soon fast asleep; but I was shortly awakened by Don Facundo, who climbed into the cart, coughing loudly, and saying, by dumb show, pointing towards the south-west, that a *pampero* had commenced blowing. The wind, which was accompanied by rain and hail, violently shook the old cart, and whistled dolefully through its reed-covered sides. The don's cough had increased alarmingly, and he shivered with cold. "*Compañero*," he continually called out, giving me a poke to signify something that his ignorance of the Spanish language would not allow him to express more intelligibly, for he spoke only the tongue of his native province — the *Quichua*. I at last handed him my overcoat — an act of generosity that I afterwards regretted, for, though I applied several times for its restoration during the journey, he would not give it up, but ate, slept, and worked in it until we had crossed the country, and it was no longer serviceable.

CHAPTER VIII.

LIFE ON THE PAMPAS — CONTINUED.

THE night passed drearily away, and glad enough was I when day dawned, and the caravan was prepared to start.

Before we began to move, I retired to my cart, and changed my clothes, appearing before my companions in the unconfined and comfortable garb of a sailor.

The moment the peons, who were clustered around the fire, beheld me, they shouted to each other "*Montenero!*" a word which at that time I did not comprehend, but which, as I learned some months later, was the name of a particular class of bandits, who, about 1817, under the leadership of Artizas, filled the republic with consternation. Probably my sailor's dress resembled that of the robbers.

As the heavy mist rolled off the pampas, we discerned two shepherds driving their flocks to another pasture; and, as there was no hut in sight, they had probably passed the night sleeping upon their saddles, a common custom of the herdsmen. As a specimen of his skill, the younger of the two spurred his horse after a ram, the patriarch of the flock, and, as he drew near it, swung the lasso a few times around his head, and the fatal noose fell over the neck of the animal.

Dismounting from his horse, the gaucho jumped upon the ram, which began to run for dear life. As they scampered over the plain, I could plainly see pieces of wool flying from the animal's fleecy sides, as the rider plied his sharp, heavy spurs.

But rams were evidently not created for saddle-beasts, for the animal stumbled in his flight, upsetting, in a most ludicrous manner, his rider, who sprawled upon the turf.

Our caravan was now in motion. · As we proceeded on our course, the pampa gradually became more undulating, and was covered with a coarser herbage, shooting up in clumps to the height of a foot or more.

Soon after sunrise we met a party of eight horsemen from Mendoza, one of whom was armed with a spear, which was ornamented with a flag. About ten o'clock we passed a miserable *estancia* house, built of burnt bricks; we halted near it for the purpose of greasing the wheels of the carts. This was attended to by the *capataz.* He first cut into thin slices a pound of white native soap, and, after pouring hot water upon it, added a little salt, when he beat the whole together with a bunch of reeds drawn from the sides of the cart. While stirring this mixture, he would not permit me to look into the pail, but, turning his back on me, leaned over the mixture, muttering to himself, and making crosses over it, acting as if afraid that I would discover the recipe for the wheel-grease.

Before noon the caravan was again in motion. Three half-starved dogs that accompanied us gave chase to several deer that appeared in sight, but they were unable to approach them. These deer (*Cervus campestris*) are very common on the pampas. They have one habit which is common to the antelopes of North American prairies. When a person approaches them, they seem anxious to make his acquaintance, drawing near, and scrutinizing him with much curiosity. They are a small species, are of a yellowish-brown color on the upper parts, and white beneath the body. They are hunted by the gauchos in parties, who pursue and capture them with the *boliadores.*

A species of parrot (*Psittacus patagonus*) was observed flying in large flocks northward. At another time, I observed one or two very small species, of a green color, with grayish-white breasts. I have seen the same species in the Banda Oriental, flying in flocks of considerable size.

The clearness of the atmosphere gave great effect to the mirages that we constantly beheld around us. Twice we seemed to see large lakes far in advance of our caravan, but they vanished utterly upon our moving nearer them.

On our right, in the distance, the mirage so much resembled the ocean, that our carpenter, who had been in Buenos Ayres, pointed to it, exclaiming, "*El mar!*" (the sea).

Since leaving Rosario, we had met, along the road, flocks of small white gulls, feeding on carrion; but they, during this day's march, became more scarce, and soon disappeared entirely, and we saw no more of them on the pampas. The little ponds of water before noticed were now rarely encountered, and it became necessary, therefore, to lay in a stock before going farther. Each cart was supplied with a long earthen jar, lashed on behind, which held five or six gallons; these jars were filled; and these, with one or two demijohns stowed inside, comprised our water supply, — enough to last several days.

About three o'clock in the afternoon a long, dark cloud of dust appeared above the horizon in advance of our troop, and the *patron*, beside whose horse I was walking, informed me that it was "*una tropa de Mendoza.*" In the course of the next half hour it made its appearance in the road before us.

The troop presented a picturesque appearance as it slowly toiled along in divisions of ten carts each. The procession was headed by four or five asses, with pack-saddles and loads, and by a number of mules without luggage, driven by gauchos. After these followed the two divisions of carts, filled to such a degree with hides that their drivers were entirely hidden by them. This troop carried, as usual, a stock of firewood, consisting of heavy branches and gnarled stumps, which were lashed to the roofs of the carts. The relays consisted of thirty oxen and a few old cows, which were also under the guidance of a crew of almost savage gauchos. At sunset we passed a little knoll, conspicuous in the midst of the vast plain, surmounted by a small dwelling; beyond it lay an extensive *pantana* (swamp), that we were obliged to traverse, although the labor it cost us was not inconsiderable. Several yokes of oxen were detached from the after carts, and connected with those of the leading ones, when, with a vast amount of uproar and merciless goading, each cart was drawn, in turn, through the mire.

We encamped beyond the *pantana*, and supped

upon sliced pumpkins, boiled with bits of meat, and seasoned with salt. I would remark here that the gauchos never use salt with roasted meat, but frequently sprinkle it into a stew, if the heterogeneous messes which they compound and boil in iron pots are worthy of that title.

Our meal was served in genuine pampa fashion; one iron spoon and two cow's horns, split in halves, were passed around the group, the members of which squatted upon their haunches, and freely helped themselves from the kettle.

Even in this most uncivilized form of satisfying hunger there is a peculiar etiquette, which the most lowly peon invariably observes. Each member of the company in turn dips his spoon, or horn, into the centre of the stew, and draws it in a direct line *towards* him, never allowing it to deviate to the right or the left.

By observing this rule, each person eats without interfering with his neighbor. Being ignorant of this custom, I dipped my horn into the mess at random, and fished about in it for some of the nice bits. My companions regarded this horrid breach of politeness with scowls of impatience; they declared, with some warmth, to the *capataz* that gringos did not know how to eat, and, "as they lived upon dogs in their own distant country, they come to the great Argentine Republic to get food and grow fat on the gauchos." I apologized as well as I could, and endeavored, during the remainder of the meal, to eat according to gaucho etiquette.

As night came on, a brilliant scene was developed before us. As far as the eye could reach, we beheld the ruddy glow of a distant conflagration of the pampa herbage. Fortunately it did not approach us, but after giving us a view of one of the most sublime and magnificent sights in nature, it faded at last away into the south.

During the night I suffered much from the cold.

I was awakened on the following morning (Sunday) by my peon, who gave me to understand, by gestures, that the *asado* was prepared. As I joined the company at the fire, the *patron* approached us with a poncho filled with watermelons, which he had purchased at the *estancia* house on the mound; of these we ate heartily, and they were delicious.

As the pieces of rind fell to the ground, they were eagerly devoured by the dogs, and by two little children that accompanied the troop. I often pitied these little neglected creatures, and shared with them my fare. I gave them a portion of my share of the melons, and their gratitude was warm and demonstrative: they were going to Mendoza with their mother, the wife of one of the drivers.

This was the first Sunday spent on the road; and as there was a plenty of thistles for our fire, and good grass for the cattle, the day was passed without leaving camp, the gauchos amusing themselves with a pack of cards.

I had with me an illustrated Testament. The peons, after gazing intently upon a picture of the crucifixion, declared that I was a *Cristiano*, and invited me to play cards with them.

During the next day we saw a plenty of wire-grass, and at least thirty deer grazed within a mile of the wagons. No cattle were to be seen. The wind, which blew from the north-east, was very warm. Our course was west.

In a halt which we made during the day's travel, I turned my blanket into a poncho, by cutting a hole in the middle, and thrusting my head through the aperture. When the gauchos saw my new garment, they shouted in admiration; and one or two, who could speak a little Spanish, exclaimed, "Gaucho, Bostron!"

At dark we camped near a corral, or cattle-yard, formed of the *tunas*, a species of wild cactus. At supper we ate our last morsel of meat brought from Rosario; the bones were heated upon the fire, then broken, and the marrow greedily eaten by the men.

Throughout the night the mosquitos and flies tormented me, until I was obliged to roll my head in a blanket.

At dawn the troop set out, in the midst of a heavy shower, without eating, and kept on until Don José commanded a halt, in order to kill an old cow which had been purchased at an *estancia* the day before.

We camped near a collection of mud-huts, surrounded by a gigantic growth of cactus, and called *Guardia de la Esquina.* It was the first place we had met that approached the dignity of a village; but its qualifications for that title were extremely limited.

Half a mile south of the *Esquina* a low brick structure, resembling in form two sugar-boxes, — one set on its side, and the other placed perpendicularly against it, — stood alone on the plain. A melancholy story is connected with this structure.

Don B., a rich *estanciero*, owned many miles of the surrounding country; and the report that he had much money buried in the earth about his brick *casa* excited the cupidity of the Indians. They came from the south in a large party, ransacked the place, and carried away the hoarded treasure, after cutting the throats of the don, his child, and sixteen peons, all of whom were afterwards buried in a common grave.

While several of the men were slaughtering the cow, the carpenter, with two or three others of the troop, guided by a man sent from the *Esquina*, visited the hole in which the bodies lay. The earth had fallen in as the bodies had undergone decomposition, for they had been buried in the usual manner of the pampas, without any other covering than the clothes worn at the time of death. On reaching the spot, the gaucho from the town conversed at length with our men; but the substance of his conversation was unintelligible to me. The carpenter threw off his poncho, and commenced digging in good earnest, with a heavy hoe, which he had brought from the carts.

Two little crosses marked the spot where father and child were laid. As his implement sank deep into the earth, a dull, crushing sound announced that it had buried itself in the skull of a man, and the digger drew forth the tool with a human head, greatly decomposed, upon it. The hoe had entered between the jaws. At the sight a sickening sensation came over me; but the *Santigueños*, who had left their work, and were grouped around the grave, laughed at my sensations, and scraped away the matted hair from the ghastly head, which was still red with blood, with their knives, which they returned to their sheaths without cleaning. It was a disgusting picture — the natives, with their bare legs and breasts besmeared with the blood of the animal they had just butchered, passing the head from hand to hand, and joking at a calamity that should have excited their pity and commiseration.

The head of the child was also exhumed, and the two were placed in a bag to be taken to Mendoza, where the priests could pray over them; for so long as they remained uninterred in the *panteon* (consecrated burying-ground), the souls that once animated them would be kept from the land of bliss.

The attack by the Indians had occurred only a short time before our visit, and the prints of their horses' hoofs were not obliterated from the spot where the butchery was done.

Our caravan continued its course until nine o'clock, and passed Cabeza del Tigre, a place well known as having been the scene of a transaction equally lamentable with the one just recorded. The facts were related to me by a gentleman in whose word I placed great confidence.

Three English merchants who had made large fortunes in California were returning to England, and, having their treasures with them, would not risk a passage around Cape Horn, but landing at Valparaiso, crossed the Cordillera to Mendoza, and there, in as private a manner as possible, engaged for the passage of their property in a large troop of carts bound to Rosario.

Far better would it have been, as it proved, had they trusted to the ocean, rather than to have attempted crossing, with their treasures, a country inhabited by a treacherous and lawless people. Despite all their efforts to keep the matter secret, it became known that a party of "gringos" from the land of gold were about to cross the pampas. The English character is proverbially daring; the three merchants pursued their course, regardless of the reports of the natives and the advice of friends. The great travesia was crossed, and they passed through the provinces of San Luis and Cordova in safety; but when they reached the vicinity of Cabeza del Tigre, several hundred Indians, mounted on horseback, and armed with spears, met them on the road and offered battle.

The *patron* ordered the carts to be formed into a square, and the peons got within its protection. The three white men and the *patron* and *capataz* fought desperately. The Englishmen were armed with double-barrelled guns, and for a time kept the enemy at bay; one of them shot a *cacique* (chief), and this for a time kept the tide of battle in their favor.

At that period, Cabeza del Tigre was a military fort; the report of the guns aroused the soldiers, but for a time they were undecided how to act, through fear of the savages. At a moment when a vigorous attack by all the peons would have decided the battle, and some soldiers were even seen in the distance, galloping towards the spot, the Indians, with a desperate effort, succeeded in despatching the Englishmen, secured their treasure, and, before the small military force arrived, hurried away beyond their reach.

The amount of money carried off by the Indians was reported to have been many thousand doubloons. Though this sum seems large, the amount taken must have been considerable, for my informant said that, for several weeks after the event had transpired, Rio Quarto and El Moro were visited by parties of Indians, who were readily admitted as peaceful visitors, their purpose being to exchange gold onzas for silver, as they obtained more in *bulk* of the latter metal by the transaction. The silver coin was manufactured into rings and other trinkets. Those intended for the ears were several inches in diameter, and so heavy that they required to be supported by fastenings to the hair of the head.

However lightly the peons regarded Indian murders at the *Esquina*, their faces assumed a very different expression from that of mirth, when, during the next day, a troop of mules from the interior passed us, and the *patron* informed our company that the savages had cut the throats of eleven soldiers not far from the very road that we were on. Their boisterous mirth was over; and during the several succeeding days I do not remember of having heard a single song, or a light word, in the company. They all looked dubious enough; one or two tried to amuse themselves by drawing their knives across their throats in a significant manner before me, but their efforts only made me smile, and provoked the other members of the party.

During the next day we passed over a country destitute of pasturage; but the road ran along the River Quarto for an eighth of a mile, and we had, therefore, some muddy water to drink.

At this place the river trended to the west; the right bank was about twenty-five feet in height, and as steep as a wall; the left side was sloping and covered with vines, thorn-bushes, and gigantic cacti, which in one place formed a natural enclosure, in which I passed fully an hour, in watching the movements of a bird resembling our turtle-dove. The river was about twenty feet wide, and had a sluggish current.

We passed at dusk the hamlet of Saladillo, but could not catch a glimpse of it, though Don Manuel wished me to visit it with him; for, said he, "*Hay mucho pan, mucho queso, e muchas muchachas tambien*"—"There is a plenty of bread and cheese, and also a great many young ladies."

Upon the pampas, winds from opposite quarters frequently meet and form little whirlwinds, that sometimes take up a large cloud of dust, which helps to relieve the monotony of the journey; but these clouds of dust not only settle upon the weary travellers, covering them with the fine powder, but render them exceedingly thirsty. Such was my condition, when, wayworn and weary, the orders were spoken to halt and prepare to camp. We had arrived at the borders of a salt lagoon, which was filled with wild fowl. The confused sounds that came from hundreds of ducks, teals, loons, white cranes, sand-pipers, and plovers, made it a second Babel. Around the borders of the lake the soil was white with saline matter, and covered with the footprints of the *bizcacha*, and I observed that the grass was trodden down into little paths leading from their burrows to the water.

Our last cow had been eaten, and we had already fasted twenty-four hours, when we prepared to camp, and I was only too glad when the directions were given to slaughter an ox; and, judging by the alacrity with which the men set about executing their orders, they were as glad as myself of the prospect of breaking their fast.

The animal was thrown down and butchered; its blood was allowed to run into a hole dug for the purpose, and suffered to clot, when it was placed in a bladder, and suspended from the roof of a cart, to be kept for the purpose of coloring the handles of the small goads — the *picanos chicos* — of the drivers. While a portion of the men were attending to this work, others were engaged in caring for their cattle, and others were lighting a fire, which, as other fuel was not to be had, was made of the argols of cattle. Soon huge pieces of the meat were steaming and crackling before the heat, and before darkness had completely enveloped us, we were luxuriating on fresh beef and some *matés*.

Supper over, we took refuge in the carts, and although the noise of the wild fowl on the lake was continued, which to my ears was a very sweet music, I confess I was soon asleep.

On the next morning, bright and early, we again took up our march, and through that day and the next pushed on over the plains.

From the hamlet of Saladillo, sixty miles westward, we met but two or three huts and a few salt lagoons. Near one of the latter, six black-necked swans flew over my head, and I noticed many other fowls that are common in North America, such as the stilt, green-winged teal, pin-tailed duck, and the great blue heron. The road was everywhere covered with saline matter,

9

and the reflection of the sun's rays upon it was painful to the sight.

As we passed a mud hut near one of the lagoons, a woman came out to sell melons and pumpkins. I visited the hut, but, although it was far neater than the majority of ranchos on the pampas, it was a miserable place to live in, for the fleas and *chinchas* were far too numerous for comfort. The hut was twelve feet long and seven feet high; it was a mere framework of sticks lashed together with strips of hide, and covered with cornstalks, reeds, and mud. It contained two beds propped against the wall; three or four bottles, a couple of spoons, and an iron kettle with the *maté*, were the contents of one corner, and the only furniture the cabin contained. I noticed long strings of sliced pumpkins drying in the sun; these vegetables keep many poor peons from starving during the winter time. They are very generally grown, and are used throughout the country.

The woman appeared to be frugal and industrious, for she had cultivated a large patch of melons, and raised numerous families of hens, turkeys, and muscovy ducks. And I would remark, in passing, that this woman was not an exception, as regards general fitness for the duties of life, to her sex throughout the republic; indeed, they seem better fitted to act in any responsible position, or attend to any duty, than the men; for of the large class called *chinos* (pronounced cheeñows), produced by intermarriage of the Spanish and Indians, that cover the pampas, and compose the lower classes in the more civilized towns, the women are the most energetic and faithful.

Our march for several days was monotonous and eventless. Late in the afternoon of Tuesday, April 10, we camped on the open plain, one mile distant from the little town of Punta del Sauce (Willow Point), so called from the scattered willows around it. It contains between two and three hundred inhabitants, as Don José informed me. The people must have been sharp-sighted, for we had hardly come in sight of the place before we saw the townsfolk approaching us.

Among the many visitors was one that very particularly attracted my attention, and for some minutes puzzled me to decide as to which sex it belonged. It was astride a one-eared donkey, which it halted before our party, without dismounting. While this person conversed with the *patron* in gutturals, I had a fair opportunity to survey its ugly features and shapeless form. The head was enormous, and the hair stuck out in every direction in wiry curls. The swarthy face, huge lips, and large bright eyes showed that the negro blood prevailed over the Indian. What added still more to its ferocious expression was the long, projecting incisors, which, when the creature spoke, caused it to resemble a wild beast more than a human being. It wore a calico tunic, unbuttoned behind, from the skirts of which protruded a thick pair of round legs, that drummed the sides of the jackass, in lieu of whip or spur. When Don José informed me that it was *una señorita* (a woman), I uttered an exclamation of surprise. But I had not seen all the beauties, for during the remainder of our journey we fell in with several others, counterparts of this woman, and, if possible, still more ugly and disagreeable. During our stay at Punta del Sauce, several young women (half Indian) brought a poor quality of salt to sell, together with cheese and melons. I gave an old Indian, who was one of our drivers, and who had on several occasions shown me a kindness, a pound of the best salt that I could procure. After tasting it, he put it carefully aside, perhaps with the intention of selling it, as he did not use any on the road. While the *patron's* back was turned, Don Facundo, my cook and attendant, sold my meat to a woman of the village for a few ears of corn; but, as I did not understand his Quichua language, it was useless for me to remonstrate. The don, with his messmates, feasted upon their new dish without extending an invitation to its should-be rightful owner, who was obliged to fast for the next thirty-six hours. The rascals told Don José some lie to account for the loss of my meat, and that was the last of it.

Again we took up our line of march. On the next day we came again to the river, and I noticed that its banks were in some places perforated with the burrows or holes of parrots. In this place the water was clear, and I did not notice any saline deposit upon its banks.

The woman in our caravan, of whom I have spoken before, on this day fell and drove a splinter into her foot; and, as she could not extract it, I offered my services as *medico*. As I was successful, she seemed overwhelmed with gratitude, and from that time she was almost the only friend that I had among the people of the troop.

During our journey on this day, as they were riding along, the *patron* and *capataz* entered upon a geographical discussion, and as their opinions differed widely, they called upon me to decide between them; but as Don José had the reputation of a great scholar among his men, I did not dare to give him any opinion of my own, and they went on in the same tone as before.

"Where *is* Bostron?" asked the *capataz.*

"Bostron is in France, to be sure," replied the other.

"That cannot be, because France is a great way off, and has not got any moon; and the gringo told me, the other night, that there is a moon in Bostron, and North America is in the same place."

"Fool!" exclaimed the scholar, "North America is in England, the country where the gringos live that tried to take Buenos Ayres."

Each was confident that he was right, and, believing that

"Where ignorance is bliss, 'tis folly to be wise,"

I left them to themselves.

The caravan dragged on its weary pace; at length, as darkness came on, the peons, looking out of their wagons, shouted, as they pointed ahead of us, "La Reduccion!" "Reduccion!"

Soon we drew near the town, which lay surrounded with fields of corn. As we approached the place, old women and young people came out to meet us, bringing soft cheese, salt, and unripe melons for sale. When we reached the outskirts, Don José wheeled his mule and dismounted; each peon cried "Sh-u-u-ah!" to his oxen, and the tired caravan halted for the night. On the next morning we again took up the march, and made considerable progress before sunrise; but the wind from the north soon came laden with a most torrid heat, and we were obliged to come to a pause, luckily close beside a river, the valley of which was filled with tall flags and willows. The water was very clear, and ran over a bed of sand, filled with scales of mica and quartz.

At dusk we prepared to cross the stream (the Rio Quarto) at Paso Durazno (Peach Pass). At this ford the river, which was very wide and shallow, has a swift current and a stony bed. We intended to spend the night on the opposite side, so that we could have a fair start next day. The men stripped themselves, and stood in a line from one bank to the other. As each cart was drawn slowly past by the oxen, the cruel fellows goaded them until the blood trickled from the punctures, at the same time yelling loud enough to be heard a mile at least. Beyond the river was a hill covered with bushes, and called by the natives San Bernardo, and to the right of the road a small collection of ranchos surrounded by patches of corn.

From the summit of San Bernardo I caught sight of the distant tops of the Cerro Moro, resembling a silver cloud in the clear heavens. During the evening we occupied ourselves in drawing trunks of trees from the river valley, and lashing them to the outside of the carts, and in filling the jars behind the carts with water, preparatory to a dry march.

While we were at supper, three pampa Indian women passed the camp. Two were very masculine in appearance, the third young and handsome. They were dressed in loose gowns. As they passed they smiled, apparently at the consternation their appearance produced among the peons, who seemed ready to sink into the ground with fear at the presence of supposed spies. The women were from the pampas, and were on their way to the village of Rio Quarto. The excitement which their advent created among our people was a long time in being lulled, and even when I sought my bed in the cart I heard the eager and animated voices of the peons, who were busily engaged in preparing for an onslaught from the dreaded savages.

CHAPTER IX.

FROM RIO QUARTO TO CERRO MORO.

ON Saturday, April 14, we unlashed our oxen before Rio Quarto. All along the road the *patron* and *capataz* had spoken of this village, which they described as being very beautiful, filled with fine white-washed houses, and inhabited by a wealthy class of people, many of whom owned thousands of cattle which were pastured upon *estancias* outside the village. Besides, it was here that the great Indian battles had taken place: both the gentlemen failed to inform me that the Indians were generally the victors, not the *Cristianos*, as they called the citizens of the village.

The woman, with her two children, who had travelled with us, set out for a visit to the village, and, bent upon exploring the place, I accompanied them.

Rio Quarto is situated upon a plain, and differs but little in its general appearance from the other towns It is laid out in a regular manner, and is shut in by a mud wall two or three feet in thickness, and five or more in height. The wall is surrounded by a broad trench about four feet deep, which serves as a defence against the Indians. It was hard for me at first to understand the value of this dry ditch; but I learned afterwards that no more formidable defence was needed against an attack from the savages; for, during engagements, they never leave the backs of their horses, and as they cannot leap the ditches, nor scramble out of them when in, they avoid the obstacles with care.

At the time of our visit to Rio Quarto, there was no little commotion among the people; for news had been received of a projected Indian attack, and the news seemed to be confirmed by the recent intelligence that the savages had drawn off from other places, and were concentrating near the town.

The garrison had been reënforced by soldiers sent by the governor of the province. These troops, in their ignorance and alarm, had loaded an old iron gun in a most singular manner; for they had first put in several pounds of lead balls and slugs, then rammed in a heavy wadding, and finally charged with powder. I judged from their manner of loading cannons, that their efficiency as soldiers, should an attack be made, would prove of little value.

The houses of Rio Quarto are built of mud, and thatched with dry grass; the streets are of mud, the walls are of mud, and the ideas of the people are muddy thick. They seem merely to exist, rather than live with any idea of what living is. The few rich men of the village own the cattle that feed in the surrounding country, while the poorer classes support themselves as best they can, living on a meagre diet of pumpkins, peaches, corn, and rarely, meat. They sometimes labor for their wealthier townspeople, but usually sleep the time away. All the persons that I met were squalid in appearance, and the children were half naked.

The gardens about the town contained but little more than quince or peach trees. At the corners of the streets were filthy *pulperias* (small shops), and the only decent building in town was the church in the plaza, which was surmounted by a dome, steeple, and cross. On the side of the building, in place of windows, hemispherical holes were cut, and covered with muslin; in fact, the only glass that I saw was in the two or three street lamps. As it was Saturday, the *vigilantes* were sweeping the plaza with a large hide, attached to the surcingle of a horse which was driven around the square.

Having fasted since the day before, I purchased some bread made in the place, and shared it with my companions. It was poor in quality, and contained no small amount of sand and sticks. The flour had been brought on mules from Mendoza, three hundred and eighty miles distant, and bread was something of a luxury in Rio Quarto.

After quite a stay, nearly a day in length, we left Rio Quarto. Our route lay over an undulating pampa, covered with long grass, but scarcely a herd of cattle could be seen, and for miles we met with no evidence that human beings inhabited the country. Water was seldom found, but the small quantities that we discovered lay in little hollows of two or three inches in depth, and was of a better quality than any that we had met with on the road.

The herdsmen are extremely dirty in their habits, and those who performed the duty of drivers in our caravan were particularly filthy; many of them, indeed, showed no token of ablutions performed for many weeks.

While the troop halted to rest the oxen close by a pool of water, I could not resist the temptation to bathe, and, stripping myself, enjoyed the luxury of a good bath, which had been denied me for more than a fortnight. I then washed my linen, and returned to the men who were sitting around the fire, solacing themselves with a round of *matés.* They laughed heartily at my ideas of cleanliness, and asked, through Don Manuel, my interpreter, what opinion I had formed of themselves, who could cross the pampas and return again — a journey of eighty days — without once applying water to their skins. I replied that it was my opinion that they were very dirty fellows, and suited for the country in which they lived. At this answer they again laughed, and replied that white skins, like those of all foreigners, were exceedingly inconvenient, because of the great attention required for retaining its color.

The next day was Sunday, but the caravan kept on its way as usual.

Throughout the whole day the sun poured down its scorching rays, and the hot wind from the north was accompanied by myriads of mosquitos and minute black flies.

We had nothing left of the ox that had been finished the day before, save the head, which had hung upon the outside of one of the carts for four days, and was in a decomposed state. The sight of the filthy cranium caused me to wonder why it was not thrown away, for I never dreamed that it was intended for any use; but it was not to be wasted.

We had not eaten anything since the morning of the previous day; but at noon a halt was ordered, a quantity of dried argols of cattle were collected, a fire was kindled with flint and steel, which the herdsman always carries in his belt, and an old iron kettle, belonging to one of the carts, was partly filled with water, and placed above the coals. When it was properly adjusted, the men piled the dry dung around the bottom so as to retain the heat beneath it, and soon the water was bubbling and beginning to boil. The old and decomposed head of the ox was now brought to the fire. Its contents — the brains, &c. — were scooped out, and thrown into the pot, and with the addition of a little salt the stew was complete. At any other time the sight of such a mess would have disgusted me, but things were changed now, and, faint with hunger, I watched the boiling of the stew with no little interest.

At last Facundo, the cook, who had stood beside the kettle during the whole time, and had occasionally tasted the dish with his horn spoon, and as often had declared it "excellent," summoned the party to dinner. I remember well that I scrambled with the others to get at it, but I only procured a very small portion, which I was obliged to swallow so hot that I scalded my tongue severely.

The meal was finished in a much shorter time than I have occupied in describing it, and soon each driver hurried off to lasso his oxen, which they lashed to the yokes, and we were again in motion.

About three o'clock we drew up beside some rough hummocks of earth to feed the cattle; the country was more undulating, and was here covered with wire-grass, which the cattle at once began to feed upon. I had here a first view of the Sierra of Cordova, the boundary line of the provinces of Cordova and San Luis.

The *patron* had purchased an old cow a few days before at San Bernardo, and having stinted the men as long as possible, he now decided to kill her. This was no easy matter, for the cow was as stubborn and furious as any bull, and had only been kept manageable by attaching her by a strap of hide to another animal equally fierce and ungovernable. These two animals had required particular care to prevent them from straying from the troop.

The strap that bound the two brutes together was cut asunder, and Don Manuel, the best gaucho of the party, set off in full chase of the doomed cow, swinging the lasso above his head, and urging on his horse by repeated applications of the enormous spurs that adorned his heels. When within eight or ten yards of the animal, the valiant don, with a fiercely uttered *ca-jo*, let fly the lasso, and at the same time wheeled his horse.

The cow, continuing on her headlong course, was suddenly brought up by the fatal noose tightening around her neck, and she went tumbling to the ground.

It was a wonder to me that the fall did not break her neck. She arose, bewildered, to her feet, and for an instant paused; but quickly divining the cause of her entrapment, she lowered her head, and made a run at the don and his horse; but the little animal that he bestrode having been well trained, was in a gallop before the cow drew near, and the lasso kept as tight as ever. The victim now uttered a loud bellow, and charged blindly at one of the cart-wheels: the force of the shock with which she struck rendered her wild with rage. She bellowed until the tightened noose choked all utterance, when she renewed her charges upon the men, horses, and carts. The *patron* now called loudly upon Maistro Ramon, one of the leading men, and, mounting his mule, Maistro galloped to the rescue.

The cow stood at bay, tossing up the earth with her nose, and stamping wrathfully with her hoofs; but her new assailant was a skilful gaucho. He started her, and threw his noose around one of her hind legs, when, galloping in opposite directions, the two men tripped the animal up, and stretched her upon the ground.

One of the peons fastened her four hoofs together with a piece of hide, and another man officiated as butcher. With his long knife he despatched her, and in half an hour she was skinned, cut up, and divided among the carts. When the meat was cooked I ate a moderate-sized piece, and strolled away from the men, who were gormandizing beside the fires, to watch the curious feast that the birds of prey were making upon the refuse parts of the cow.

Whether some of the birds of prey discover their food by means of sight or scent, has long been an unsettled question, some naturalists affirming that the former sense is their principal guide, and others that the latter is the only one.

Audubon, in his Ornithological Biography, gives some accounts of interesting experiments that he made with the turkey-buzzard, proving that this bird is attracted only by the organs of vision to its food. Other writers have offered other observations, corroborative of Audubon's position. And I would here present a fact that came to my observation, concerning one of the most common South American birds, helping to show that Audubon was correct in his opinion.

Before the cow was butchered, I searched the plain, but not a single caracara (*Polyborus Brasiliensis*), the well-known carrion-lover of the pampas, was visible. There was no wind stirring, and had there been, the scent of the fresh offal of the cow could certainly not have been carried to any distance. But the cow had hardly been butchered when a single caracara was seen on the horizon. He had hardly alighted beside the offal when another and another were distinguished, coming in the path of the first. For half an hour they continued to arrive, all coming from one direction, and as one alighted upon the carcass another came in view, flying straight to the spot where the others were collected. I remained watching them for a long time, and when I left there were at least fifty birds on the spot, and the line of flight was still unbroken; each new comer being greeted by the others with their indistinct guttural ca-ra-ca-ra! Now, of course, all these birds had not been attracted by the sense of smell, for the supposition that the scent of the newly killed animal could have travelled miles in a few moments is simply preposterous.

The birds must have been flying in air, on the look-out for food, and, as they are gifted with a most wonderful vision, on seeing the first one hurrying in one direction, the natural inference must have been — if birds draw inferences — that he was hurrying to something to eat. The birds nearest him followed him, others followed them, and they arrived at the slaughter-ground in the order in which they started for it — the nearest first, and the farthest last.

Perhaps a more extended account of the caracara will not be uninteresting to the reader.

The caracaras feed upon anything that comes in their way, gleaning carrion like the buzzards, and killing other birds like the hawks. I even once saw one attack a lamb, but the old dam interfered, and after receiving some rebuffs from the bird, succeeded in protecting her offspring from her enemy.

This bird possesses an unenviable reputation as a thief among the gauchos, and, as it kills young birds, lambs, even seizes the game that the hunter has just killed, it is far from being a favorite with any class of the people.

It inhabits an extended geographical range. I have seen it in south-western Texas and in most parts of South America. This species is the "Mexican Eagle." A fine bird, indeed, for the emblem of a nation! — it is emblazoned upon the Mexican flag; but we of the North must not be too critical, for we still retain upon our banner and coin that selfish thief, the bald-headed eagle — the most relentless robber and pirate of our rapacious birds.

The caracara is sometimes found in company with

the *Gallinazo* (*Cathartes atratus*), also known to the people on the Plata as the carrion crow. This latter bird is found north of the Rio Negro in various localities, not being met with except near the rivers and damp places. I did not observe them about Buenos Ayres, but found them afterwards common dwellers about the vicinity of Mendoza, along the bases of the Andes. The habits of the turkey-buzzard are so well known that I will not dwell further upon them here. I have noticed that the species seems to be tamer on the southern continent than it is on the northern. It has the extended range of one hundred degrees of latitude.

Though somewhat repulsive from the offensive odor which it receives from its food, this bird is one of the most useful species. As a scavenger and remover of decaying animal matter in the tropics it is invaluable, and it is properly protected and cared for in many cities.

At noon, April 6, we reached the mountain range that had loomed up before us for several days, and camped at its base. The sierra terminated in low hills, barren and destitute of verdure, save where occasional clumps of dwarf trees grew about their bases. A little rivulet, taking its rise in the mountains, flowed down through a deep fissure in the soil, and afforded good water for the cattle.

We remained at this comfortable camp through the remainder of the day and night, but started early the next morning.

The monotony of our journey was disturbed by the arrival and passing of a troop of sixty mules loaded with little barrels of sugar and hide bales of *yerba* (tea). This troop was driven by six men, and was bound to Mendoza. Like similar parties, the troop was headed by an old mare carrying a bell, the sound of which keeps the animals from straying away.

Though the mule is a stubborn creature, it has a very strong affection for the *madrina*, as the mare is called, and follows her like a colt. I have often watched two large troops approaching each other from opposite directions, in some place where the road was very narrow, as in a mountain defile, and have been surprised to witness the absence of all bewilderment on the part of the animals. Though both troops were crowded together, each mule kept with his own party, and followed the sound of the *madrina's* bell, even in the darkest night.

Having wound around the point of a sierra, our caravan kept on until dusk, when we camped for the night, supping upon beef and four armadillos, which the peons had caught during the day in the grass.

The armadillo is a singular animal, both in appearance and mode of living. Four species are found upon the pampas. In Buenos Ayres they are known by the general name of *peluda*. Darwin applies this term to a particular species — *Dasypus villosus*.

The gauchos call the female armadillo *Mulita*, which name Darwin uses to distinguish a separate species. The male is called *Cinquizcho*.

As my readers doubtless are aware, the body of the animal is protected by a coat of hard scales, consisting of several divisions, adapted to the locomotion of the animal. Its head is pointed, and is scantily clothed with little tufts of hair which grow out between the scales. The feet and legs are short, giving the animal, when walking, a waddling gait, similar to that of the tortoise. The toe nails are sharp, and admirably shaped for rapid burrowing in the ground.

All the armadillos, with the exception of one species, which is nocturnal in its habits, are diurnal, retiring to their burrows at dusk, and coming forth at dawn to feed upon the roots of grass, insects, worms, &c.

Their burrows do not exceed eight feet in depth. In these retreats the female brings forth four or five young, which follow her, soon after birth, in her journeyings upon the plains. When man approaches them, if near a burrow, they retire into it; but when they are distant from home they endeavor to hide in the grass until all danger is past. While in most localities these animals were found, to the south of Rosario and Mendoza they were very numerous. The females of one species that I frequently met had two mammæ. I think the others had four or six.

The flesh of the armadillo is white and delicate, and has the flavor of young pork. The peons cook the animal by dividing the two shells at the junction, and burying the whole in hot ashes and coals, and allowing it to bake until thoroughly done.

Darwin, in his account of these animals, says that three species of armadillos are found in this country, while a fourth species, the *Mulita*, does not come as far south as Bahia Blanca. Of these first mentioned are the *Dasypus minutus*, or Pichy; the *D. villosus*, or Peludo; and the *D. apar*, or Mataco. The Pichy is found several hundred miles farther south than any species.

The Apar, commonly called mataco, is remarkable by having only three movable bands, the rest of its tessellated covering being nearly inflexible. It has the power of rolling itself into a perfect sphere, like one kind of English wood-louse. In this state it is safe from the attack of dogs; for the dog, not being able to take the whole in its mouth, tries to bite one side, and the ball slips away. The smooth, hard covering of the mataco offers a better defence than the short spines of the hedgehog. The pichy prefers a very dry soil, and the sand plains near the coast, where for many months it cannot taste water, are its favorite resort. It often tries to escape notice by squatting close to the ground. In the course of a day's ride near Bahia Blanca several were generally met with. The instant one was perceived it was necessary, in order to catch it, almost to tumble off one's horse, for in the soft soil the animal burrowed so quickly that its hinder quarters would almost disappear before we could alight. It seems almost a pity to kill such nice little animals; for, as a gaucho said, while sharpening his knife on the back of one (the gauchos often use a portion of the armadillo's armor for a knife hone), "*Son tan mansos*" (they are so quiet).

Another writer informs us that the armadillos "burrow to the extent of thirteen or fourteen feet, descending in an abruptly sloping direction for some three or four feet, then taking a sudden bend, and inclining slightly upward. Much of their food is procured beneath the surface of the earth. They possess carnivorous tastes, and feed upon dead cattle, insects, snails, snakes, as well as upon roots. The giant armadillo, according to one writer, digs up dead bodies in the burial grounds."

"When hunting these animals," says Waterton, "the first point is to ascertain if the inhabitant of the burrow is at home, which is discovered by pushing a stick into each hole, and watching for the egress of mosquitos. If any come out, the armadillo is in his hole. A long rod is thrust into the burrow in order to learn its direction, and a hole is dug in the ground to meet the end of the stick. A fresh departure is taken from that point, the rod is again introduced, and by dint of laborious digging the animal is at last captured. Meanwhile the armadillo is not idle, but continues to burrow in the sand in the hopes of escaping its persecutors. It cannot, however, dig so fast as they can, and is at last obliged to yield."

While we were lying behind the fire, after supper, a loud, creaking noise in the distance announced the approach of a caravan from Mendoza. As it drew near our dogs commenced barking, and were answered by the mule of the captain of the caravan with a loud bray. While the concert continued, other mules and asses took up the strain, and our camp was "vocal with melodious sounds" as the caravan came in sight. As they passed I counted sixteen wagons heavily laden with cargoes of hides.

A fresh breeze from the east was springing up as I lay down on my hide amid dogs and sleeping natives, and as I dozed away, it seemed difficult to decide which of the two was the most agreeable bedfellow; for as it grew colder, and a sharp frost came on, one dirty fellow crowded me off my hide, and a still more filthy dog, covered with fleas, crept under my blanket, from the shelter of which no moderate effort of mine could remove him. At last, becoming desperate amid dirt and flea-bites, I dislodged the intruder by a kick sharp enough to cause him to cry out, and arouse his master Facundo, who waxed exceedingly wrathful at such demonstrations on his dog by a "gringo."

Early the next morning the caravan was on the march, and for an hour our course led over high hills and across one small stream that flowed from the sierra behind us. After crossing these hills I observed beyond, along the bases of some low mountains, a few fields of corn and a number of mud huts, where dwelt, in all their indolence, a party of natives — half Indians, half Spanish, or Christians, as Don Manuel called all his countrymen on the pampas.

As our troop trudged slowly along, some fifteen men, women, and children followed in our track, offering to sell corn, soft cheese, and a few loaves of bread, very small, and containing a goodly proportion of sand. These loaves had not been baked in the ashes after the more primitive fashion of the country still practised in many parts, but in Egyptian-shaped ovens, built of adobes (sun-dried bricks), and plastered within and without with mud. I purchased a sample of the bread, which proved even tougher than the meat of the old cow, and was not half as clean; but being a new article of food to us, it proved a luxury not to be despised. One woman, who exchanged corn with the drivers for meat, presented me with nine ears of the corn. Knowing from the experiences of the journey, that after a feast comes a fast, I hid the corn inside a pair of boots among the rest of my baggage in one of the wagons, and felt well armed against the hungry time that was sure to follow.

An hour later the caravan halted. While the cattle were grazing, overpowered by the long walk under a hot sun, I lay down to take a short siesta, from which, on awakening, I discovered that somebody had carried off my little stock of food.

From this occurrence I never afterwards *stored* food, but ate whatever came into my possession.

At dusk two well-dressed travellers, who proved to be Frenchmen, came up to our encampment, and made inquiries regarding the road. They reported that serious trouble had occurred near San Luis among the farmers, the Indians having cut the throats of fourteen persons! This intelligence caused much speculation among the drivers, and, as before, a general gloom pervaded the whole company.

As soon as everything was arranged in camp for any emergencies that might occur, I rolled myself up in my blanket, and soon forgot all troubles in sleep.

CHAPTER X.

FROM RIO QUARTO TO CERRO MORO—CONTINUED.

WHILE all around me seemed to offer danger in some form, I grew lighter at heart every day that we further penetrated the country, for everything was novel and captivating to the fancy. I was at last among a strange people, and their habits and mode of life, and the many incidents that were constantly occurring, were full of interest to me. Although my heart was light, and I trudged along cheerfully and with courage, my companions in the caravan were but little calculated to make the trip a pleasant one; and I must say that they did not try to change their evidently disagreeable nature.

The rations I received from the tall Santia gueño, my "protector and firm friend," were selected from the toughest and driest portions of the meat, while he devoured my living, and at the same time, at meals, called the attention of the whole company to the unsuccessful attempts I made at mastication.

At times, when indignation caused me to reply in no gentle terms to their conduct, in a tongue different from theirs, I perceived my folly, for it only served to draw out more jibes and greater insults from the fellows.

When we were in motion, to avoid uncongenial company, I started in advance of the troop, and kept far ahead of it. Sometimes I improved these opportunities to brood over the ill-treatment of the men; but at sight of a wild animal, or a gaucho pursuing a colt across the plains, an instant revival of my spirits took place, and my whole senses were awakened to things around me.

I usually had enough to occupy my mind; sometimes I was studying the habits of birds or insects, at others following with my eyes the movements of a herd of cattle, or gazing upon the mirage in the distant horizon, in which our caravan was reflected with wonderful distinctness.

I have said that the peons had not treated me with great friendliness lately; but since we left Rio Quarto their coolness grew more noticeable, and at length I began to fear that we should not part without a collision, in which case I knew I could depend on but two people in the whole caravan, the old Indian and the woman spoken of in a preceding chapter.

These two had always treated me kindly, while all the others had given me uneasiness in some way or other.

Before the troop had left Rosario, my friend, Señor G., cautioned me against showing money, and I had followed his advice, having departed from it only on one or two occasions. When near Rio Quarto, not wishing to be thought penurious, I had imprudently purchased more than my share of the pumpkins and melons, which served to regale the peons at night, when collected around the camp-fires; and this had caused the ignorant fellows to suppose that there was *mucha plata* (much money) in my possession. And this was the cause of their ill-feeling towards me.

Several times they were particularly anxious to know if I had friends in Mendoza, and who were the persons that would receive me on the arrival of the troop in that town. I at last found it necessary to introduce to their consideration a character as new to myself as he was to them. One night, when we were lying around the fires, I, after describing my home and friends, casually remarked that one of them, a medico, the distinguished Dr. Carmel, of Mendoza, was anxiously awaiting my arrival, and that his apprehensions for my safety would increase until I reached the town.

To the reader whose conscience has never been subjected to violence, this subterfuge may appear unmanly; but, in justice to myself, I was obliged thus to impose upon the peons, and the result fully proved it.

Under Dr. Carmel's strong (prospective) arm and influence I found more peaceful hours, and suffered less from annoyance than if his name had never been mentioned, or if the villanous fellows had been left in their first belief, which at the same time was correct, that I was a friendless *gringo*, to whom they might offer any insult without fear of punishment. In what manner was I, a solitary stripling, to protect myself against more than a score of barbarians, in the very heart of a country to the languages and localities of which I was a total stranger, unless by subterfuge?

But my troubles were not yet over.

While walking, as usual, one day, in advance of the carts, which came slowly creaking behind, my attention was directed to Juan, the little son of my female friend, who came running after me. Juan spoke only broken Spanish; but upon reaching my side he commenced a voluble discourse, which, however, I gave little notice to, supposing it to be merely childish prattle. At length the boy took my hand, and demanded my attention.

From what he said, I could, indeed, glean but little; but it was enough to confirm my suspicions, which I had had for some time, that some rascality was being planned by the drivers. From mispronounced words and broken sentences, I received warning not to eat with the *capataz* at the fire, — " *Sta malo no come con él*," — and to be cautious when with the men. Juan said that his mother had sent him to tell me this. The little fellow was about to communicate something further regarding his mother, when he suddenly became silent, and squeezed my hand. I looked around, and beheld *Chico*, the servant of the *capataz*, close upon our heels; he had stealthily approached, without attracting our notice.

" Why do you walk ? " interrogated little Juan.

To this question the swarthy Chico, half Indian, half negro, made no answer; but he uttered a sly laugh, that meant a good deal. We walked on for upwards of an hour, during which time the half-breed kept close behind us.

Watching favorable opportunities, Juan informed me that the *capataz* had sent his servant to prevent us from conversing; and seeing that he was determined to remain by us, I at length, with the boy, rejoined the troop.

When the caravan halted for the night, I walked over to the fire where the China woman was seated; but two or three gauchos from our own fire followed me, and engaged the woman in conversation.

In the aspect of affairs now, I confess I was somewhat alarmed, and more than ever felt the want of a companion on whom I could depend. The words of a foreign merchant, with whom I had conversed in Buenos Ayres, were recalled most forcibly to me. "My boy," he said, "you don't know whither you are going. When you get among the gauchos, you will find much trouble and danger." And I acknowledge that I now felt he spoke the truth.

The men still kept the woman aloof from me. I determined to take things coolly, and await events.

Don Manuel came to the fire late in the evening, and, taking his meat in his hand, galloped off in the dark to see to the cattle. I now missed Don José, the *patron*, whose protecting arm was to be my support in danger. On inquiring of Facundo, my cook, he pointed off into the gloom, and uttered the Spanish word "*Estancia*," by which I understood that the *patron* was at some one of the great cattle-farms lying off the road.

I now felt that I was unprotected, indeed; and when the hour arrived for our lying down to sleep, I was uncertain as to whether or not I should remain unmolested through the night. But the time for the attempt on my purse, if not life, had evidently not arrived. I was permitted to fall asleep, which I did at last; and our whole party evidently accompanied me in my visit to the land of dreams, for nothing was heard among us, and no one moved (if they had I would have been awakened in an instant) until daybreak.

When the sun was just appearing above the horizon, the *capataz* came galloping up to the carts, and soon the word was spoken to get up the oxen and mules, and prepare to start.

I remained in the cart to write in my journal until the ugly-visaged Facundo appeared to inform me that my breakfast was ready. As I approached the group that was huddled about the fire, not one of them deigned to notice me, save one big fellow, who, with an obsequiousness that I knew to be assumed, pointed to the breakfast.

The strips of meat had been removed from the fire, and the spit, in a separate piece, was stuck into the ground, waiting for me. This was an unusual attention, for I generally shared my meat with the *capataz*, or with Facundo. The *capataz* sat smoking by the fire, but the *patron* had not yet returned from the *estancia*. I offered my steak to Don Manuel; but he courteously declined, appearing to lack appetite. He refused a second similar offer, and continued smoking.

Determined not to be balked by him, as I wished to prove my suspicions that mischief was afoot, I informed him that he lacked politeness, and that I would not eat without him. The effect of my words upon the company was of such a character that I could no longer doubt their intentions.

At length Don Manuel, seeing that I suspected something, cut off from the extreme edge of the steak a mouthful or two, and ate it, upon which I cut from the opposite side a little larger piece, and ate it leisurely. I then cut off another piece, and, pretending to eat it on the way, left the party, and retired to the cart to finish my writing, throwing the meat in the grass on the way.

Fifteen or twenty minutes passed, at the end of which time I was compelled to put aside paper and pen, for a strange sensation of weakness came upon me, rendering me unable to move — a helpless prisoner in the cart.

Violent pains, that racked my head, were followed by strong vomitive symptoms; but I was still helpless.

While the oxen were being harnessed, I made a second effort to leave the cart, but I could not rise. Soon the villanous Facundo entered, and, bidding me, in no gentle tones, to keep quiet, and not kick around, he started his oxen, and, with the rest of the caravan, we were again in motion.

I soon fell into a delightful sleep, and dreamed most pleasant dreams. At one moment I was moving through the air, light, free from human bonds, a very spirit; my whole senses were intoxicated with most delicious sensations. Again I beheld most beautiful visions and most gorgeous colors. At last I seemed to have been transported back to my native village, and kind friends were grouped around me. The voice of welcome greeted me, all trouble seemed ended. A clear, sweet voice sang a well-remembered song, which seemed to be the very essence of melody, so ravishingly did it fall upon my ear.

Gradually the voice grew indistinct, then loud and harsh, and I returned to consciousness to recognize the tones of Facundo, who was singing to himself. His discordant words were uttered in a long-drawn cadence, commencing in a low, mournful strain, and ending with a couplet and groans.

The following syllables will give an idea of his song. They were repeated so many times that I shall hardly forget them: —

"Que pur ma no yepe — *oh* — AH — OUGH.
Ya, ke, pur, se, va, yah — *oh* — OH — AH — OUGH."

Facundo continued groaning, either for his own pleasure or for my discomfort, during the greater part of the time that I lay sick in the cart.

At our first stopping-place, about two hours after breakfast, the woman sent me, by little Juan, a tea that she had prepared from some herbaceous plant of the pampas, to gather which she had walked all the morning behind the carts.

I felt much better after drinking the tea, but did not entirely recover from my sudden illness for several days. I subsequently learned that it was not unusual for the Santia gueños to revenge a fancied insult, or to annoy one whom they have a dislike for, by administering poison, sometimes in sufficient quantities to destroy life, and at other times in a quantity sufficient to produce only sickness. They had undoubtedly taken advantage of the absence of the *patron* to treat me as they did.

The first time I sallied forth from confinement I was received in a characteristic manner by the drivers, who clapped their hands to their stomachs, and questioned me with impudent gestures if I was not ill, and what was the trouble. The good woman only said, compassionately, "*Pobre cito*" (poor fellow).

During my sickness I continued to write daily, much to the annoyance of Facundo, who looked threateningly at my notes, as if he suspected his name was there. I even went so far as to ask him how he spelt his name, which was a useless question enough; for had he been disposed to inform me, he could not, since he knew not one letter from another.

My illness cost me but little time, and I was soon able to resume my pedestrian journey, and by night of the same day I was nearly well.

Our journey had been through the day across a hilly country. As evening drew near, we reached a watering-place, which afforded an abundance of feed around it, and the caravan was halted, and camp prepared.

At supper I was cautious to eat only of the food that I saw the others partake of, which they observing, I noticed that glances and meaning smiles were exchanged among them.

Early the next morning we were again in motion.

The country was still broken, and we met several deep gullies, which we crossed with great labor, it being necessary to attach extra yokes of oxen to the carts to effect a passage. One of these gullies was so dangerous, on account of the steepness of its sides, that a pair of oxen were fastened behind the cart to prevent it from gaining too great a velocity in its descent.

Near this latter pass was a five by six stone hut, roofed with sticks and mud, which served as a post-house, where the galloping courier receives his fresh horse. Two women, with low foreheads and heavy features, came out of the cabin, followed by an old man, the postmaster, to stare at us, and inquire if the drivers had any sugar or yerba to exchange with them. For what articles they proposed to barter I could not conceive, as the open side of the hut showed an interior destitute of everything like comfort; for it contained only an old hide and bedding, and one cheese, that rested upon a swinging shelf made of canes bound together with hide thongs.

Like many of the poor gauchos, the postman smoked bad Tucuman tobacco, rolled up in a narrow piece of corn-leaf, a material that is preferred by some to the coarse linen paper manufactured in Europe for the South American market.

Among the hills that bounded our northern horizon, and which some travellers would classify as mountains, the wind blows almost constantly with great force from various quarters. The smallest of the hills were well grassed over, and wherever the ruts entered the soil near them it showed a sandy gravel. Upon the plains to the south was the richer pasturage, with a soil better fitted for cultivation.

At night we encamped close by the hamlet of El Moro, situated, as I believe, not far from the foot of Cerro Moro, a chain of low mountains.

At daylight the next morning the caravan wound down among the hills to a level pampa, with barren mountains to the north.

The Mendoza diligence passed, drawn by six tired horses. Besides drawing his share of the weight of the carriage, each animal carried upon his back a postilion, who did not fail to use whip or spur as necessity demanded.

The plain that we were upon was covered with immense piles of decomposed granite, how placed in such positions it is difficult to surmise. The thorn and algarroba tree grew abundantly. Our course for the remainder of the day continued over the pampa, with hills growing more distinct each hour in the distance; a strong wind blew steadily from the Cerro until dark, when it died away, and a calm, lovely night succeeded.

The following day we left the plains, and travelled through a hilly country, which gradually became more and more irregular as we approached the River Quinto, which stream we reached about noon, and halted on its banks for dinner.

The country near the river was sandy, and covered with scattered thorn-bushes. The banks of the Quinto, at the ford where we camped, were high, and almost perpendicular. The bed of the river appeared to be formed of quicksand in agitation, and the current was very strong. A few mud huts were close to the river on each side, and their occupants had a great quantity of beef cut in strips, drying for winter use, together with sliced pumpkins, which two articles of diet form the principal support of the people; the sterility of the soil will not support a healthy crop of corn.

Large flocks of parrots, of a species that dig holes in the banks in which to deposit their eggs, like our northern bank swallows (*Cotyle riparia*), filled the air with loud cries, and gave some appearance of life to the scene. The town of Rio Quinto was not far off; but as the road lay in a different direction, I did not get a glimpse of it, but, judging by the few lazy natives that I saw, who appeared as if laboring under mental derangement, with two prominent traits visible, — selfishness and idleness, — I did not feel that I was losing much in not visiting the place.

Dinner over, we prepared to move. Crossing the river, we found the ascent of the opposite bank the most difficult to surmount of any obstacle we had met on the road; great exertions were made to get the carts up the rise, and the oxen were most terribly goaded by the drivers. One peon, with loud imprecations, thrust his goad into an animal so far that it could not be withdrawn until the iron was pulled out of the goad-stick, when the man caught it, and jerked so fiercely, that when it came from the wound the blood followed it in a little stream. This exhibition of brutality afforded satisfaction to the other drivers, who laughed at the fellow as he cursed the ox for being the cause of the breaking of his new picano. At last we were all across the river and in motion.

The high plain upon the opposite side was covered with thorns and algarroba, save here and there some spot more fertile than the rest, which sustained a growth of coarse grass. In crossing this tract the wheels of the carts sank into the deep ruts to the hubs, and raised clouds of dust that were almost choking.

I covered myself with a woollen poncho, for I well knew that it was doubtful if an opportunity to bathe would again present itself before we reached San Luis, the great town of the interior. During the afternoon a little boy passed us, driving to his house by the river a flock of goats and sheep; the last-named animals looked very ragged, from the custom of the people, who still adhere to the old practice of *pulling out* the wool from the skin instead of shearing, at such times and in such quantities as they need it.

As the moon was a few days old, the caravan kept

on until eight o'clock, when it encamped on the travesia.

The cattle were driven a long distance from the road to feed, but no pasturage was to be had, and at about one o'clock I was aroused by the approach of the cattle, and the loud cries of the drivers, who shouted "*Fuera! fuera!*" as they drove the teams to the carts.

The moon had set, and the night was very dark; but the necessity of moving at once was obvious, for there was no water nor grass to be had for many miles, and both must necessarily be obtained at the earliest moment for the hungry and thirsty beasts.

We got under way at once, and travelled by landmarks with which the drivers were acquainted. As we moved along the plain, the noise of the caravan aroused hundreds of parrots from a roosting-place among the branches of a clump of algarrobas. An Indian stampede could not have created a more confused or louder noise than that of the frightened parrots, as they hovered over us in a cloud.

CHAPTER XL.

SAN LUIS AND THE SALINE DESERT.

WE travelled through the remainder of the night, and until near eleven o'clock on the following day, when we encamped at a place in which there was a fair pasturage and some water. Here we tarried until the morning of the next day, when we filled our vessels with water, harnessed up the teams, and started.

Our course lay through a country that was dreary in the extreme, and we had no incidents or experiences that were worthy of a notice here.

My readers have found in these pages so many mentions of a certain individual, the *capataz*, that they, perhaps, would like to know him better.

As *capataz*, Don Manuel Montero commanded the troop when the *patron*, or owner, was absent, and his services as *baqueano*, or guide, were of the utmost importance to the welfare and success of the caravan. Don Manuel had not the swarthy complexion of the Indian peons, but could prove his superiority of birth and family in comparison to theirs by a hue that would have been pronounced in the United States decidedly yellow, that is, if his physiognomy could have been divested of dirt so as to exhibit the true color; for the don loved not pure water externally applied, and would have been but a poor patron of hydropathy, even could he have been convinced of its wonderful virtues. He was of middle stature, and sat with great dignity upon his pampa steed, which he rarely left during the day; for, being a true gaucho, he always kept the saddle except when he was eating or sleeping. These two necessary duties he attended to while reclining on the ground — a position that he always assumed when off duty. To sleep within a hut or cart was beneath his gaucho dignity.

His hair hung in long black locks, excelled in jettiness only by those of Facundo, my cook. His toilet was attended to at such times as the same operations were necessary for the comfort of his dog Choco, when master and animal shared the use of the same toilet articles. I might write a treatise upon his comb, in which I could speak of its decayed and broken parts; of its lusty and lively inhabitants that played hide-and-seek between the teeth; of a brawny, lively creature from the hair of Don Manuel struggling for mastery with another from the shaggy coat of dog Choco.

As a guide the don's skill was unrivalled. Like most *baqueanos* he was grave and reserved in manner, and conversed but little with the other gauchos.

He was familiar with every mile of the road from the banks of the Paraná to the rocky bases of the Andes. He could not, like the geographer, tell the exact longitude, in numbers, of the principal towns of the republic, but he knew where they were situated, and could travel towards them without missing the true direction in the darkest nights.

Don Manuel never offered his advice in a boisterous manner, as though in authority, but quietly said to the *patron*, "Three leagues to the right of the road are about thirty squares of good grass, and farther on to the left is a small lagoon of water not yet dried up." His word was always respected, and the usual answer of the *patron* was, "Do as you please, Don Manuel; I have confidence in your judgment."

A native author gives the following description of the *baqueano*, which will correctly apply to Don Manuel: —

"If lost upon the plain, he dismounts, and by examining the soil decides upon his latitude, and tells his companions the distance that they are from habitations. If this is not enough, he pulls grass from different localities and chews the roots, decides upon their proximity to some pond or rivulet, fresh or salt, and departs in search of it, to decide upon his position.

"General Rosas can tell by taste the grass of every farm south of Buenos Ayres.

"The guide likewise announces the nearness of the enemy when within ten miles of him, and the direction from which he is coming, by means of the movements of birds, and by the deer and wild llamas that run in certain directions. When the enemy is near at hand he observes the dust, and by its thickness counts the force. He says they number two thousand, five hundred, two hundred, as the case may be, and the chief acts under this instruction, which is almost invariably correct.

"If the condors and vultures flutter in a circle in the air, he can tell if there are any persons hid, or if there is an encampment recently abandoned, or if the cause of their movements is merely a dead animal."

Such is the true *baqueano*, and such was Don Manuel. At noon we halted near a couple of *cerros*, the commencement of the San Luis chain of mountains. The peons killed an ox, but as there was no grass for the cattle we did not remain long enough to cook an *asado*. This was the more aggravating, since we had none of us eaten anything since the morning of the previous day.

At two o'clock the caravan again halted — this time to water the animals from a stream that flowed through a *quebrada* (valley), along which were scattered a few ranchos, whose inhabitants lived on pumpkins and porridge, the latter being valued at one *real* per quart. A troop from Mendoza passed us at this encampment, and I took advantage of the opportuuity to get rid of some cut *reals*, that are current in Rosario, for several bunches of grapes. This troop had also packed in wicker baskets oranges and figs, a quantity of which I purchased to divide with my friends, the old Indian and the squaw. I offered a bunch of grapes to Facundo, but his sour disposition would not allow him to accept.

From the river the road wound over a plain abounding in thorn trees and cacti. Here also grew a low plant bearing red berries, and resembling peppers in taste. The fruit was eagerly sought for by the peons, who, throughout the remainder of the journey, seasoned their stews with it.

At the end of the plain the barren mountains of San Luis rose abruptly, and seemed to form a barrier to farther progress. We entered a narrow cleft in the chain, and wound through it for an eighth of a mile, the voices of the drivers echoing among the rocks with fine effect. But great was my surprise when we passed from the defile to an elevated plain, to see stretched out below us the town of San Luis, with its white plastered dwellings, half hidden, and shaded by tall rows of poplars, and groves of green willows. It brought to mind the days of the conquest, so finely described by Prescott, and I pictured the city below me as another *Cuzco*, inhabited by the children of the Incas.

But this was not all. Another sight caught my eye, and filled me with joy. Far in the distance a dim, blue line, pencilled upon the heavens, told me that I had obtained my first view of the Andes — that mighty range of mountains which traverses two continents and a dozen countries, though known by different names.

What emotions were aroused within me as I gazed at that faint streak that seemed floating in the air, for below it all was enveloped in clouds! What visions it awoke of steep precipices, dark gorges, and rushing streams of water falling in cascades from heights unattainable by man! I pictured myself in the act of toiling up a narrow path, or sliding down the sides of a *cerro* on the snow. I longed to be there, and wondered whether from the lofty summit of the Cordillera I should be able yet to gaze upon the distant waters of the great Pacific.

Above the hazy line two points arose into the clearer heavens, and from their sublime appearance particularly attracted my attention. The highest of these peaks, which lies to the north of west of Mendoza, was the famed Aconcagua, which, rising above the line of eternal snows, attains an elevation of twenty-three thousand nine hundred feet: higher by two thousand five hundred feet than that monarch of the Andes, Chimborazo. The other peak lies to the south of Aconcagua, and runs up sharply into the heavens. It has been measured by a recent traveller, who gives it an elevation of twenty-two thousand four hundred and fifty feet above the level of the sea, or not so high as Aconcagua by fourteen hundred and fifty feet.

As I viewed the distant picture with enthusiasm, the caravan that came lumbering behind was forgotten, until a rough shake, and the words, "*Esta dormiendo?*" aroused my attention. Looking around I beheld the grinning features of the *capataz*, who exclaimed, "*La Cordillera de los Andes, que cosa tan rica!*" (The Cordillera of the Andes, what a rich thing!)

As we descended to the town, a party of equestrians, male and female, passed on the canter, and entered before us. The caravan encamped alongside the mud wall that defended the property of the inhabitants, and I remarked that the women who visited the troop did not come as venders of produce, but as visitors. These females were gayly and tastefully dressed, but their morals were questionable. As there were no seats near the fire, our *capataz* gallantly offered one of the fair visitors his hat for a substitute; but she, with the others, preferred their own mode of sitting, and squatted, *à la Turque*, upon the sand, where they made themselves sociable, and when supper was ready joined in the meal, eating their meat without knives or forks, but using their fingers instead.

San Luis is the largest town upon the road from Rosario to Mendoza. It is the capital of the province of the same name, and contains about two thousand inhabitants. This place has varied greatly in its population within the present century. In 1825 it had two churches, now it has but one, and this, I afterwards learned, was not well supported — which fact accounts for its being so immoral a place.

For many years San Luis had been governed by an old, ignorant fellow, just such a man as Rosas was accustomed to place over the interior provinces, in order that they might remain in a degraded state, and thus be more submissive to his power. A new governor, a man of education and energy, had taken the place of the old one just removed, and under his influence it was hoped that the condition of the people of the province might be improved. Formerly a tax of five dollars was imposed upon every cart that passed through the province, but it has been lowered to a more reasonable sum.

No town on the pampas has suffered from the depredations of Indians as San Luis. While I was in San Juan, two or three months later, I became acquainted with several Puntaños, as the people of this place are called, and from them received much information regarding these encroachments.

The Indians usually surprise the town about an hour before daybreak, and not only seize what property they can remove, but also carry off into captivity the wives and sisters of the male portion of the inhabitants. While one party is engaged in sacking the town, another party drives off all the mares they can find, as mare's flesh is used as food among them, and if they take horned cattle, it is only to sell them to Chilenos, who cross the Andes by the most southern pass — the Planchon. Great numbers of women and children have been carried off during these frays.

There was living in San Luis, at the time our troop passed through the place, an old woman who was stolen when a child from her friends. She lived many years with her captors, serving them as a menial, or slave. Twice she attempted to escape, but each time was retaken, and for both attempts her feet were skinned by the brutal savages. She made a third attempt, however, which was successful. Her captors were away, hunting guanacos, a species of llama. Secreting about her person a quantity of dried mare's flesh, she set out for a little lake, telling the squaws that she was going to draw water. As soon as the lake was reached she struck out boldly into the pampas, shaping her course in the direction of San Luis.

The Indians, fortunately, did not overtake or find her, and after many days of wandering, she fell in with some gauchos, who took her to San Luis, and restored her to her friends.

Another occurrence that was related to me will not be without interest to the reader.

During the California excitement a great number of foreigners accompanied caravans from Buenos Ayres to Mendoza, *en route* for the land of gold. Two or three of these caravans were troubled by the Indians while on the passage to San Luis.

At last one troop of twenty carts, which was accompanied by a large number of foreigners, mostly French and English, started from Buenos Ayres, and as the men were armed with double-barrelled guns and six-shooters, they were continually on the *qui vive* for an opportunity to test their weapons against the long spears and boliadores of the Indians.

Scouts were always on the watch, but not an Indian was seen. At length, just before they reached the mountains of San Luis, they were met by flying horsemen and terrified women from the town, who informed them that the savages were among the mines of La Carolina, some sixteen or eighteen leagues to the north, and were plundering without mercy. As the party were debating as to their proper action, the news was brought that the Indians, harassed by a few troops sent by the governor, were on the retreat. The caravan was at once drawn into a defile of the mountains, and the white men prepared for action.

Soon the Indians were descried coming at a rapid rate, in one body. Behind each savage were one or more female prisoners lashed to the rider. "It was an awful sight," said the narrator of the story to me, "when we beheld the strangers point their long guns at the approaching party, among which were our friends, bound to their relentless captors."

Unaware of the proximity of strangers, on came the galloping party. Suddenly they fell back in confusion, but too late for retreat, for the discharge of nearly two hundred guns scattered death among them. In an instant the horses were freed from their savage riders, who lay upon the plain in the last agonies.

Great credit was given to the foreigners who had done such service to the province; and, followed by hundreds of the natives, they marched the carts into the plaza of San Luis, and there remained several days, feasting daily upon eight oxen that were presented them by the governor. My informant said that such was the skill of the strangers in the use of fire-arms, that not a bird flew over the plaza but it was shot while flying, much to the astonishment of the townsfolk, who will never forget the visit of the strangers.

At San Luis de la Punta the pampas end. On the next morning, the 27th of April, when we left the town, our course lay over a *travesia* (desert), which was wooded, for the first few leagues, with the black algarroba (*mata-gusano*), and many other species of low thorn trees and bushes. The road was filled with deep ruts, and as the heavy wagons passed along they raised clouds of dust, that made travelling an almost insupportable task. At night the cattle had to be driven some miles from the road to a place where a little pasture was found. We did not eat meat during the day, but I found that many of the cacti bore a fruit at the top, which, though nearly tasteless, was better than nothing. Near where we encamped, three peons were loosening a patch of land with the rough plough of the country. They were preparing to dig a receptacle for the water that falls during the summer time, and just behind two or three ranchos were two of these old pools, out of which our oxen and men drank, the *capataz* paying six and one fourth cents per head for each animal. The water could not have been a foot in depth, and what kept it from soaking into the ground I could not tell, as the soil was porous rather than clayey.

We resumed our march on the following morning without any breakfast, and kept on until noon, when the cattle were driven to a distant pasture, and the peons cooked an *asado*. We again watered the oxen at another dirty pool, paying the same price per head. I was thirsty, but before I could get at the water the cattle were crowded in the pool, and I returned to the cart without any. Don Facundo furnished me with a bottle to fill. I gave it to a dirty urchin, who seized a stick, and wading into the muddy pool, drove the oxen right and left until he had space enough left to fill the demijohn. This he succeeded in doing, but the contents were such a mixture that, to avoid swallowing dirt, sticks, &c., I was obliged to strain it through my teeth.

I noticed in this part of the country a species of cactus that had previously escaped my observation. It grows about eighteen inches high, spreads out in large, broad leaves, and is fed upon by cochineal insects, which the natives gather, and sell at a low price. It bears a fruit which resembles, in form and color, the pine-apple, and is about twice the size of a hen's egg. Inside the skin is a white pulpy substance, filled with small black seeds, and pleasant to the taste.

The little pepperish berry became more abundant, and, taking advantage of the opportunity, the peons put large quantities in their stews, which rendered it so fiery to the taste that I was frequently obliged to go supperless.

The *travesia* which we were now upon was covered, in greater or less quantity, with a peculiar saline mineral which was new to me. I saved a small quantity of it, and when I returned to the United States, presented it to a scientific association, with the following account of the locality in which it is found: —

"This peculiar mineral is found mixed with the soil, in greater or less abundance, from San Luis de la Punta (a town on the western side of the pampas of the Argentine Republic, where the grass plains properly end, and the *travesia*, or desert, commences) to the foot of the Andes.

"San Luis lies in latitude 33° 16′ south, longitude 66° 27′ west, and is the capital of the province of the same name. From this town westward the soil is almost worthless, until the River Mendoza is reached, where irrigation commences.

"The soil is very light and dry, and not in the least compact. This is probably caused by the dryness of the atmosphere and absence of water; for when I crossed that part of the country, no water was found save that which had been caught and retained in holes in the ground by the natives. Stones are rarely met with, and where they are found I did not observe the salt.

"There are several spots on the *travesia* between San Luis and Mendoza furnishing a poor quality of grass, which is fed upon by the cattle which are driven across the continent to the coast.

"With the exception of these spots the country between the above named towns, and extending many leagues to the north and south, is a desert waste, covered with a low growth of thorn bushes and a few species of gnarled trees, some of which bear pods.

"The mineral penetrates the earth from a few inches to a couple of feet in depth. It is particularly abundant at certain places east of the town of San Juan, where the ground is covered with a thin incrustation. It is here that the reflection of the sun's rays is exceedingly painful to the eyes, and the inhabitants are constantly affected with inflammation of those organs.

"The soil for cultivation must first be prepared, and the mineral removed. The native method of doing this is very simple. The water is conducted from the Rivers Mendoza and San Juan (which take their rise in the Cordillera) through an *acquia*, or canal, around squares of level land, at irregular intervals of time, and, to use their own expression, they wash off the *salitre* (saltpetre). Then a plough, constructed of two pieces of wood, is brought into service, and it turns up from six to eight inches of the soil, which goes through the same washing process as the first.

"After two or three repetitions of this operation, a shallow soil is obtained, partially free from *salitre*, in which wheat, clover, pumpkins, melons, &c., are raised. The remaining *salitre*, according to the belief of the natives, is exhausted by successive crops, and after several years of tillage the soil is suitable for the vine. Oranges, peaches, quinces, olives, figs, &c., flourish. Within a few years large tracts of land have been made exceedingly fertile by the process above described, and could the New England plough be introduced there, the process would be far more effective."

The following analysis of the salt was made by Dr. A. A. Hayes, of Boston, a gentleman well known in scientific circles for the care and accuracy with which he conducts all analyses: —

"The specimen was a white, crystalline solid, formed by the union of two layers of salt, as often results from the evaporation of a saline solution, when the pellicle formed on the surface falls to the bottom. Along the line of junction crystal facets are seen, but the forms are indistinct. These crystals readily scratch calc spar, and dissolve without residue in water, affording a solution, which, by evaporation at 150° Fahr., leaves the salt with some of the original physical characters. It readily parts with a portion of water by heat, and when the temperature is raised to redness, it fuses quietly into a transparent, colorless, anhydrous fluid. On cooling, an opaque, white, crystalline solid remains. In this climate the specimen attracts moisture, and therefore has not a fixed amount of water constituent.

"It consists of water, sulphuric acid, soda, magnesia, chlorine. Mixed with it are traces of crenate of iron and lime, with sandy grains of earth.

"One sample afforded —

Water,	16.420
Sulphuric acid,	49.658
Soda,	23.758
Magnesia,	9.904
Chlorine,	.260
	100.000

"Three fragments from different masses were taken, and the following substances found: —

Water, ...	16.42	18.84	19.60
Sulphate of soda, . .	48.00	45.82	45.74
" " magnesia, .	34.20	33.19	33.31
Chloride sodium, . .	1.21	1.79	1.16
Crenates lime and iron with silicic acid,	0.17	0.30	0.13
Sand, ...		0.06	0.06
	100.00	100.00	100.00

"The varying amounts of water given are illustrative of the absorptive power of the salts in the atmosphere of this place. Dried at 90° Fahr., the amount of water was 15.20 in 100 parts, which exceeds by four parts the proportion necessary to form proto-hydrates of the two salts present.

"Analysis does not show the two sulphates to be in definite proportions in the masses, but the crystals may be a double salt, composed of one equivalent of sulphate of soda and one equivalent of sulphate of magnesia, each retaining an equivalent of water. In the masses, the closest approximation is 42 parts of sulphate of magnesia found, instead of 46 parts required."

The communication presented embraces interesting facts. These saline deserts cover extended areas in different parts of South America, and, so far as the author has been able to learn, the saline matter differs in kind at the different points. The tendency of saline matter contained in any soil is to rise through the aid of moisture to the surface, where, the water escaping, the salt is deposited. This effect, contrary to the gravitating influence, is the most common cause of deserts, and may be exerted everywhere when the evaporation of water from a given surface becomes much greater than that surface receives in the form of rain and dew. The cultivation of saline deserts, by washing down the saline matter, exhibits the opposite action of water in restoring fertility, and it is by no means essential that the water should contain organic matter to insure the full effect, as the soil of deserts generally contains all the organic matter of many years' accumulation.

An interesting inquiry naturally presents itself to the traveller while crossing this peculiar desert. By what means was the salt deposited? Two theories have been advanced by gentlemen who have visited the *travesia*, both to account for its presence.

Mr. Bland, the North American Commissioner, who visited the Argentine Republic in 1818, thinks that these plains "may have been gently lifted just above the level of the ocean, and left with a surface so unbroken and flat as not yet to have been sufficiently purified of its salt and acid matter, either by filtration or washing."

Sir W. Parish's idea of the origin of the salt is different. He says, "But is it not more likely to have been washed down from the secondary strata, which form the base of the Andes, in which we know that enormous beds of salt abound, particularly in those parts of the Cordillera where the greater number of the rivers rise which run through the pampas, and which are almost all more or less impregnated with it?"

While crossing the pampas I occasionally noticed that the water of some of the streams was brackish, but as we approached the Andes the water of the rivers was pure, and free from salt. The San Juan and Mendoza Rivers, both of which may be called great torrents, bring down alluvial mud in their currents; but I never was able to detect any saline properties either in the mud or water. The natives, however, have assured me that there are many salt mines in the Andes.

CHAPTER XII.

ON THE TRAVESIA.

ON the 28th of April our caravan crossed the River Desaguadero, and upon the western bank the peons killed an ox, and we ate for the first time since the morning of the previous day. At noon we reached the limits of artificial irrigation, which is carried on extensively in the neighborhood of Mendoza. Along the road ran a shallow ditch, four feet wide, and containing about two inches of water, which, when the canal is full, fertilizes the soil in the vicinity.

Beyond the Desaguadero, forty leagues from Mendoza, lay the hamlet of La Paz, upon the outskirts of which we encamped for the night. Very different was this hamlet from the others we had passed, which looked old and squalid, the houses seeming ready to crumble in pieces, and little vegetation, save in San Luis, was to be seen. Here everything looked neat, and a degree of comfort prevailed that was refreshing to the eye of the traveller who had just crossed a dreary country. This comfortable and fresh appearance was the result of irrigation, for very little rain falls on this great travesia, which covers many thousand miles of territory in the provinces of San Luis, Mendoza, and San Juan; and wherever the water of rivers can be

The Caravan at Rest. — Page 182.

turned from their natural course to fertilize the broad waste lands, there little spots of verdure appear, and the labor of the farmer is crowned with success.

The whole township of La Paz was divided into square pastures, around which ran a wide canal. Along the borders of these grew tall poplars, that served to fence in and protect the herds of cattle that had been brought from San Luis to fatten on *alfalfa*, a species of clover. Our *patron* was so parsimonious that he refused to purchase good pasturage for the cattle, which were growing weaker each day on miserable fare, but ordered the *capataz* to drive them to a piece of waste land, upon which grew a scanty supply of dry grass.

The next day we encamped a few leagues beyond the village, where I bought, and shared with the peons, a couple of pumpkins, some coarse bread, and a quantity of dried figs, that had been brought from Mendoza. Our road the next day led through woods of thorns and algarrobas, and occasionally over an open plain.

Just before dark we had a fine view of the distant Andes, which were now distinctly visible. The most lofty peaks were covered with snow, although in many places dark lines showed where the rocks remained yet uncovered.

The wind blew direct from the west, and coming from the snowy mountains, was very chilly. All night I turned and rolled upon my hide in great discomfort from the cold that benumbed my limbs. On the next day, May 1st, the peons stopped to kill an ox close to Las Casitas, a village larger and better than the last one we passed three days before.

While the troop rested, a broad-faced, good-looking

fellow beckoned from over a fence of thorns and cornstalks for me to come and dine with him. I accepted his kind invitation, and he showed me his hut and grounds; the former was built of cornstalks, and was well thatched.

Upon the rafters, that projected, and formed a platform outside the hut, were piles of dried pumpkins, melons, &c.

He informed me that he had commenced improving the land one year before, and by hard labor, he, together with his wife and children, had a home, and were more plentifully supplied with the comforts of life than any other rancho on the road between Rosario and Mendoza.

The canal that ran past his hut watered beds of onions, beans, garlic, and many other vegetables not often found on the road.

His wife, a dark-complexioned woman, with "*para servir à vd*," welcomed me to their cabin, and spread upon a trunk of an algarroba a small piece of white cloth, and upon this placed a dish containing a stew of beans, onions, corn, and meat, well-seasoned with garlic. They would not receive anything for their kindness, but when I left presented me with a fine pumpkin, which I in turn gave to the peons.

From this place we travelled very slowly until four o'clock, when we halted to feed the oxen. The peons, though they had eaten heartily three hours before, roasted large slices of meat, and ate a quantity during the next half hour that would have astonished the followers of Graham. These people can go without eating for an astonishing length of time; but when an opportunity offers for gormandizing, they will rival Claudius Albinus himself. I dare not mention how many steaks, each averaging two pounds, Facundo could devour in a day; nor should I wish to state that he thought nothing of eating three pumpkins at a single meal.

At dusk the creaking of wheels and loud cries of men announced that a troop from Mendoza was approaching, and a young man came galloping in advance, and greeted our *patron* as an old acquaintance. The oxen of the troop, fresh from Mendoza, contrasted strangely with our lean animals, some of which could scarcely walk.

The next morning we were on the road very early, for it now became evident that unless our journey was soon terminated our cattle would give out; and the carts thus situated would be in an unlucky situation.

The next town was Santa Rosa, once the headquarters of the Jesuits, who held religious sway over all the pampa territories when the country was under the control of Spain.

The place was nothing more than a collection of mud huts and corn ranchos. The inhabitants, however, supported a small store.

The only signs of life in the hamlet were from a party of women weaving, and two or three half-Indian girls chasing a flock of goats and sheep. The country around the place was covered with low bushes, and, judging by appearances, I concluded that the place had seen its best days. Many poor families were supported by a flock of twenty or thirty goats and sheep, the latter providing sufficient wool, from which their garments were made; and as the goats breed twice a year, they had plenty of animal food to satisfy their wants. Beyond this place our caravan entered a straight, broad road, shaded with tall poplars, which were planted in regular rows on each side of the street, and afforded a pleasant shade for the traveller.

Following the road for two or three miles, we encamped for the night in Alto Verde, where were the best houses seen by us since leaving Rosario. The frames were of poplar, and were well put together, the roof projecting sufficiently to form a veranda. All articles of food were cheaper here than at any of the towns passed by our troop. Three or four large watermelons were given for a medio (6¼ cents), and two loaves of bread for the same amount of money.

During the day following we passed scattered houses, and large pastures of *alfalfa*, separated from each other by fences of growing poplars. Our *patron* now felt compelled to purchase fodder for the oxen, and he obtained the privilege of pasturing them for the night, and until the day following, for three dollars; which, considering the number of animals (over one hundred), was a very small sum.

As we encamped in the highway, we were disturbed in our slumbers all the night by the numerous troops of mules and racing gauchos who were continually passing and repassing, while flocks of wild fowl flew over our carts, shaping their course to the south. The following morning we reached Villa Nueva. The roads were very sandy, which gave great trouble to the oxen. Before taking our last meal we halted for the night.

On the next morning we started very early, following a lonely road, without seeing a rancho. About noon we crossed the River Mendoza, which, at the place of crossing, was narrow, with a current setting to the northward. I had some difficulty in effecting a passage without getting wet.

While the carts were forming a double line, and commencing other preparations for halting, I disrobed, and, under cover of some stunted bushes, bathed in the cold stream.

This was the third bath that I had enjoyed since leaving Rosario. The peons laughed derisively at a gringo who could not travel eight hundred miles without washing himself. These disgusting fellows, with one or two exceptions, had not applied water to their skin for more than forty days, and did not intend to cleanse themselves until the troop was close upon Mendoza.

From a few mud houses beyond a rising ground, not far from the river, came several men and women, bringing peaches and melons in their ponchos, together with baskets of native manufacture, filled with two kinds of grapes, one variety of which was the white Muscatel. At different points near this river my attention had been attracted by a disease very prevalent among the people, which exhibited itself in the form of a large swelling upon the throat, and was called by the natives the *coté* (goitre).

One poor fellow, who had a very large *coté*, informed me that it was caused by drinking the water of the stream, and that large swellings had come out upon his thighs, from laboring several weeks in the water.

A young cow that had been purchased on the road was the only tender meat that we had eaten since leaving Rosario. The peons gorged themselves until they could eat no more, and ate, perhaps, more than they would have done had not the *patron* been absent; he had gone to Mendoza in order to advertise in the only paper in the province that his troop would make its *entrée* into the Plaza Nueva on the following day.

Owing to our proximity to the great town, several of the Santia gueños changed their minds about ablutions, and busied themselves in making preparations for the *entrée.* I watched their movements with considerable interest, for in making their toilet the comb of Don Manuel passed around the group, and received generous patronage, the little dog that belonged to my friend and the woman coming in for their share of its use.

The ball having once been set in motion, the excitement to appear neat became so great that some of the peons actually shook the dust out of their *chiropas*, and put on clean drawers, that had been long kept for some great occasion. While the men beat their ponchos upon the wagon-wheels, the woman entered a cart to make her toilet; and so changed was her appearance an hour after, when she appeared clad in a new calico dress, with her hair neatly plaited in two braids, after the fashion, formerly, of young girls in our own country, that I involuntarily raised my sombrero, which attention she very pleasantly acknowledged. But, as is usually the case with mothers, she had expended the principal part of her labor and finery upon her little girl, whose appearance had been greatly improved.

An hour before she had run along the banks of the river barefooted, and with hair streaming in the wind;

but now, with hair smoothly combed, and little body decked out in a gay tunic, her black eyes sparkling with fun, she seemed to have been transformed from a wild Indian girl into an interesting little lady.

After again eating, the troop moved on until sunset, passing several dilapidated houses, and two or three dirty *pulperias* (stores). Our camping-ground proved to be a bad selection, as it was on a low plain, part morass, and covered with tall weeds. The peons tried to compel me to fill the jars with water at a pond, the direction of which they pointed out to me in the dark; but I informed them, through a little fellow that spoke Spanish, that, as I was aware of our proximity to Mendoza, all further orders from them would be disregarded. Furthermore, I stated that there were people in the town which we were soon to enter who could converse equally well in English and in Spanish, and if they, the peons, attempted any more insulting acts, the matter would be exposed. This answer they evidently did not relish, for they became very angry, and conversed among themselves in their own language, evidently making threats of some kind against me.

Before retiring, I conversed with the old Indian, who was my friend, and he promised to receive my little property, snugly packed in a canvas bag, into his cart.

The night passed without any incident, and when daylight came we were already on the march. As the troop was not to enter the town until the following morning, I partook of an *asado* for the last time, and, discarding my pampa costume, and dressing after the fashion of civilized men, I set out in advance of the company for Mendoza, which was twelve miles distant. The whole plain, over which our road lay, was covered with a curious bush, growing in clumps from three to six feet in height, and bearing a yellow pod, resembling in shape a screw. The houses that were scattered along the road were built in the old Spanish style. When within three or four miles of the town, a continuous line of buildings commenced, which was broken only by green pastures of *alfalfa*, surrounded by mud walls and extensive vineyards, the vines of which bent to the ground from the weight of the fruit they bore.

Upon the walls of the houses, suspended from canes, hung, drying in the sun, bunches of the fruit just mentioned; and, seeing a great number of casks and barrels in almost every yard, I judged that each farmer manufactured his own wine.

Oranges, lemons, limes, peaches, and olives were everywhere abundant, while occasionally the eye rested with pleasure upon a pomegranate, or palm-tree.

Within the yards, surrounded by high enclosures, were piles of melons and pumpkins; and ranges of jars, filled with olives just stripped from the trees, stood beneath the verandas of the houses.

The people seemed very hospitable. Twice the proprietors of different *quintas* came out, and persuaded me to enter their residences and partake of food, saying that everything they possessed was at my disposal, and that the foreigners received their great respect.

"How knew you that I was a foreigner?" I asked.

"By your countenance and your walk," was the reply.

An old man detained me a long time to inquire the prices of North American goods.

"What is the value of this article in your country?" he asked, holding up to my view a cheap earthen mug.

"About a medio," I replied.

"What rogues!" he exclaimed. "In Mendoza they charged me three times that sum. Tell me, friend, why did you neglect to bring some with you? You would have been a rich man soon."

The day was the Sabbath, which is regarded as a holiday in this country. The *pulperias* by the road-side were thronged by the gauchos, some gambling, and others dancing to the sound of the guitar, while a few lay drunk upon the ground. About two o'clock, after leaping several streams of water that ran along the streets, I entered Mendoza, and, after many unsuccessful inquiries, found myself in the *calle de comercio*, where I luckily met with a Frenchman who spoke a little English, and to him made known my wishes regarding my proposed journey across the Andes to Chili.

The Frenchman informed me that an English physician, Dr. D., who had resided several years in Mendoza, and had ingratiated himself into the favor of the government, was just the person to apply to, as he could give me any information relative to the Chili road. At the moment the doctor himself came up, mounted upon a fine horse, and returning from a visit to the country.

I handed him the letters given me by Mr. Graham, and inquired if either of the two persons to whom they were directed were in Mendoza; he returned them to me, rather brusquely saying that *he* was not an *American* physician; and as for Mr. Allen Campbell, he had left two months ago for Santa Fé. In as delicate a manner as possible, I informed Dr. D. of my object in visiting his adopted country; that I was a stranger, and unacquainted with the language, and hinted that if some person conversant with the dialect would make inquiries regarding troops of mules that might be leaving for Chili, he would be doing me a favor that I could not too highly appreciate. To this the doctor drew himself up stiffly, and replied, impatiently,—

"If you wish to cross to Chili, the only method of procuring necessary information is to inquire of the native merchants, who often send troops across the Cordillera. According to the last accounts the mountains were passable, though the Chili mail has not yet arrived."

I answered, "Doctor, I am unacquainted with the language, save the little I have acquired upon the road; and if several days are lost by me in fruitless inquiry, the mountains will be closed, and I shall be obliged to remain here for the next six months."

"Very well," he answered, touching his horse at the same time with his silver spurs. "It is only among the merchants that you will receive the information." And he was soon out of sight.

The Frenchman, who had been a listener to the conversation, exclaimed, energetically, "Vat a tam fool! He might speak one word, and find plentee mules going to Chili: he much puffed up with practeese. Come to my home, and I will find you a troop of mules to-morrow. I loves the Americans; they is tam goot fellows!"

On our way to his lodgings, my new acquaintance

suddenly remembered that there was a party of North Americans in town, and at my request he led me to their house. They were professional gentlemen, my guide said, but of what particular branch of science he could not tell. Never was I more surprised than when the Frenchman introduced me to four young men, whose flag, as it waved above their house, announced them as the Circo Olimpico (Olympic Circus), from North America. The director of the company, Mr. Daniel H., of Utica, New York, had left the States for Mexico thirteen years before, and was with the American army through the war between the two republics.

After peace had been established, he freighted a small vessel, and, landing upon the northern coast of South America, had since travelled over nearly all the countries of the continent

Of the original number that left with him, he was the only survivor. As soon as one performer had died, or retired from the profession, some strolling *provistero* was always found to fill the vacancy.

While the company travelled in the upper countries of Bolivia, Peru, New Granada, and Ecuador, success followed them; for silver is more plenty among the middle and poorer classes of those republics that abound in rich mines than in the Argentine Republic. Here their good fortune deserted them. They had crossed over the vast pampa country, and, by giving here and there a *granfuncion*, had taken money enough to enable them to reach Mendoza. Mr. H. informed me that he should follow along the sierras of the Andes, and cross the great travesia that covers several of the upper provinces, until he reached Potosi, and from Bolivia the company would cross the Cordillera to Peru, where better luck would surely meet them.

Being the latest arrival from North America, I had to answer many questions, as they had not heard from that country since leaving the Paraná, twelve months before. At dusk a negro band played an air that was very popular in the United States nine years before. With all the facilities of communication that exist between the two countries, the song and accompanying music had just reached Mendoza, a town supposed by its inhabitants to be first in the scale of civilization and refinement.

The following morning I visited the Plaza Nueva, where the carts of our caravan were discharging their cargoes, and received from the old Indian my bag.

We parted pleasantly, and I only regretted that my present to him could not have been as great, proportionately, as my regard for him. The *patron* and *capataz* commended me to the care of my Maker, and wished that many years might be added to my life, to which civil speech I made an appropriate reply. As for the peons, they said nothing, nor even comforted me with a single glance or nod of good feeling.

CHAPTER XIII.

MENDOZA.

TWO or three days were passed in inquiring for a troop of mules bound for Chili, but no information could be obtained of any, and I afterwards learned that the last troop of the season had left Mendoza on the day after my arrival, and had barely succeeded in reaching Chili with their lives.

For twenty-one days the Andes were enveloped in clouds, the dark and portentous appearance of which was terrible to behold. I passed hours of each day in watching the fierce *temporales*, as the natives called them, that came rolling along the summit of the sierras from the regions of Cape Horn, covering, in their mad career, whole ranges of mountains in a mantle of snow. To have attempted a passage at that time would have been certain death; so with all the philosophy that could be drawn from irremediable disappointment, I became resigned to my fate to remain in the interior of the country until the genial sun of another spring should melt the snow-drifts that blocked up the passes of the Andes.

The old Spanish town of Mendoza is situated in latitude 32° 51′ south, longitude 67° 57′ west, at the foot of the eastern declivity of the Andes. It was laid out in *cuadras*, or squares, the sides of which were one hundred and fifty yards long. It contained, at the time of my visit, nearly ten thousand inhabitants. Of the two plazas the Independence was the most celebrated, because of the fountain it contained. This fountain, however, was dry when I was there, the aqueduct having become choked with leaves and stones; it had been permitted to remain in this useless state for some time, and I was of the opinion that it would still continue dry, as no attempt was made to clear it out, and no plan was discussed by which it might in the future be again in operation.

The *Alameda*, a much-talked-of public walk on the side of the town nearest the mountains, was resorted to by all classes. An artificial canal flowed beside the principal walk, watering a row of fine poplars, beneath which were a few stone seats, where I often sat and watched the different classes of the Mendozinos promenading after the *siesta.*

In a little mud hut, kept by a Chilino, I was surprised to find a luxury not often met with in southern countries. Ice was brought from the mountains on mules, and the inhabitants were enabled to enjoy their creams at a trifling expense. It was in the *Alameda* that I sometimes had a glimpse of the governor of the province of Mendoza — Don Pedro Pascual Segura. He was a man small in stature, and this characteristic seemed to be general in the different traits of his character, for he was of little energy, and had, consequently, little of the rascality of his predecessors. He was literally small in everything, as the following incident will show.

The Mendoza band belonged to the government, and Don Pedro had disposed of their services by contract, for a certain sum of money, to the theatrical company of Señor Rodenas, who had established himself in the town a short time before my arrival. The North American Circus Company came into the place soon after, and the director presented the governor his compliments and a season ticket to the performances. As the circus company wished to perform on the same evening as the company of Señor Rodenas, and by so doing could not obtain the services of the band, the governor, without further ceremony, broke the contract with the theatre, and ordered half the musicians to the house of the North Americans. This unjust act greatly injured the native performers, who were poor, and had but just arrived from a distant part of the country.

The houses of Mendoza were one story high, and, unlike those of Buenos Ayres, were built of *adobes*, which were covered with mud and whitewashed. These, like the dwellings of that city, had a dreary, prison-like appearance. The *patio*, or yard, was in the centre of the building, and was accessible by a large, heavy door, called the *puerto-calle*. A door from each room opened into the yard, where, in the summer months, the household, including servants, usually slept, for the climate near the mountains has not the heavy dews of the pampas. The roofs were generally of mud, plastered upon canes, bound together by strips of hide, which rested upon a rough frame of willow, poplar, and a hard kind of wood resembling the *algarroba*. The *adobes* were made near the spot where the building was to be erected when sufficient material could be procured. Mud, trodden fine by horses and mixed with straw, was placed in moulds about twenty by eight inches, and four or five deep, and, after being removed, the adobe was allowed to dry in the sun's heat for two or three weeks. Outside the town a rough, square brick was made, which served to floor the houses of the rich, and was covered by a carpet of European manufacture.

The town, at the time of my visit, was liberally supplied with churches, and had a convent. The priests bore a much better character than those of the northern countries of the continent, as in most places where Catholicism exists they have a strong influence over the lower classes, and fill the narrow streets of the town with processions, much to the annoyance of every one who is obliged to kneel uncovered as they pass along. One foreigner told me that when he entered the place for the first time, he halted his horse in the plaza, through which a crowd of people were hurrying with lighted candles and crucifixes. The priest observing that he did not recognize, by humiliating himself, the respect due them, sent a vigilante, who threatened to run him through with the bayonet if he did not dismount from his horse and kneel upon the ground. There being no protecting power nearer than Buenos Ayres, or Santiago in Chili, a foreigner must go through these debasing forms, do homage to man, or feel the point of the bayonet or sword, "for there is no protection for *gringos* in the provinces north and west of Buenos Ayres."

This I had told me more than once by officers of the

government of this republic that pretends to copy the principles that have been expounded by Washington, Jeffèrson, Adams, and Lafayette. I always kept a bright lookout when abroad, and the instant the shaven heads of the good fathers appeared I turned the first corner, and stopped not until two squares were between us.

At a certain season of the year a mock Christ was crucified by the priests. The deluded people, believing it to be the true Savior, wept as they beat their breasts, and cried out with compassion. At these and other services of the church, as the mass and vesper prayer, the men formed a very small portion of the congregation, but the women were constant attendants, and were continually at the confessional.

One young lady with whom I was acquainted made it a rule to confess three times a week. This she continued to do for the space of one year, when good Father Maximo became so weary of her appearance or of her sins, that he told her to come once in seven days, and he would pardon the whole at once. Every morning the early riser met with little parties of females returning from early mass, chatting pleasantly as they proceeded to their homes. Each female who could afford it had a servant, who followed behind with an *alfombra* (mat), upon which the lady sat while in church. The children always went on before, that they might be under the eye of the matron who watched them, particularly if they were young ladies, with a degree of vigilance equal to that of the dueñazas of old Spain.

While speaking of churches and church-goers I will

not omit mentioning a few facts relative to one Padre A. and his family, whose fame is wide-spread in the other provinces of the republic. This A. was a priest in the church of San Domingo, and, breaking his vow, acquainted Rosas with the thoughts and actions of those who had unbosomed themselves to him.

His villanous character began to show itself, and throwing aside the padre's cloak, he took the sword, and became one of the bloodiest generals that Mendoza had ever supported. His deeds of cruelty made him known throughout the country. His family, which had, during his career, enjoyed a notoriety, sank into obscurity after his death.

Several years since, a daughter of the padre, who had distinguished herself for her licentious conduct, performed a journey, in company with her sister and another young lady, — all wild girls, — that proved no less disastrous than it was foolish in design.

The three girls, attired in gaucho costume, set out on horseback, and *not* with side-saddles, to cross the Cordillera of the Andes. The trip was successful. They entered Chili without meeting any obstacle to mar their happiness, and after having passed a few weeks with friends, started to return to the Argentine Republic. The guides warned them of coming *temporales*, but they had tarried from home too long to protract their stay; perhaps to be obliged to remain in Chili until the winter's snows were gone. They entered the mountains, and somewhere near the Cumbre pass, a storm broke upon them, and only two of the females escaped with their lives.

Each church in Mendoza had several bells, which

were far from melodious, having a tinkling sound, and the manner in which they were rung reminded me of our national air. But the people were well satisfied with these discordant sounds, and one of the priests, who had returned from a visit to England, on being asked how he liked that country, replied, —

"England is a fine country, superior to ours in everything save one — the English do not know how to chime their bells."

A theatre of two stories in height had been built under the supervision and at the expense of a certain "scientific gentleman," and though the building was but a whitewashed structure, it raised the gentleman to enviable fame. He was pointed out to me as a profound man, a geologist and astronomer, and furthermore the government would not raise a wall or dig an *acquia* without first consulting Don Carlos's opinion. Though a native of the country, he assumed to be an Italian, but did not succeed in convincing the people to that effect when I left Mendoza. I was told that the don had acquired his principal knowledge of engineering, &c., while assisting Lieutenant Archibald Macrae, of the United States Naval Astronomical Expedition, two or three years before, in taking the altitudes of certain places in the Andes. Don Carlos occasionally turned aside from his researches in science, and amused himself, or became the amuser of the more talented portion of the Mendozinos. Once he collected an eager crowd of people by mounting the roof of a house, and pretending, by means of the needle of the compass, to determine the course and distance of a comet, which, with fiery tail, looked so ominously as to cause many of the gaucho population to believe that the town was about to be destroyed.

I was convinced that the Mendozinos were the most peaceable and hospitable people of the republic, and showed more respect to foreigners than was customary where the old dogmas and customs of the Spanish prevailed. I could not perceive any difference between the higher classes of this town and those of Buenos Ayres in the matter of complexion.

They had as light skins as any Spaniard that I had met in the last named city, and generally retained the purity of blood. The lower classes differed, however. They were of every type that exists in the republic west of Paraná and south of latitude 28°, being composed of peons of the different provinces, while the blood of the Indian and negro courses through the veins of many. They were very immoral and exceedingly ignorant, but were kind-hearted and courteous to strangers. Much time was wasted in dancing and other frivolous amusements. The females of all grades embroidered with skill, and showed great taste in the selection of their patterns. The bonnet was not worn, but a shawl, covering the head and falling gracefully about the form, supplied its place, the temperature being so mild and uniform that no warmer head covering was needed.

I noticed that the ladies painted their cheeks in an extravagant manner; a custom that we should not suppose would have gained entrance to such an isolated place. In San Juan, one hundred and fifty miles to the north, I saw nothing of this, and was told that it was of rare occurrence.

Mendoza was a very healthy place at the time I was there. I learned that many persons, troubled with complaints that usually end in consumption, after residing there a few years were restored to health.

But there was one form of disease which was said by the physicians to be incurable, and which in our own country would lead to a desertion of the site.

This was the goitre of the medical fraternity, and, as I have before mentioned, is known among the people as the *coté*. The disease appeared in the form of a large swelling on the throat, which was caused by the mineral qualities of the River Mendoza.* The canals that supplied the citizens of the town ran through nearly every street, and each family procured their water from them.

The richer portion of the inhabitants had filters, or drip-stones, through which the water was allowed to pass, and become free from all vegetable matter. Now the question presented itself to me, Did the water, in passing through the fine drip-stone, rid itself of any of its mineral properties? and I was led to the opinion that it did, from noticing the fact that the richer classes, having their water thus filtrated, were rarely troubled with the goitre, while the poor people, who drank from the canal itself, presented the disease in all its forms upon them. In fact, the goitre seemed to be a part of their person, for every sixth or seventh female, and now and then a man, that I met during a morning walk, exhibited the disagreeable symptoms.

At San Vicente, a small village, four miles from the

* Undoubtedly the miserable food upon which the poor people subsisted helped in encouraging the growth of this excrescence.

town, the goitre could be examined in all its forms; "for," said an individual to me while in Mendoza, "I fully believe that every fourth woman in the place is affected by it." It was not a rare thing to see a large swelling on both sides of the throat, so large as to be absolutely disgusting. There was in the neighborhood of Mendoza a spring of fine water, but only a few of the citizens took advantage of its existence.

Mendoza had, when I was there, a good school for the instruction of the young, who, like most creoles, acquired knowledge very quickly. A young Englishman was at the head of the establishment, and in all respects the school seemed prospering. Besides the school there was a public library containing three or four thousand volumes, which, if consulted, could not fail to be of benefit to the inhabitants, who were extremely ignorant of things unconnected with their immediate vicinity. The people had recently started a newspaper, "El Constitucional," and, judging by the pompous leaders of the gentleman who occupied the editorial chair, a stranger would have been led to believe that Mendoza was the greatest and most important city on the globe.

For their press, types, etc., they were indebted to Mr. Vansice, formerly of Utica, N. Y., who came to this country several years before, and by his energy became of great assistance to the government of the province. He remodelled many old forms, and liberalized the ideas of the people to such an extent that they encouraged him to revisit North America, and obtain many articles, the introduction of which have facilitated the different kinds of labor in which the people were engaged; and following out this plan to a greater extent, a company was forming, the object of which was to send to the United States for machines, tools, &c. Mr. Vansice furnished two other provinces, also, with printing materials, and used all possible effort to establish a public press on a substantial basis.

After filling offices of dignity and honor, he retired to the miserable little village of San José del Moro, where he resided with his native wife, carrying on a profitable business in English goods, which were brought from Valparaiso.

While I was in Mendoza, the celebration and festivities of the 25th of May, the independence day of the republic, took place, and were celebrated with unusual enthusiasm. For several days previous the people were engaged in preparing for the festivities, though not half of the lower classes knew for what reason the celebration was made, so ignorant were they of their country's history. The government, for one hundred dollars, secured the services of the North American performers, and under their direction a ring of adobes was constructed in the centre of the plaza, and close beside it a rostrum for the governor, his suite, and the musicians. The news of the *gran funcion* that was to take place spread far into the country, and three days prior to the 25th the gauchos came galloping into town from all parts of the province. At sunrise, on the great day, I visited the plaza in which the populace was pouring, the whole forming a most picturesque scene.

Gauchos, gayly attired, were mounted upon horses decked out with silver ornaments, and tails braided with ribbons, and galloping about in little parties. Some farmers came into town, accompanied by their wives and daughters, and it was no uncommon thing to see two women, each with a child in her arms, riding on the same horse with a man. At such galas one sees a degree of life and animation not to be met with at other times; for, as soon as the festival is over, the people sink into a most indolent state, and remain so until the next *dia de fiesta* arouses them to life and action.

The school-boys sang the national hymn, and the governor swore to support the constitution, after which a military review took place. The several companies, as they marched around the plaza, were preceded by a trumpeter, who blew terrific blasts as the occasion required. All the foot soldiers carried old English muskets, the cavalry being armed with short carbines or lances.

Two cannon, the only pieces of artillery in the province, were drawn by foot-soldiers, dressed, like the others, in white pantaloons and jackets, and from beneath the former hung the frill of the gaucho drawers. While the review was taking place, the bells of all the churches were pealing in their usual manner, and rockets were constantly sent off, though the sun shone brightly, which, of course, did not heighten the pyrotechnic display. Nearly every house showed a flag, and among them I observed the English colors floating from the house of the courteous (?) English physician.

During the day many of the gauchos attempted to climb a greased pole erected in the plaza, upon the top of which money had been placed; but not one succeeded in gaining the coveted prize. The only decoration in

PATAGONIANS. (From a Photograph.) — Page 207.

the plaza was a hexagonal figure, resembling a Chinese lantern, and covered with white cloth. Upon each side was painted a figure, one of Liberty, one of Justice, and another, a portrait of General Urquiza and our own Washington, side by side.

The stand was decorated with the flags of the South American republics, and the only foreign one was that of the United States, which floated over the figure of Washington, beside which was a quotation from one of his speeches delivered to the American people.

The circus performance passed off to the delight of all, and the equestrians who could so skilfully perform upon a galloping horse were declared by the gauchos to have been trained for the occasion by his satanic majesty.

Just after the 25th, the Mendozinos were thrown into a great excitement by the announcement that a cacique, attended by fifty of his men, had left his native plains of Patagonia, and was rapidly approaching the town.

Upon the receipt of the news, the governor called together all the musicians, and sent them to escort the savages into Mendoza. The chief encamped outside the town, and, having obtained an interview with the governor, presented, in the most barefaced manner, a petition from his tribe which any other government would have recognized as an insult, and treated it as such. He wished to be told how much per month his tribe would be allowed if they would not steal any more.

Instead of sending them off about their business, or seizing them, the governor treated them like spoiled children, promising them an allowance if they behaved well, and distributing presents among them, after which they were escorted to their own country, fourteen days' travel from Mendoza, by a party of soldiers commanded by an officer.

A day or two before the departure of these Indians, while I was transacting some business in a store, the chief entered, followed by two of his tribe. This beardless savage was dressed in a full English suit, that he had undoubtedly stolen somewhere, as his tribe were notorious robbers.

He addressed me, through an interpreter, in broken Spanish.

Probably suspecting that I was a foreigner, he asked if "Ropa" (Europe) was not my home. He had no knowledge of any other country, but supposed that all foreigners came from the same land on the other side of a great water. I told him concerning my native land, and in the course of the conversation remarked that we had a great many Indians, but that they generally used fire-arms; at which he probably set me down as being as great a liar as himself.

According to his own story, he was a good man, a rich man, and a friend to humanity, and to foreigners in particular. He had the same hypocritical way of talking as the natives of Mendoza, and I came to the conclusion that they had mutually assisted each other in their education.

After scrutinizing the various objects about him, he at length asked me, with a grunt, to lend him four reals. Of course I refused him; but I was curious to learn more of him, and my refusal was not made in the most decided tone possible. He smiled grimly, and commenced telling a long story of his beautiful house (?) far away in Patagonia, where I should always be a welcome visitor. He had vast numbers of ostriches and guanacos running about his grounds, all of which should be at my disposal if I would but accompany him back to the pampas. He liked foreigners, because they were braver than the gauchos. Pausing in the midst of his harangue, he gave me a punch in the ribs, and asked to be accommodated with three reals. I again refused. Taking up the thread of his story, he continued at great length, finally promising to bring me a tame guanaco when he returned to Mendoza. Here followed another poke, and a request for two reals, then one, and finally promising to be content with a medio. I gave it to him, and he left me.

The circus performers intended leaving Mendoza for San Juan, a town lying one hundred and fifty miles to the north, and earnestly wished me to accompany them. To me it mattered little whether I remained four months in Mendoza or any other place; but before accepting their invitation I called upon the *correo*, or Chilian courier, to see if I could possibly cross the Cordillera with him. The *correo* was away on the passage, and the postmaster-general believed that he was detained by the *temporales* that had been raging, and would not return for several weeks.

In crossing the mountains during the winter season, four men form the *correo*. One carries the mail, another wood, another provisions, &c. They do not leave either side oftener than once a month, and are sometimes a whole month in performing the journey, as they are frequently shut up in the snow-huts that are scattered along the road for many days at a time.

The *casuchas*, or snow-huts, are scattered along the trail at irregular distances. These huts are built of brick, with an entrance so constructed as to be above the drifting snow. The post party left Mendoza on mules, or horses, and proceeded into the mountains as far as the depth of snow would permit. Peons then took back the animals, leaving the *correo* to continue the journey on foot. This was the custom at the time of my visit. Upon reaching the main chain of the Andes, the state of the atmosphere was carefully studied, and if the result proved favorable they ascended the Cordillera.

When upon the western side of the chain, the party sometimes adopted an ingenious method for facilitating their progress. Each man carried with him a square piece of hide, upon which he sat, and descended the inclined surfaces with much ease and great rapidity. After reaching Santa Rosa, the first town upon the western side, the *correo* mounts a horse, and gallops to Santiago, the capital of the republic, which is about twenty leagues from the village.

Upon the 5th of June the *correo* had not returned; and as there was no possibility of my crossing into Chili, I consented to go to San Juan, and set out about dusk with the circus manager and one of his men for a *quinta* outside the town, from which we were to start the next morning. The owner of the *quinta* had agreed to take charge of the company's mules and baggage, and act as guide to our party while crossing the dreary *travesia.* We passed, by moonlight, the burial-ground on the outskirts of the town, and reached the muleteer's house, where we found the family sleeping in the yard, — men, women, and dogs, promiscuously.

As I probably shall not in this volume again have occasion to refer to the town of Mendoza, I will here speak of its destruction, which, as my readers doubtless are aware, occurred in 1861, from an earthquake. This most terrible catastrophe, in which thousands of human beings lost their lives, has rarely found a parallel in the history of the western hemisphere.

A recent traveller, who visited the place after the calamity, says, in describing the ruins, —

"I arose at an early hour, and sallied forth to see and contemplate the ruins of the doomed city.

"I walked along the fine avenue of poplars (the Alameda) for about a hundred yards, and turned into the right; a few paces brought me into the nearest street, where I was absolutely struck dumb and immovable with horror at the scene which presented itself.

"As I gazed along the whole length of that street, not a single house was there to be seen standing; all was a confused mass of 'adobes,' beams, and bricks.

"The street was filled upon a level with what remained of the walls of the houses on either side, which at a glance accounted for the fearful number of victims — upwards of twelve thousand — entombed beneath the ruins of that fatal 20th of March, 1861.

"From the plaza I turned towards the north, and there saw the only edifice, or rather portion of one, that had remained entire: it was the theatre, which, having had a considerable quantity of timber in its construction, remained partially uninjured. I ascended to the roof, and got a fine view of the entire city. For a mile around on every side nothing but a chaotic mass of ruins was visible, — the *débris* of a large city razed to the ground in an instant! On the left were the ruins of what had been once a fine church, 'Santo Domingo,' the altar and a portion of the arch being the only remaining traces of its former sacred character.

"Looking away towards the south might be seen the still partially-erect walls of 'San Francisco,' another fine church, which boasted of the largest bell in the city. This bell was pitched from its position to a considerable distance by the shock, and stuck between two towers on the north side of the building, where it may be still seen, wedged in so firmly that all attempts at removing it simply by lifting have failed. On approaching 'Santo Domingo,' in order to examine it more closely, I saw lying about its 'precinct' several human skeletons, and portions of the human form protruding from beneath the masses of masonry. I was almost sickened by the sight, and moved quickly away. In many parts of the city I saw the same horrible exhibition, — skulls, arms, legs, &c., lying about, some still undecayed, especially near a convent on the south side of the city."

A gentleman who was buried under the ruins, and afterwards extricated, in describing his experiences, says, —

"I stood at a table (about half-past eight, P. M.) in the centre of the room, and was in the act of lighting a cigar, when the shock, preceded by a low, rumbling noise, was first felt. It was slow for a moment in the beginning; but from the noise, I concluded it was going to be something more than ordinary; so I rushed into the street, and ran down the middle, intending, if possible, to reach the Alameda. I had run only some twenty paces when I felt as if I had been struck a heavy blow on the back of the head, and was borne down to the earth in a moment. I knew that the town was infested with rats and vermin of all kinds, and that, sooner or later, they would not fail to find me out amongst the thousands of victims entombed, like myself, beneath at least six feet depth of 'adobes.'"

Mr. Hinchliff, who visited Buenos Ayres, in writing of the earthquake, says, —

"M. Bravart, a French *savant* of some eminence, who had foretold the destruction of the city by an earthquake, was himself among the victims. The principal watchmaker in Buenos Ayres, which is about eight hundred miles distant from the scene of this awful calamity, told me a curious fact in connection with it. One day he observed with astonishment that his clocks suddenly differed twelve seconds from his chronometers; and when the news arrived, about a fortnight later, he found that the pendulums of the former had been arrested at the moment of the destruction of Mendoza."

Since my return to the United States I received a letter from Don Guillermo Buenaparte, of San Juan, in which he spoke at considerable length of the earthquake. He wrote me that when he approached Mendoza, three or four days after the catastrophe, the stench rising from the dead bodies beneath the ruins was perceived at a distance of several miles from the town. He found gauchos from the plains robbing the wounded, and searching among the rubbish for plunder. When he reached the public square of the city he found more than a hundred women, all mentally affected, many entirely bereft of their reason; all were praying on their knees, asking the Holy Mary to intercede for the lost souls of their countrymen who had, prior to the fall of the doomed city, united with others from San Luis, and had attacked and butchered many of their political enemies (some four hundred) of San Juan. The unfortunate lunatics seemed to think that God had overthrown their city to avenge the murder of San Juaninos. A political conspiracy was being planned in the city at the time it was destroyed.

Such a spectacle as the above needs no comment.

At four o'clock of the next morning after our departure from Mendoza, the muleteer aroused us, and bade us prepare for the journey; and an hour later we were journeying along the base of the lofty Andes, that towered above our heads.

Two hours' ride brought us to the *travesia*, over which we journeyed, passing close to a great lake that is supplied by two streams that flow from the Cordillera.

Much of the water is absorbed by the soil about the lake; and as but very little escapes through one or two outlets, it has been called by the natives "El Guana Cache," or the Consuming Lake.

I afterwards saw specimens of fishes that had been taken from its waters, which were offered for sale in San Juan by the half-starved peons during the winter season, when provisions were very dear. If the specimens did not belong to the genus Nematogenys of Girard, they were closely allied to it.

At night our party stopped beside a rude hut, inhabited by a poor gaucho. The hut contained a curious family of men, women, children, dogs, goats, and fowls. The poor owner begged for a little sugar as a *remedio.*

Throughout the following day our course was over the same dreary desert, and at night we were glad to arrive at a post-house within a few leagues of San Juan.

By noon of the next day our party entered the town, which is still more isolated than Mendoza, being one hundred and fifty miles north of the principal road to Chili.

CHAPTER XIV.

A WINTER IN SAN JUAN.

AS soon as I arrived at San Juan, I made inquiries for parties who were about crossing the mountains; but owing to a most severe snow storm that set in, the clouds of which were plainly visible from the town, I was forced to the disagreeable necessity of remaining until the snows melted. The people told me that the winter had proved to be the most severe of any season within the last thirty years. They said that after ten dry or mild winters there always succeeded a similar number of wet or severe seasons, and that the present was the first of the hard series. The apparently settled weather that greeted me was but the precursor of most severe storms in the mountains. They said I could not cross; to attempt it would be madness.

While the time hung heavily on my hands, I heard much about a strange person, yclept Don Guillermo Buenaparte, a North American by birth, and a second father to the poorer classes of his immediate vicinity. So many were the charitable deeds of this man, and so frequent were the eulogies pronounced upon his character by the natives, that I felt a desire to visit him in his own castle, which he had constructed of mud and sticks, some eight or nine miles distant, in a small *villa* called Causete.

Before I could find an opportunity of going, I was favored with a call from the gentleman himself, who rode into the *patio* of my dwelling one evening, mounted upon a powerful white horse, and covered with a long *poncho*, which, with a broad *sombrero*, gave him a truly patriarchal appearance.

Don Guillermo, having heard of my arrival in San Juan, had come to invite me to his estate in Causete, where he carried on a little flour mill, and followed a number of other occupations. A day was appointed for the visit, and when it came around I set out with a peon for a guide for the *villa*. We soon, on leaving the town, came upon a plain which gave support to a few stunted trees, peculiar to the *travesia*. With the soil was mingled the peculiar saline mineral described in a former chapter, which, with the dryness of the atmosphere (for it seldom rains in this part of the republic), made our journey a disagreeable one.

In crossing this tract the reflections of the sun's rays upon the white surface affected my sight, and obliged me to follow the practice of my guide, and, like him, cover the face with a large cotton handkerchief, *à la gaucho*. The first human habitation that I saw was a rancho built of cornstalks; and here reposed a peon with his wife, children, and dogs, while a huge buck goat, with a formidable pair of horns, stood at the entrance as if to receive us.

I soon came to a place where a liberty pole was standing; and knowing that such a thing could not be the work of the natives, I concluded that I must be near the residence of my new acquaintance. I was not mistaken, for he soon appeared over a little rising ground. After greeting me cordially, he led me across the canal, that furnished his mill with water, to his house, where he introduced me to his wife and four children, the youngest of whom could not yet lisp its father's name.

I remained through the day with them, and when night came on, so interesting had been Don Guillermo's recital of nine years' residence in the Argentine Republic, that I was easily prevailed upon to remain until morning. The next day came and passed, but still I was an inmate of my countryman's house, and finally was persuaded to promise that I would not leave it until the snows began to melt upon the Cordilleras, when I must hasten to Chili, and from its principal port, Valparaiso, sail for home.

I accepted the offer of Don Guillermo's hospitality only upon the condition that I should be of service to him by taking charge of his mill; for the natives were so dishonest that he dared not employ one in any office of trust, and I felt that it would be but a pleasure for me to aid him. I was accordingly installed, after fifteen minutes' teaching, as *molinero*, or chief miller.

I felt proud of my office, though it was but a humble one. My mind was fully occupied, and I became contented. When opportunities offered, I took an old condemned English musket, which I charged with powder and a few pebbles, and made explorations in the surrounding country for the purpose of making collections in its *fauna*. I often captured many a rare specimen, and laid the foundation of an ornithological collection; but although I had no difficulty in getting specimens and preparing them, — for taxidermy was familiar to me, — I found one great obstacle to their preservation that I could not surmount. As my readers doubtless know, arsenic is very essential for preserving the skins of birds and mammals, and I found I could do but little without it. So one day I mounted my horse, — a present from Don Guillermo, — and galloped into town in quest of the mineral; but not one of the druggists would sell me an ounce of poison; it was a crime to vend the article. I applied to the physicians, but to no avail. I next tried some of the officers of the government, but failed again. I even offered *three dollars* for one pound. The doctors and officers exclaimed, "What does the boy want? He's mad! Where did he come from?" &c.

Despondingly I returned to the mill, and my fine collection, intended for a scientific society at home, was destroyed in a short time by a minute species of red ants, which ate the skins almost entirely.

A pair of burrowing owls, a dove, a stilt, and a few eggs were all that I succeeded in bringing home with me.

At the mill the season proved to be a busy one. Merchants from other provinces visited San Juan, and, after disposing of their goods, generally invested their returns in wheat, which was sent to the mill to be ground. There were no water privileges in the interior, and the merchants and farmers of Cordova and San Luis frequently sent wheat three or four hundred miles by troops of mules. My office, therefore, proved an advantageous one, as I was enabled to have direct intercourse with people from several of the northern and eastern provinces. Among the numbers that I became acquainted with were the old-fashioned Riojano, who came from his distant home to the north of the desert, clothed in a heavy *frasada*, manufactured from wool of his own shearing by the industry of his wife or daughter. Sometimes the Indian-looking Santiaguenian, or Catamarcan, and the crafty yet polite Cordovese, traded at the mill; and many were the little gifts that the most respectable portion of my customers brought me from their estates far back in the irrigated *travesia*, or along the bases of the Andes. The press of business demanded that the mill should be run night and day. This compelled the poorer classes that came from a distance to sleep in the mill. And at night, when all was quiet, save the restless hum of the revolving stone, it was a curious sight to peep in at the door, and behold the ground covered with sleeping forms of men, women, and children of many types and complexions — here the offspring of the negro and Indian; there the child of a Spanish father and Indian mother. It was a study worthy the attention of a profound ethnologist to separate and classify the various crosses and mixtures of the different races of the genus *homo* that came to the mill of Don Guillermo Buenaparte.

Leaving the dusty atmosphere of the mill, I frequently wandered out into the night air to gaze upon nature by moonlight. The canal that watered the district of Causete branched off in a different direction from the main *acquia*, and could be traced, as it wound along the *travesia*, by the willows and clumps of reeds that grew upon its banks. The Andes towered above the plains a few miles to the west, while on the east the solid range of the mountains of Cordova, stretching far to the north, gave an additional grandeur to the scene. The nights were bland and lovely, excepting when the wind called the *zonda* (a sort of sirocco) came from the Andes, when the natives suffered from its parching heat, and those affected with diseases of the heart trembled in expectation of sudden death.

While I strolled along the banks of the canal the mill hummed on as usual, for Don Guillermo had constructed an ingenious method of alarm, by means of which the absent or sleepy miller was warned of the state of affairs within the building.

Such was the delight that I took in these rambles upon the *travesia*, that duty was in one or two instances neglected, and I found, on returning to the mill, that some villanous male or degraded female was stealing the "millings" from the miller's box, or purloining flour from the hide sack of some countryman who was fast in the embrace of the drowsy god. Once or twice, on such occasions, I became so vexed as to attempt clearing the room of the thievish fellows; but to accomplish this required a stronger arm than mine, and one attempt almost resulted in a general *mêlée;* but as the female customers always took sides with the gringo, I came off in good condition, and attained my object: thus the good name of the mill was not forfeited.

The gauchos love to gamble, and while waiting for the mill to do its work, they generally spent the time in playing their favorite games, always staking small sums of money upon the chances in order to make the time pass more profitably. But whatever might have been the rules of the other mills, Don Guillermo soon put a stop to what he called a degenerating practice, and by various small skirmishes with the gaucho peons, he fully demonstrated that *his* was a North American institution, and that, therefore, gambling could not be permitted upon his premises. The peons remonstrated, but the don was firm. They threatened to ruin his business by patronizing the other mills in preference to his own; but as their masters respected the policy of my friend, they were restrained from carrying out their designs. Thus law and order were firmly established, and North American principles were triumphant. It requires no small degree of firmness and knowledge of human nature to carry on the flour and grain business in the Argentine Republic.

Peace and quiet did not last long before a second innovation was attempted, although upon a new plan. A band of thieves and loafers erected a hut of cornstalks and briers upon the opposite side of the canal, in the district of Anjuaco, and the place was once more disturbed by midnight revels, and by frequent raids upon the grounds of neighboring farmers. Sheep, calves, and, even horses, disappeared in a mysterious manner. At length Don Guillermo became exasperated, and watching an opportunity when the rascals were absent, he attacked the shanty, levelled it to the ground, and, collecting the ruins into one pile, set fire to it, and burned it to ashes.

The party returned, and, on seeing the condition of their house, would, in their rage, have demolished the buildings of the don, had not fear prevented them; for they well knew that the law-and-order man possessed fire-arms, dogs, and a stout heart.

During my stay at the mill I occasionally visited the town of San Juan, and passed a few hours with some acquaintances. I found, to my surprise, among the wealthier citizens, a class of society, which, for dignity of deportment, strictness in etiquette, and generous hospitality, would favorably compare with any class that I have met in the United States or in Europe. The young men were intelligent and full of generous ardor, and the maidens — how shall I describe them? Since returning to North America, my friends have sometimes asked if they resembled our Indian women!

"Most certainly not," I have almost indignantly answered. The higher classes of San Juan boast of a pure descent from the old Spaniards or Portuguese. The fine, clear atmosphere of the Andes provinces has affected favorably the complexion, and most of these people have a skin as light as that of the inhabitants of the southern states of the Union.

Many of the females, particularly the younger ones, have complexions that, in clearness and beauty, would rival the blondes of the north. In addition to personal beauty, the ladies of San Juan can boast of varied attractions. The guitar is used with a grace and skill that give evidence of careful study and long practice. Many play upon the piano, using instruments that have been carted a thousand miles over the pampas, from the port of Buenos Ayres.

All can embroider with skill and elegance. Poetry appears to be assiduously cultivated among them, and many specimens of true inspiration came to my notice that would be considered worthy of the name of Tennyson or Longfellow.

Altogether I know of no situation more pleasant, or containing more elements of interest and romance, than San Juan. It combines every description of scenery, from the arid plain of the *travesia* to the sublime alpine ranges; and it has a climate, during many months of the year, of surpassing loveliness.

The San Juaninos are a most hospitable people; and when the remembrance of their unaffected and genial kindness comes to my mind, I feel the keenest regret that we are so widely separated.

The town is said to contain about nine thousand inhabitants; but I think the estimate high, although many persons have given a larger population. It certainly, in numbers, falls below Mendoza. The town is laid out in the same manner as was Mendoza, and is watered by the canals that run from the River San Juan, a stream rising in the Cordillera.

No goitre exists in this vicinity. I saw only one case of it during my stay, and the subject had lived many years in Mendoza.

About the town are large pastures of clover, which serve to fatten the numerous herds of cattle that pass through the town on the way to Copiapo or Coquimbo, in Chili. Soap, raisins, and cattle are among the exports to the latter named state. Flour is forwarded to the pampa towns, and to the villages on the *travesia.* Wine is made in large quantities, but does not now pay a sufficient profit if sent to any considerable distance, although it was exported largely in by-gone years. All the fruits that grow in Mendoza thrive better in this province. The oranges of Mendoza seemed to possess an acrid taste, but I did not detect this in any of the fruits of San Juan. The vineyards surpass anything that I have ever seen, — not in the culture of the grape, as but little is done to the vines, but in the quality of the fruit. I distinguished eleven kinds of grapes in the *quintas* around San Juan.

The iron plough and other improved implements of agriculture were unknown, and when I described to the *quinteros* the facility with which the celebrated Prouty and Mears centre draught plough is handled, they fairly overwhelmed me with questions, which had, at least, the merit of artlessness.

There is at San Juan a Board of Water Commissioners, who have charge of the irrigating department. These officials are seven in number. They have labored hard to extend the main canals beyond the *villas* of Causete and Anjaco, even to the very base of the *Pié de palo*, or wooden foot — a sierra some fourteen miles east of San Juan. By these means the sterile saline *travesia* is gradually becoming clothed with verdure, and spreading pastures of clover, surrounded by poplars and willows, cover spots that three years since were occupied only by scattered thorn-bushes.

As I have already mentioned, the situation of miller, that I filled, was the means of giving me many opportunities for meeting and studying different phases of character.

One of my customers, whom I have set down in my journal as Don José, the penitent, was indeed a study.

15

He was a large-limbed, long-winded, courageous old fellow, of the pure Spanish stock, and descended from the original conquerors of the Argentine Republic. I had frequently heard his name mentioned by the gauchos, one or two of whom delighted in telling of his prowess during the last revolution. The town of San Juan had been taken by an armed band while the illustrious Benavides was outside the place, and Don José, who was then an *arriero*, or muleteer, felt it his duty to rescue it from what he considered the wrong political party. The *cuartel* had been taken, and no soldiers could be enlisted for the purpose; but Don José's energy did not fail. He scoured the country about San Juan, and collected twenty-five gauchos, who followed him to the town. The precipitate entry made by the gallant little party struck fear and consternation into the revolutionists, and Don José was hailed as deliverer for many weeks.

The rich people, who had never before noticed him, now touched their *sombreros*, and honored him with their praise and approbation. But, as Don José said, this did not give him money, and he therefore was no better in station than before the revolution. He was still a peon. After the excitement had died away, and rich dons no longer doffed their hats as he passed, he sat soberly down and meditated upon how he could raise money enough to rent him a farm, for he well knew that his industry would soon make him independent, provided he could hire a spot of land fit for cultivation. Nobody would loan him a *peso*.

Our hero, nevertheless, did not despond. He sought relief in religion, but in a different manner from that which is usually practised. The don knew that several of the churches of the town had large endowments. People dying, and wishing to enter a better world, there to enjoy a life of bliss, had left sums of money to the church, surely not to be applied to charitable purposes, for the priests generally require nine dollars for saying mass over the body of the poorest child of the church. The priests will sometimes lend these moneys upon good security, and to pious people, at the low rate of five per cent.; and we may well call this a low rate, when, in business transactions, the people of the interior towns rarely charge less than eighteen per cent.

The don, knowing that he had not attended mass regularly, did not feel satisfied that his application for money to the priests would meet with success, and he therefore commenced a plan that, if carried out, would insure him all the money that his wants required. He resolved to become a penitent. He looked back over his past life with sorrow. "I have sinned — have sinned more than all others," he said to the other penitents. "I am resolved to change my mode of life, and now I will live for some good purpose."

Each day his phiz lengthened. "How solemn he looks!" said the friends of his family; "poor Don José!" He lost flesh rapidly, and the brave deliverer of the town became feeble as a woman. He attended church regularly, was always at the masses, and never absent from the confessional. He was, in short, a model church member. The priests were his friends, — not the jolly, fat, laughing padres, but the frizzle-headed, stern old fellows, that rarely smiled, and then only at the follies of the world. Don José fasted a great deal, and then, after advising with his confessor, determined to scourge himself, and to pass three days in solitary confinement. He bade adieu to his friends, and locked himself into a little domicile that belonged to the church. Here, in communion with himself, he passed three long days and nights without food. With a short piece of raw hide he chastised his body, — vicariously, probably, after the example of his illustrious Manchegan countryman, — and spots of blood (from the arteries of an ox) were observed upon the floor and walls of the chamber when good Father R. entered, and who declared that his son had done his duty nobly.

Don José had accomplished his object. He could be trusted by the clergy now, and it was with pleasure that the treasurer-padre gave the sum required by our hero. With the borrowed money he rented a farm, and I can so far attest to the success of his operations, that as I passed his residence I often filled my saddle-bag with the fruits of his penitence, which I took to the mill to make happy the little cherubs of Don Guillermo.

CHAPTER XV.

A WINTER IN SAN JUAN—CONTINUED.

WITH the approach of spring, the desert around the mill became a constant source of study to me. The lagoon near the house was filled with seven or eight species of ducks and teals, and occasionally a pair of white swans might be seen upon the water, where they frequently staid for several days in succession. The ducks remained throughout the whole year; and before I left Causete, the *China* or half-breed girls were frequently seen swimming into the lagoon, where they captured great numbers of the young fowl.

The green-winged teal, pin-tailed duck, and other species of the northern continent, were far from uncommon.

One day, while standing in the doorway of the mill, attempting to get a glimpse of a dim line of the point of the *Pié de palo*, where I had been told that a beautiful region, called the "Fertile Valley," lay embosomed in trees, my attention was attracted to a dark spot in the sierra, which seemed to be a hole in the rock. On the following day, at sunset, I again distinguished the same dark spot: each day it grew larger; and one morning an old miner came into the mill, and informed me that a company of Chilenos were opening a vein;

the situation of the *sierra*, the peculiarities of the rock, &c., led him to doubt of the practicability of the undertaking. How the party succeeded in their search for gold I have not yet learned; but the antecedents of the mountain are bad, for when the *sierra* was discovered by the early adventurers, in expectation of finding gold, they named it *Pié de Oro*, or "Foot of Gold," and afterwards, when they had been disappointed in searching for the ore, they dropped the first name, and called it that by which it is known at the present day — *Pié de Palo*, or "Wooden Foot."

The llama and other animals are found in the *sierra* of this section, which are also known — for what reason I never could learn — as the mountains of Cordova. I had not time to visit the range when in Causete, though I much desired to do so, as the old guides and miners told many strange stories regarding it.

One evening, as I was in the mill at work, a servant came from the house, saying that Don Guillermo wished to see me, and give me an introduction to a guest who had just arrived. I repaired to the house, where I made the acquaintance of the celebrated gaucho, *Diablo* McGill. As he has quite a local notoriety, I will speak of him more fully here than I otherwise would.

McGill was celebrated above most gauchos for his skill in using the lasso, knife, and *boliadores*, and in the management of wild colts. He was the handsomest herdsman that I ever saw, and was so polite and easy in his intercourse with strangers that I at first doubted if he was really the wild gaucho of whom I had heard so much. McGill was the owner of a troop of mules; he left his native province to follow the wandering life of a pampa merchant, because he despised his own countrymen, and declared that they were all peons (laborers), and not gauchos; for the province in which he was born, being situated upon the desert, at the base of the Andes, contained very few cattle-farms, and consequently the inhabitants were mostly traders, laborers, and "loafers."

He visited the province annually, and while in his native town invariably played some mad prank to astonish the natives, and keep his reputation as a *diablo.*

On feast days he dressed himself in the full habiliments of a herdsman, a showy *chiropá*, finely-wrought drawers, heavy silver spurs, &c. His horse was selected with care from his corral, and bedecked with silver ornaments from the head to the tail, and a costly *recado*, or country saddle, placed upon its back. Thus equipped, he would sally forth to visit the various *pulperias*, or drinking-shops, where the gauchos crowded to listen to his songs, and tales of mighty deeds transacted while accompanying his troop of mules across the lonely pampas.

All the señoritas felt happy when McGill asked them to accompany him through *la samba cueca*, *el gato*, or *la mariquita*, as the three principal dances are styled, and she who could keep the wild gaucho by her side for one half hour felt more gratified than if she had made a dozen ordinary conquests. But the wild gaucho could not love a fair señorita, though she might be the belle of the province. Horses, wild colts, wild bulls, and wild gauchos were his chosen companions, and the fair sex tried, but in vain, to find some uncovered spot upon which to make an impression: he was impenetrable to the shafts of Cupid.

The story is told that, during one of his last visits, Don Antonio Moreno, who had always envied the success of McGill, challenged him to prove his skill in the use of the lasso. McGill accepted the challenge, and entered, lasso in hand, the corral of the jealous Don Antonio.

"I will do more than you challenge me to attempt," said our hero, coolly. "Here are five hundred mules in this circular yard, and as you drive around the circle they run eight or ten abreast. Now, I will stand in the middle, and as they pass around me you are to call out which mule you wish lassoed, and upon what leg or part of the body the animal is to be noosed. This you must do when the particular beast is in front of me, so that I can throw the lasso *when she is behind me.* As fast as one is caught, you are to remove her from the corral. Thus will I catch each of the five hundred mules, without missing a single throw, and catch them while they pass BEHIND MY BACK. Will that satisfy you, Don Antonio Moreno?"

The other party looked incredulous. Don Antonio was himself a first-rate gaucho and *rastreador;* he had seen good lassoing, but this offer seemed preposterous.

"Go on, McGill," he said, with a contemptuous shrug of the shoulders. "When you have caught five hundred mules behind your back, I will pay you well for your trouble."

The gaucho took his place in the centre of the yard, and, as the mules were driven around the circle, threw his lasso with unerring skill; first one, then another, then a third, rolled over upon the ground, always falling upon the head in a particular manner.

Don Antonio suspected the gaucho, and perceiving his object in throwing the mules upon their heads, protested against it.

"You will break the necks of half of them!" he exclaimed to the gaucho, who at the same moment, with a dexterous jerk on the lasso, sent another mule, stunned, upon the ground.

"Stop!" he shouted. "McGill, what mean you by throwing the mules in that manner?"

"What do I mean?" replied the herdsman, as another mule shared the same fate of the last one. "What do I mean? Why, man, I mean to break the necks of all your mules, that I may give you a certain proof that I *can* throw the lasso equal to, and better than, any San Juanino."

"Enough! enough!" replied the excited don. "You have proved it; there is no necessity of further effort. Besides, these mules are to be driven across the Cordillera into Chili, and if you break their necks it's money out of my pocket. Had we not better enter the house? I believe Doña Trinidad is ready to serve *maté*."

When McGill rode forth upon a feast day as Gaucho Porteño, or Buenos Ayrean herdsman, the peons of San Juan gazed with astonishment upon his rich trappings. I have the list of articles that he and his animal wore. Upon his favorite black horse were first placed three *bageras*, or skins, to preserve the animal's back from the chafing of saddle-gear. Upon these were laid a heavy, fine-wrought *jergon*, or blanket, to absorb the perspiration; over these were laid, first, a *corona de vaca*, or cow's hide covering, to give firmness to the saddle; secondly, a *corona* of fine leather, to hide the rougher pieces beneath.

The latter article, which was richly embossed, was very ornamental, and drew from the gauchos many admiring remarks. Upon this platform, or foundation, the *recardo* was placed, and kept firmly in position by a wide *cincha*, or girth, cut from softened, untanned hide. A *pellon*, or sheepskin, was laid upon the saddle, and kept in its place by a smaller girth. The *pellon* was then covered with a small piece of embroidered cloth, worked by the hands of some fair damsel. The lasso lay upon the animal's croup, behind the rider, and was attached to an iron ring in the broad *cincha*. A pair of *alforjas*, or saddle-bags, were thrown across the peak of the saddle, and around the animal's neck hung a leather rope, the *biador*, used to tie him when feeding, though the lasso is generally employed for that purpose.

Upon the peak of the saddle were swung the *chifles*, two cows' horns, in which was carried wine or water,— fluids absolutely indispensable upon the *travesia* of San Luis.

From beneath the left side of the *coronas*, close by the peak of the saddle, peeped the three balls, the well-known *boliadores* (called in most works of travel *bolas*), with which the gaucho secures game while upon the road.

Hanging from the *fiador* was a pair of *manes*, or shackles, for the horse's fore feet, which serve the same purpose as a pair of handcuffs. If the rider wishes to leave his horse in the street, where many travellers are passing, he places the *manes* upon the animal's fore legs, and it is only with great difficulty that the beast can slowly move about. Lastly, the bridle, a magnificent article, formed of leather, and thickly studded with silver plates, and the horse was equipped. McGill was dressed in the gala costume of a Buenos Ayrean gaucho, with drawers of the finest needlework, and the *chiropá*, that covered his loins, of costly silk. From this description the reader can gain some idea of a fast man among the gauchos, for such was the guest of Don Guillermo.

In this connection I may devote a few lines to a character well known throughout the Provinces of La Plata — the *rastreador*, or trailer.

While the mill was in operation one afternoon, I had occasion to leave the building, in order to let on more water from the *acquia*. While attending to the floodgate, I saw an old man slowly approaching the mill, with his eyes bent upon the ground. He frequently stopped to inspect the soil; then, continuing his course, he passed the mill, and crossed the rude bridge that spanned the canal. Continuing along the *travesia* in the district of Anjuco, he was soon lost among the thorn trees and thickets of *mata-gusano*. I thought no more of the old man, supposing that he had probably lost some article, and was searching for it. An hour later he returned to the mill, and said a few words to Don Guillermo and several gauchos, who were waiting for their respective turns at the hopper. In an instant the room was vacated; the party dispersed along the road, and as they occasionally came together near the mill, I could see the old man giving some advice, upon which the gauchos again dispersed. The party returned about eight o'clock, and from the peons I learned that the old man was a trailer. He had been walking along the road, and had noticed a footprint that struck him as "deceitful." He said that a man had passed the mill about three o'clock, and that the man was a robber. "For he was dressed," said the trailer, "in woman's clothes. There are places along his trail that prove he held the dress up with his hands; in others it trailed along the ground. He wore a woman's shoe, which did not fit him; his foot was broad, the shoe long and narrow. He walked in some places, and ran through the thickets. No man dresses in woman's garb without some bad intent."

"He is somewhere among the ranchos of Anjuco."

Wonderful to state, news came from town the next day that several men had dressed themselves in female attire, and in that disguise had visited the stores in the Calle Ancho, or Broadway, where they had purloined many articles, which the rogues had hidden beneath their dresses. It was the trail of one of these dresses that the old *rastreador* had struck.

The patriot Sarmiento, a San Juanino by birth, says of the characteristics of these men, the trailers, —

"Once, as I was crossing a path that led into the Buenos Ayres road, the muleteer that conducted me cast his eyes upon the ground, as was his custom, and said a very good black mule passed here yesterday; she had an easy gait, and was saddled; she belongs to the troop of Don ——. This man was coming from the *sierra* of San Luis; the troop was returning from Buenos Ayres.

"A year had passed since he had seen the black

mule, the track of which was confused with those of a whole troop, in a path not more than two feet wide. But this keenness of perception, so apparently incredible, is a faculty common to every gaucho; this man was a mere muleteer, and not a professional trailer."

He also describes another trailer in *La Vida de Juan*, Facundo Quiroga, as follows: —

"I knew a trailer by the name of Calibar, who had practised his profession in one province during forty successive years. He is now nearly eighty years old, and though bowed with age, still retains a venerable and dignified appearance.

"When they speak to him of his fabulous reputation, he answers, 'I am now useless; these are my children.' It is said of him that during a trip that he made to Buenos Ayres a saddle was stolen from his house.

"His wife covered the robber's track with a wooden bowl. Two months later Calibar returned home, and saw the almost obliterated footprint, that to other eyes was imperceptible, and nothing more was said of the occurrence. A year and a half afterwards Calibar was walking along a street in the suburbs of the town, with his head inclined towards the ground. He entered a house, and found a saddle, blackened, and almost worthless from use; he had found the trail of the robber after a lapse of two years.

"During the year 1830 a criminal had escaped from jail, and Calibar was charged to find him. The unhappy man, knowing that he would be tracked, had taken all the precautions which the fear of the scaffold could invent.

"Useless precautions! Perhaps they only served to

insnare him, for Calibar felt that his reputation might be compromised, and self-pride caused him to acquit himself well.

"The runaway took every advantage of the unevenness of the ground so as to baffle his pursuer; but his efforts only proved the marvellous sight of the *rastreador*.

"He walked the whole length of streets on tiptoe, then climbed low walls, crossed a pasture, and returned in his own track.

"Calibar followed without losing the trail. If he momentarily missed it, it was soon recovered. At last he arrived at a canal of water in the suburbs, where the fugitive had followed the current, to foil the trailer. But in vain! Calibar followed along the shore without any uneasiness, and at last stopped to examine some grass, with the words, 'At this place he came out; there is no track, but these drops of water in the pasture indicate it.'

"The fugitive had entered a vineyard. Calibar surveyed with his eye the walls that surrounded it, and said, 'He is within.' The party of soldiers that attended him sought in the vineyard without success. At length they became tired of hunting, and returned to report the uselessness of their search. 'He has not come out,' was the brief answer which the trailer gave, without moving himself, or proceeding to a new examination. He had not come out, indeed; another search discovered him, and on the following day he was executed."

CHAPTER XVI.

VIENTE DE ZONDA.

IN a preceding chapter I made reference to the *viente de zonda*, or zonda wind; and as the history of it is imperfectly known in the northern continent, I will here speak of it to some extent.

The *viente de zonda* may be called a local wind, as it blows only in the vicinity of the province of San Juan, the town where the following observations were made.

San Juan, the capital of the province, lies at the eastern base of the Andes, three or four leagues distant from the outer sierra, south latitude 31° 4′ (Molina), longitude 68° 57′ west (Arrowsmith). Behind the first range in a valley are four or five farms, which constitute the hamlet of Zonda, from which the wind is named. It blows at all seasons, though during July and August (midwinter) it is most frequent. This wind is hot and parching to the skin, and brings with it clouds of dust and fine sand.

All persons leave their work, and seek refuge in their houses, while frequently the huts of the gauchos are blown down by the force of the wind. Most persons are troubled with severe headaches. Those who have been suffering from diseases of the heart find their complaints greatly aggravated, and frequently there are cases of sudden death. Three or four years since, five persons fell dead during the *zondas* in the month of August. The wind lasts sometimes two or three hours; at other times, forty-eight hours, though this long duration is rare. While the *zonda* is at its height, a few puffs of cold air from the south announce a change, and immediately the weather-cock veers from east and west to north and south, and a cold wind, equally as strong as the hot *zonda*, then prevails from the south. All nature is refreshed by the change, and men resume their abandoned labors.

In searching through the works of the very few authors who have visited the interior of the Argentine states (all but one or two of whom were Europeans), I find that only one mentions the existence of this phenomenon; and he did not, probably, visit the town where my observations were made, which locality is considered by the natives as the northern limit of the *zondas*.

John Miers, the author of an interesting work on the Provinces of La Plata and Chili, remained a short time in Mendoza. He states that this southern locality is annoyed by winds that blow during the summer months from the valley of Zonda, and notes the fact that two dark clouds came from the north-west, and hovered over the town during the greater part of the night, and in the morning everything that had been exposed to the air was covered with fine sand, which was of a light gray color, and slightly magnetic. It was Miers's opinion that "a *souffrière*, or active volcano," existed to the northward of San Juan, from which the hurricanes and showers of sand originated. Had Mr. Miers visited San Juan, his view of the position of the volcano would, undoubtedly, have been changed; for though the *zondas* reach Mendoza to the south, the direction of the wind when it strikes that place differs from the line it follows when it rushes with violence upon the northern town. At San Juan it comes due west from the Andes. Hence the starting-point of the *zonda* cannot be to the north of the town, as Miers conjectured. According to the account of the natives, the *zonda* of San Juan does not cover a broader space than ten or fifteen miles after it leaves the sierra of Zonda.

Taking this into consideration, in connection with Miers's statement that the Mendoza *zonda* comes from the north-west, differing, as it will be seen, four points from the northern town, we may infer that the Mendoza and San Juan *zondas* do not blow at the same time. If this is true, it is an interesting fact, showing that this peculiar wind does not always follow the same track.

Miers further states that these are summer winds in Mendoza. From personal observation, and by reliable accounts of educated San Juaninos, I found that they were more particularly the winter winds; at least they are more frequent during that season. Invalids suffering from pneumonical diseases and complaints affecting the heart and liver, anticipate the month of August (midwinter) with consternation, and their anxiety is not quieted until they have passed through the dreaded ordeal.

While passing the winter in San Juan, I noted the

courses of upwards of twenty *zondas*. Some were of short duration; others lasted eighteen or twenty hours.

During the latter part of August, as I was standing upon the saline desert, a few miles east of San Juan, my attention was attracted by a cloud of dust that appeared to roll through the air as it approached me. I started for a shelter, and had hardly reached it when the *zonda* swept past, filling the air with fine yellow sand. The temperature of the previously sultry atmosphere suddenly rose many degrees, and the occupants of the neighboring huts were affected with severe headaches. I noted, with a compass, the course of the wind, which was west. All night and through the following day and night, the wind continued blowing with undiminished force. Each hour the vane beside the hut was consulted, and the same course as at first was always observed. A few hours before the wind ceased the sand showers were exhausted. The greatest heat was during the first few hours; and this is always the case if the *zonda* commences during the day. After continuing for thirty-six hours the change came. It was instantaneous. The hot wind seemed cut off at right angles by a cold wind from the south. The change could not have occupied more than forty seconds. The south wind lasted twenty hours, and was as violent as the hot *zonda*. In speaking of the Mendoza *zondas*, Miers does not mention the succession of the south wind. It is easy to comprehend that, after so large an area has become filled with heated air, the effect will be felt in the cooler regions of the south, and a strong current from that direction will rush in to restore the atmospheric equilibrium. Hence the cause of the south wind succeeding the *zonda*.

Miers believed that the origin of the *zondas* was volcanic, and a corroboration of his views is found in the work of Sir Woodbine Parish, in which he states that the volcano Penguenes, which is situated about one hundred miles south-west from Mendoza, and reaches an altitude of nearly fifteen thousand feet above the level of the sea, emits clouds of ashes and pumice-dust. This dust is carried by the winds as far as Mendoza, but these clouds do not strike the town with the force of the San Juan *zonda*. The pumice-dust is *borne* along by variable winds. From this fact we may infer that the fine sand of the *zondas* comes from a similar source. The most important question is, *Where originates the hot and parching wind that always accompanies, and is peculiar to, the zondas?* The old guides, who are familiar with the valleys of the Andes, informed me that these winds blow from off the main snow-clad ridge of that great chain of mountains, and expressed their surprise at the fact "that from a cold region comes a burning wind."

Strong and steady winds generally follow a direct line. This fact is characteristic of the *zondas*. If Miers's conjecture be true regarding the origin of these winds, the position of the volcano, or *souffrière*, might be found by observing the following suggestion, bearing in mind that the Mendoza wind comes from the *north-west*, and the San Juan *zonda* from the *west*. That point where two lines — one running west from the northern town, the other *north-west* from the southern town — will intersect, is the starting-point of the sand clouds, if not of the accompanying hot wind.

Looking upon the map of South America, we find in the Cordillera of the Andes, between the latitudes of San Juan and Mendoza, four peaks marked as doubtful volcanoes: Limari, directly west of San Juan; Chuapu, thirty miles farther south; and near the half-way point of the two towns, Ligua. To the north of west of Mendoza stands prominent the lofty Aconcagua, that has been estimated by two English captains to have an elevation of twenty-three thousand nine hundred feet. The point of intersection of the west and north-west *zonda* lines is in the vicinity of Limari and Chuapu, and, if not either of these, the *zonda* volcano is a near neighbor to them.

CHAPTER XVII.

ADVENTURES OF DON GUILLERMO BUENAPARTE.

DURING the months that I remained with Don Guillermo, I studied well the character of mine host; and so generous were his sentiments, and kind his heart, that each day my attachment for him increased. His life had been a curious one; and as we sat by the table, one morning, imbibing a *maté*, I urged him to give me some account of his peregrinations since leaving his native land. Grasping my hand, with tears visible in his eyes, he said, "My friend, if you will promise to search out my relatives, when you return to North America, and give them my history, I will willingly answer your request." A *brasero* of coals having been placed beneath the table, around which the members of the household were seated, Don Guillermo commenced his recital.

"At eighteen years of age, certain family troubles occurred, and being a proud-spirited youth, I changed my quiet life on shore for an adventurous one upon the ocean. From my own village I proceeded to the great metropolis, New York, and was directed, after some inquiry, to a shipping office, the proprietor of which informed me that he was procuring a large crew for a vessel, owned, and then lying, at New

Bedford. The first question asked by this gentleman was, 'Have you been round the Horn?' As this was to be my first trip upon salt water, I informed him to that effect. 'Well,' continued he, 'that's bad enough. Now, you see, I have already shipped all the green hands that are wanted, and the old man sent word down from Bedford forbidding me to take any others than such as have made one or two voyages. But don't get discouraged at trifles; we will settle that matter: follow me.'

"In the centre of the room was a post or pillar, upon which was a cow's horn; and round this he walked twice, I following close upon his heels. 'Now,' said the shipping master, 'if any man, sailor or monkey, says that you haven't been round the Horn, just give him the lie. You can sign these articles, and go up to Bedford to-morrow morning, with a dozen likely young men, who are going to sea for their health, and they will enjoy themselves, I don't doubt, as there are several gentlemen's sons among the crew.' I was amused at this comical way of weathering the Horn, and asked him if it would not be advisable to inform our captain of the quick passage I had made; but the old fellow silenced me by stating that he had shipped hundreds of sailors (?) in the same way, and they had all given satisfaction.

"I left New Bedford, a few days later, in the Golconda, and, after a good run round the Horn, we touched at several places on the coast of Chili, at one of which I left the vessel, and secretly joined a pearl and whale ship that was bound to the Galápagos Islands, with the intention of procuring supplies of wood and tor toises, the latter being a good remedy for scurvy. The first land made after leaving the coast of Chili was the *rock* of Dunda, which rises some hundreds of feet above the level of the sea. Here the boats were lowered to catch a species of fish that weighed about six pounds, and found in large schools close in to the rock. With pieces of pork and white rags greased, we caught in a few hours several barrels full, which were taken on board the ship and salted down. While fishing, the mate caught on his hook a large serpent, eight or nine feet in length, covered with scales, and nearly as large as a man's leg. It came into the boat with severe struggles, during which it knocked the mate senseless, and two Dutchmen, from fright, jumped into the sea. This rock is supposed to have once belonged to the Galápagos, being in the same range, and, with a fair wind, is but a few hours' sail from the principal members of that group.

"The ship, which had been lying off and on, was now put before the wind, and we steered for an uninhabited island of the Galápagos, called Terrapin Island, and, when near it, a party of picked men were lowered in the boats, with orders to collect all the wood and tortoise that could be procured. The three boats' crews, upon landing, found the island to be composed of pumice-stone, probably thrown from a volcano in its centre. Next the beach was a narrow strip of land, covered with a light growth of wood, which did not extend forty rods inland; and though immediate search was made for water, not a drop could be found. One of the crew asserted that inland grew a stunted prickly pear, and dwarf camphor tree. We were full of fun, and each boasted that he knew where to hunt for the largest tortoise; and a party of four, including myself, set out together, each promising to return with a gigantic one. As we journeyed inland, the surface of the island became more irregular, and was filled with deep cracks or chasms, the bottoms of which, in many instances, could not be discerned. These fissures descended far below the level of the sea; and, hoping to discover fresh water, we descended into several, but they were all dry and warm as ovens. The rocks around us were porous, and therefore must have absorbed the water that fell when it rained, which, in these parts of the world, is a rare occurrence. Among the rocks abounded a sort of lizards, with long tails, called iguanas.

"After wandering several miles and not meeting with tortoises, a portion of the party concluded to ''bout ship' and return, when a dispute arose regarding the true direction to the bay where the ship lay, and we parted, I following the course that appeared to be the true one, while my three companions set out upon an entirely different one. I continued on until the shades of evening enveloped the island, and made the volcano look like a grim giant. Here I should have rested until morning, as much suffering would have been prevented; but, feeling confident that my course was right, I travelled on in the dark, and, as I afterwards learned, passed the bay without being aware of its proximity. At last, exhausted with walking, I lay down to sleep upon the pumice-stone; but the heat was so great, that I was obliged to turn from side to side with the torture it inflicted; for the sun's heat had been absorbed during the day by these rocks, and it was now given off with an intensity that was truly astonishing. I lighted my pipe and tried to forget my troubles; but, almost dying with thirst, and scorched with the slow fire beneath me, the night wore heavily away. When morning came, I examined my stock of matches, and found that three remained, besides a little tobacco, and, carefully putting these in a safe pocket, I directed my steps to the tall mountain, which appeared to be but a few miles distant. By so doing, chance might favor me, as the men had said, the previous day, that the prickly pear grew in the interior; but my great object was to find water.

"When the sun had reached the meridian, a pair of new double-soled shoes, which I had on, were worn or burned through; I had found no water, and the mountain appeared farther off than it did when I saw it the previous morning.

"Thanks to a good Providence, this misery was soon to be ended, at least for a time; for while journeying along late in the afternoon, with feet bleeding at every step, I espied a little green hill that peeped above the rocks, and with renewed energy I pushed forward, and sank fainting at its base.

"I soon recovered from the exhaustion caused by my sufferings, and as darkness came on, sleep overpowered and wrapped me in its embrace. It was after midnight (so I judged by the height of the Southern Cross) when I woke with a curious feeling caused by suffocation. Recalling my scattered senses, I beheld a huge pair of jaws and two horrid eyes close to my face, while a clawed foot rested upon each shoulder. I trembled in every limb, but did not lose my self-possession; and now I laugh to think that the cause of my trepidation was nothing more than a harmless iguana — a large species of lizard. A single movement of my body caused him to slide from his place and drag his ugly form away; but he did not choose to end his antics here; several hours he continued the annoyance, and determined to make the best of his affectionate ways. I threw a piece of pumice-stone at him, and Mr. Iguana lay senseless among the rocks. Cutting the reptile's throat and catching the blood in the heel of my dilapidated shoe, I drank it as if it had been a beverage of cool milk. With refreshed vigor I ascended the hill. It was covered with grass, and little trees resembling the American beech grew upon it. Flocks of birds were flying about, and their songs revived my spirits.

"Commencing a search for water, I discovered a deep fissure, at the bottom of which some shining substance attracted my attention, and feeling certain that it was water, I descended into the chasm. Again was I doomed to disappointment. A soft, damp mud covered the bottom, in which hundreds of tiny tracks told me that birds had visited the spot, and that the water which had fallen from the clouds had been drank or absorbed by the soil. Had I been a student of natural history, an hour could have been whiled away in the study of ornithichnites; but, dropping all thoughts of science, I made balls of the mud and sucked the moisture they contained, then climbed into the open air. The birds were exceedingly tame, and suffered me to approach and knock them down with a stick. In this I beheld the beneficence of Providence, for here was food for many days. After killing several, I attempted to light a fire with the three matches before mentioned. All three failed. I ate two birds in a raw state, and went in search of an iguana to procure more blood to quench my thirst. The sides of the hill were perforated with the burrows of this animal, into which it crept, leaving the tail outside. I caught hold of one lusty fellow's appendage, but was too weak to pull him out; he beat me from side to side, and I sat down upon a rock in despair.

"The next day, when about to leave the hill, a singular fact attracted my attention. The birds left in flocks, and winging their way towards the big mountain, returned in twenty or thirty minutes.

"Following them for some time with my eyes, I concluded that it was for water that they left the green hill; and carefully marking their flight, I followed them; but, weak and exhausted, after travelling nearly a mile across ridges that became more and more difficult to surmount, it seemed advisable to return. An attempt to capture a young iguana was successful, and this quenched my thirst, while a few birds' legs kept starvation at a distance. Another night's rest revived my courage, and I determined, come what might, to make one more effort to reach the sea-coast. Another day's travel being over, I slept upon the pumice-stone a few miles from the hill. One more day of suffering, and when Night spread her mantle over the island, I knew too well that mental derangement was coming; but still one idea had possession of my mind — Onward, onward!

"I crossed a little ridge, and saw something white at its base; for the moon had risen, and shed its light over the burning island of pumice-stone. I lowered myself into a chasm, and examined it. My brain became settled and attention fixed; and with horror I laid my hand upon the skeleton of a man lying upon his face, with a large tortoise bound to his back by a piece of ratlin. Poor fellow! he had, undoubtedly, while making his way to his ship, missed his footing, and fallen in such a way that he was wedged in and kept down by the great weight upon his back: perhaps the fall itself killed him." "But," said I, "why did not his captain send men to search for him?" "By asking such a question, my friend," begun Don Guillermo, "you show your ignorance of the character of a captain of a whaler. Do you think, if the captain wished to make sail, he would wait even *one* day to seek for one of his crew? If you wish to satisfy yourself on this point, try a voyage in a New Bedford whaleship, and you will soon be assured that my opinion is true."

Don Guillermo continued his narrative.

"This affecting sight filled my mind with thoughts both joyful and dismal — joyful, because I knew that the coast was at hand, for the experience of the few days past had taught me that the tortoise does not wander far inland — dismal, because it might be premonitive of my own fate. With a giddy head I continued on my way. Of the events which occurred from that time I have but a dim recollection. I faintly remember wandering on for many hours, and sleeping upon the heated rocks — the light of day coming again, when my journey was continued; the sound of rushing waters — and then my vision became clearer. I remember the white sandy beach that seemed covered with eggs, and the ringing noise in my ears — the screaming of the sea-birds. All this passed through my brain with the rapidity of lightning; then, rushing frantically to the sea, I swallowed greedily large draughts of water. The cove was filled with other swimmers, that gnashed and gritted their teeth, as if mocking my suffering. They were, in reality, seals; but, almost a maniac, I jumped about among them (so others afterwards informed me), cutting all kinds of pranks; at which the whole school retreated with fear. All then became a blank to me.

"I was next aroused by the voices of people engaged in conversation, together with the strong smell of liquors, and, opening my eyes, I found myself in a comfortable berth in the cabin of a vessel, which, by a perceptible motion, I knew to be under way. 'He has come to,' said a rough voice; 'there's nothing like an internal as well as external application of brandy.' Two or three persons came to the berth, and questioned me regarding my 'island excursion.' Their various applications had restored my system to a comparative degree of vigor; and, assisted by the second officer, I went on deck to behold the shores of Terrapin Island sinking below the horizon.

"The name of this vessel was Henry Astor; she was a Nantucket whaler, and her captain, my deliverer from a melancholy fate, was Pinkham. I would give his name in full, every letter of it, had not nearly sixteen years of wandering obliterated it from my memory.

"A few days' sail brought us to the Marquesas Islands, and by that time the sea air and good living had perfectly restored me to health, and I was eager for new adventures. Our captain proposed remaining here a few days, in order to procure fresh provisions, and trade was commenced with the natives by bartering hoop-iron, knives, beads, &c., in exchange for pigs, yams, cocoanuts, and other fruits. A small, uninhabited island near by was resorted to by the islanders for fishing, and our captain sent our boats to secure a supply for the men. We met a party of natives with canoes on one side of the island, and we became very friendly in our intercourse with them.

"The boat returned to the ship without me, but conveyed a message to the effect that I should not return. The reason for so doing was satisfactory to the sailors. Our second officer was a Portuguese, and a vile fellow. He so exasperated his watch while on the passage from Terrapin Island, that they were now ripe for mutiny; and having no interest in their affairs, I did not wish to be one of their number longer. The Henry Astor would not return to North America for two or three years, and homeward-bound vessels (whalers) sometimes touched at the Marquesas. Thus, if I remained with the natives, there was a chance of my being taken off by a better-omened ship than the one I had just left. The next day a *pearler* hove in sight, and ran close in to land. I raised a signal, and was soon taken on board. The vessel steered for Hiva-oa,* sometimes

* Hiva-oa is about seventy miles south-west of Nukuheva, the island upon which Mr. Herman Melville, the author of "Typee," passed four months among the islanders.

called Dominica, and commenced business in good earnest. The natives were employed to dive for us in four or five fathoms of water. In this they were very expert, and some of them could remain four minutes under water. They swam off to our boats every morning, and worked all day, receiving in payment for their labor pieces of red flannel and bright-colored calico.

"Strict orders were repeated to us every morning regarding our duties for the day. We were forbidden to go within a certain distance of the shore, as the natives were very treacherous, having captured and eaten an English boat's crew a short time before (1840 or '41). Three days passed very pleasantly, when, upon the fourth, word was given to be diligent, as the vessel would sail for the coast of Japan with the first fair wind. 'What!' exclaimed one of the boat's crew to which I belonged, 'are we to leave without setting foot on Hiva-oa? Shiver my timbers if I don't go ashore to-morrow night, after work is done! and the old man may send the whole ship's company after me, if he likes.' To this expression the other two agreed, and, not wishing to be behind my comrades, I consented also; and before retiring to sleep we had made arrangements for a visit to the dreaded cannibal islands.

"The next morning the boats' crews commenced work as usual, and at four bells in the afternoon returned to the ship. This was the time agreed upon for carrying out our design. The natives, who were with us during the day, had swam ashore, and disappeared among the cocoa-nut groves, and the only living objects in sight were a party of women, and two or three old men, the former engaged in various diversions, and the latter sitting like statues near them. It was the custom of these females to collect in groups near the sea-shore during the day, and watch their husbands and lovers, who were hard at work diving for the pearl-oyster; and taking advantage of this circumstance, we came prepared for the party. Upon landing, we distributed from our well-filled pockets various little presents, and were at once treated with the greatest kindness. The looking-glass that we brought filled them with astonishment, and Cram, a young Pennsylvanian, was endeavoring to teach them the philosophy of it by all sorts of gestures, when a low murmur caused us to look seaward; and lo! a long line of men, the fathers, brothers, and lovers of the female party, were advancing towards us, and as we hastily rose to depart, they pointed towards the interior, and made signs for us to go inland.

"Too late we perceived our boyish error; the boat had been secured, and there was no chance for retreat, and sullenly we marched on in advance of the islanders. All the way Cram grumbled at the fate that might be ours. He blessed his top-lights, then cursed them, the women, who followed, laughing all the while at his curious physiognomy. As we drew near the end of a beautiful valley, in which the natives dwelt, Cram felt quite at home, and remarked that it was not 'much of any consequence where a person lived. These fellows,' said he, 'have plenty to eat, and don't have to turn to every morning while in port, or every watch when at sea. If the king here will give me his daughter, I will settle down on a farm after swallowing my sheet anchor;' and putting a quid of tobacco in his mouth, he squirted the juice right and left among the crowd, who became wild with mirth.

"Thanks to our previous kind treatment to the islanders, upon arriving at their village they gave us to understand that we should receive no harm. We did not go through any trial, or appear before any council; but by gestures they made known to us that each of our number could choose a place of residence from among the two or three hundred habitations in the valley. I fancied that of an old man, who must have been, in his younger days, a great warrior, as his body was covered with scars, and one longitudinal one, that, commencing upon his forehead, and ending with the chin, excited my amazement, for the skull had evidently been split by some weapon, from the effects of which he sometimes labored under temporary insanity. At Cram's suggestion, we christened him 'Old Split Head.' The three other sailors were quartered in habitations near my own, and for a few days we lived contentedly enough, every wish being anticipated and satisfied by these kind people.

"One morning, about a week after our capture, while talking together, the conversation was suddenly interrupted by the booming of cannon, and we arose to go down to the beach, but were prevented by our captors. Report after report followed, and echoed among the hills that divided the island into separate parts. I was convinced by these sounds that our ship had got under way, and was exercising her two or three rusty guns for our benefit. But what seemed stranger than all was, that these reports came from the opposite side of the island, and from an entirely different direction from her former anchorage. Cram laughed at my opinions, and harangued the other two after this fashion: 'He says that it's our craft that's making all that noise. I'll sell myself for a sea-cook if it isn't one of those parlez-vous French men-o'-war that's come along, and heard that we are among this confounded set. Now, shipmates, what say you? Here we have been loafing about like a set of lobster marines, doing nothing, nor serving mankind, and it's a certain fact that we have got to be laid up here until we get away. Now, I, for one, am heartily tired of this wasting of energies; and as for living here listening to these cocoa-nut eaters, who expect to tattoo us into Davy Jones's locker, I won't; so come along. We can make a straight course across those big hills yonder, and then hurrah for Johnny Crapo's boats. If you will all start, I'll agree to steer my trick to-night, if it *is* aboard a French man-o'-war.' The two sailors were overpowered by Cram's eloquence, and swore roundly that they would follow him, if he set out instantly.

"Now, all the while the natives had been watching us, and when the orator, during his speech, pointed to the hills, they at once comprehended their prisoners' intentions, and, coming forward, an old man, better dressed than the others, gave us to understand, through signs, that upon the other side of the mountain dwelt other savages, who were their enemies. Nothing daunted, Cram and his associates set out for the mountain, followed by a party of islanders, who continued expostulating with them until they reached its base.

"The old man, whom I now took to be the chief, in an authoritative manner, despatched a second party;

but Cram and the other two showed fight, and, rolling down large stones upon the chief's men, prevented them from advancing. As the three reckless fellows neared the summit of the mountain, they were watched with intense interest by the people below. A few minutes more, and they had disappeared on the other side, where they met the savages of whom they had been warned, who drove them back, fighting with great fury. The men in our village ran for their arms, and a loud shout resounded throughout the valley. Twice I started to join in the affray; but those near me prevented my departure. The fight lasted about fifteen minutes, and was ended by the death of the white men, my companions. The captors retired to their own territory, while I wept for the first time since leaving my native land. I was but just nineteen years of age, and was, perhaps, a prisoner for life, destined to live apart from my countrymen. I had been nurtured in refinement, and trained under the holy influence of a mother's prayers; and now a most miserable life was before me, indolence and barbarity.

"The fate of my friends was a cruel one. The natives around the base of the mountain saw them fight bravely until overpowered by superior numbers, when one by one the three sailors were felled to the earth. Cram was seen struggling with an islander until another native, with his spear, broke the poor fellow's jaw, and he was obliged to surrender.

"About noon the next day came a deputation from the people of the territory behind the mountains to make peace with our 'Tehoke' (principal chief), which caused a great palaver among our natives. To appease our chief, a gift was presented him by the committee. It was rolled up in cocoa-nut leaves, the first layer of which was green, as if just gathered from the trees. While they slowly unrolled the present, the natives clustered around it, and as wrapper after wrapper fell to the ground, a sight was disclosed that caused me to shudder. It was a fitting present from cannibals, the leg of poor Cram, browned from the effects of fire. I identified the limb by means of a tattooed ring upon the calf, that still retained the original color. But this gift, instead of soothing the ire of the haughty 'Te-hoke,' produced an entirely different effect; for he called a council, and, after a palaver, the cannibal committee were dismissed, and war formally declared. The islanders were wild with excitement, and I was made to sing, in the midst of the rabble, a grand *hoolo-hoolo*, and to dance, which I did to the music of a drum, made by stretching human skin across the ends of a short, hollow log.

"At dawn on the following day, an army of nearly three hundred men ascended the mountain, and disappeared over the summit.

"The day of battle was one of nature's loveliest. The rays of the sun, with trembling light, pierced the dense foliage of the groves around the absent warriors' homes, and sparkled upon the cool streams of water meandering along the valley, and falling in little cascades among the rocks. It would seem a time and place for quiet thoughts and pious meditation. But my mind was not in a fit state to appreciate the beauty that reposed around me. I wandered through the valley, thinking of my curious situation, of the strange beings who were my companions, and my isolation from civilization. I thought of the happy American home that I had left, and my memory went back to a beautiful Sabbath morning (the day prior to my departure from home), when, taking the hand of my sister, I led her to a little wood behind the house, and there she sang to me a song, the words of which have since rung in my ears, through all my wanderings, over sea and land, and have kept me from the errors that have caused the downfall of thousands.

"Perched upon the top of a cocoa-nut tree, Old Split Head kept on the lookout for news. Beyond him another dark head peeped above the foliage, and still nearer the mountain another and another native could be seen. This was a telegraphic line of communication.

"Soon after the natives had disappeared over the mountain, the reports of a few muskets, obtained from the English boat's crew that was captured some months before, together with distant shouts, told me that the game was up. After this, a long silence caused me to doubt as to who were the victors, for I believed that if our party were successful, they would return quickly with what booty could be obtained.

"About four o'clock in the afternoon, a courier appeared on the brow of the mountain, and a telegraphic message came quickly to Old Split Head, who was beside me at the door. Now, as my guardian attempted to communicate the intelligence to me, he became so excited that he could do nothing more than jump high in the air, roll over and over upon the ground and shake his long spear at a tree. He then caught me by the arm, and led me to the beach, where the army arrived, an hour after, in six large war-canoes, each holding about fifty rowers. These canoes, together with three men, and many pigs and weapons, had been captured during the engagement. The three captive warriors lay bound in the bottom of the boat, and were unable to move hand or foot.

"Now commenced a great hoolo-hoolo, during which I was embraced by the Tehoke in presence of the multitude. The three prisoners were removed to a little square formed by a wall of stones, and left under a guard for the night, and I was informed that upon the next day I should receive a high *taboo.* This is a mark of distinction and privilege, differing according to the grade or class of the taboo — some causing the person tabooed to stand above those who have a low mark upon them. This favor is only given to men; the women do not receive it, and are, therefore, in one sense, slaves to their husbands. The next morning the Tehoke performed the process of tabooing, by passing over my head a piece of *tappa* (native cloth), and pronouncing several words not comprehended by me. After this the Tehoke presented me with two wives, one of whom was his own daughter, and Split Head, with two ingenious fellows, built in the course of the day a new habitation, in which I was to dwell.

"Now came the hour in which the prisoners taken during the battle were to meet their doom. They were seized by a party of natives, and each one placed erect, with his back against a cocoa-nut tree. Around the neck of the victim, and trunk of the tree, was wound a short piece of native rope, and a stick being placed in the bight, it was turned around several times, until the tongue protruded from the mouth, and the prisoner was dead. Deep holes were dug and lined with stones, upon which a large fire was kindled, and allowed to continue burning until the stones were very hot. The ashes and sticks were raked out, and the bodies of the prisoners, which had been previously wrapped in many layers of cocoa-nut leaves, were laid in the cavities, and hot stones placed upon them. There was no chance of straying from the spot, as I sat close by the Tehoke; but I sickened and my head grew dizzy at the horrid sight. The horrors of a cannibal feast I will not describe. Suffice it to say that the natives became in my eyes as wild animals devouring prey.

"I now led a more agreeable life than I had formerly enjoyed, that is to say, if enjoyment consists in having a mind free from care or trouble. Before the taboo had been placed upon me, there were times when some of the natives attempted great freedom with my person, and were a source of trouble to me. Now I lived as the chief's son-in-law, and as a person of distinction, as I possessed a high taboo. I was ingenious, and by repairing the old flint-lock muskets of the chief, took a new stand as a man of superior endowment. As month after month passed away, I became more accustomed to my situation, and felt, at times, almost contented with my lot. I began to acquire the language, and took part in the councils of the chiefs, where my word was valued. During all this time I passed but one ordeal, that of *tattooing*. I was taken by force from my dwelling, and, being laid upon my back, underwent an operation, the effects of which I shall carry with me to the grave."

So saying, Don Guillermo divested himself of his shirt, and there were visible upon his breast two curious specimens of Marquesian tattooing. "This figure on my left side," said he, "is intended to represent the moon, while the one on the right is the sun." Upon his thighs and arms were other figures equally curious as those upon his breast. He then continued: "Once I was dragged out to be ornamented upon the face; but I struggled and begged so hard to escape from the hands of the artists, that Old Split Head, whose influence was considerable, interceded with the islanders, and I was permitted to go free. Having acquired the dialect, the natives placed more confidence in me than they had previously done, and I walked along the sea-coast two or three times a week with the hope of seeing a vessel. Once or twice I descried ships in the distance, but was doomed again and again to disappointment, as they did not approach the island; and for eleven long, weary months, did I remain a prisoner among the cannibals of Hiva-oa.

"In conversing with the islanders, they had often spoken of a foreigner, who, by some accident, had been a resident among them. They called him Oorie, and though I questioned them regarding his escape, they would not give me any clew by means of which I could ascertain the method he used to obtain his freedom I afterwards comforted myself by believing that as *one* person had been taken off the island, another might meet with the same good fortune; and from the time I received the above information, my eyes were always gazing over the surface of the ocean for a glimpse of a distant sail.

"As the eleventh month of my life among the cannibals drew to its close, a whaler from North America dropped anchor in the little bay, and almost in the same spot where, nearly a year before, I had gazed with admiration upon the tropical scenery of my new island home, the prison-ground that debarred me from civilization. The rare event of a ship visiting Hiva-oa threw its inhabitants into a state of great excitement, some of whom were for having me closely guarded, while others, too much occupied in getting ready their fruits for a market, only laughed and shouted to increase the confusion that everywhere prevailed. During the hubbub and clamor of voices, I conversed with some of the females, whose ideas of a ship and the uses to which one is applied, were of the most primitive kind. 'Where does the great monster live, and from what country does it travel?' they asked, gazing at the same time eagerly into my face, as if expecting to receive an incorrect reply. 'It comes from my own country, which is a long way off,' I answered. To this one young girl gravely responded, 'Then your home is in the clouds, for this thing (the ship) rains down; we have seen the same before two or three times.'

"The men swam off to the vessel, and, while absent, I endeavored to persuade some of the chiefs to allow me to go upon the same errand the next day; but in this I was unsuccessful. They sternly objected to my appeals, and, urged to desperation, I projected an escape, but was twice foiled in the attempt.

"The second night after the whaler arrived, I left the hut before the islanders arose from their slumbers, and, though my movements had been watched, I reached a branch of the valley stream, and, wading along its course up to my chin in water, soon entered the sea, and boldly struck out for the vessel that lay at her anchorage.

"The man who had the anchor watch saw the gleam of light in my wake, caused by the displacement of the water, for the moon was high in the heavens, and the smallest object could be easily distinguished. Thinking I was a savage on a predatory excursion, he called the mate, who in turn aroused the captain. A rope was thrown to me, and half an hour after leaving my hut of canes and cocoa-nut boughs, I was surrounded by a half-naked group of down-east greenhorns, who kindly presented me with a suit of clothes, in place of my island one of tappa.

"The next morning, the master of the whaler, Captain Brown, thinking that my escape might exasperate the natives, mast-headed the topsail yards, and heaved short our cable, to be in readiness to leave in the afternoon, at the moment the heavens gave indications of a breeze. While these preparations were under way, Old Split Head came down the beach, and loudly shouted my name. To prove his affection for me, I did not answer his call; whereupon he danced about for some time, clutching his hair, and then rolling upon the sand, appearing to be in hysterics.

"Towards three o'clock came the wished-for breeze, and with it the order to 'fill away the topsails.' Springing to the sheets, a party of us hauled them home, while others heaved up the anchor, and as we slowly stretched away from Hiva-oa, I breathed a prayer of thanks for my safe deliverance. The long line of natives upon the beach, at sight of our departure, could restrain themselves no longer, for above forty threw themselves into the sea, and followed after us like a school of porpoises. I threw out a rope for Old Split Head, and the rapidity with which he ascended the ship's side drew many remarks of admiration from the sailors, who declared that 'no salt could have done it better.' The instant he touched the deck he embraced me, and, refusing to be comforted, pointed over the ship's side at one of my wives, who was *treading water*, and softly uttered her name many times — 'Cuahoo! Cuahoo!' Captain Brown gave the old fellow several pieces of red flannel, and a few pounds of tobacco, and, rolling the latter in the cloth, he lashed the bundle to his head, and with a long, tearful embrace, we parted.

"This was the last time I saw Old Split Head, who was the truest and best friend I ever had; and many times since we parted, when amid trials and sufferings, my thoughts have turned to our little hut beneath the cocoa-nut grove, where so many hours had been passed in his company, savage though he was; and I have regretted leaving that romantic island. Then reason and the voice of duty have said, 'You were born among civilized people, and it is your duty to act manfully against vicissitudes; but to live a life of ease and pleasure, surrounded by things that injure rather than strengthen the noble faculties of the soul, is sinful, and is not in accordance with the principles of truth and of the Bible.'

"From Hiva-oa a breeze wafted us into Talcahuana, the port of Concepcion, Chili, where I remained for some months, working at different trades, in nearly all of which I was able to compete with the native workmen. I could relate to you many interesting stories of the Araucanian Indians, who occupy the south of Chili, and often come to Concepcion to barter their ponchos, mantas, &c., for English articles; but having occupied much of your time, I shall draw my narrative to a close as soon as possible.

"While residing in Chili, I made the acquaintance of two young men, who, having visited Juan Fernandez, spoke encouragingly of the chances that existed for making money upon that island. And they proposed that we should purchase a boat and repair to the island, where thousands of goats run wild, and there pass a few months in securing the skins of these animals, after which we were to sail to Masafuero, an adjacent island, where there were a large number of seals.

"I had earned by this time a sufficient sum of money to accept of their offer, and they being supplied with like amounts, we purchased a large whale boat, a stock of provisions, and three dogs, besides guns, ammunition, and all the accessories necessary to insure success to our enterprise. We bargained with the captain of a vessel that was about leaving Talcahuano for a sperm whale cruise, to leave us to ourselves when the ship hove in sight of Juan Fernandez, near which his course lay. One thing more was yet to be done; we had no person to do the drudgery of preparing and cooking our food.. Our choice, therefore, fell upon a stout negro, called Pedro, who was fluent in the use of the English and Spanish languages, and for a low sum we secured his services.

"The ship put to sea with a gentle breeze one fine morning, and early on the fourth day the rough peaks of the island were seen above the horizon.

"Preparations commenced immediately for disembarkation. Our little craft was launched, the masts stepped, her cargo carefully adjusted, and quickly tumbling in our dogs and Pedro, we bade adieu to the whaler.

"Though the breeze blew fresh at the time we left the ship, and our party spread every stitch of canvas, it was not until night set in that our boat grounded amid the surf upon the white sandy beach of the romantic Robinson Crusoe island, and we all crawled on shore drenched with spray to the skin.

"A few days after, a hut was completed, and our party commenced business in good earnest; and while the three whites were occupied in capturing the goats, the black, Pedro, officiated as cook and housekeeper in our little dwelling. Among the cliffs the goats scampered about singly and in little parties. It was our object to concentrate all stragglers, and driving them into some little nook or valley, from which there was no escape, we shot them down, or, when practicable, captured them with the lasso. In collecting the stray goats into parties, we were greatly assisted by our dogs, which had been trained for the purpose.

"When the animals abounded in places where the valleys were large and did not afford opportunities for capturing them, we built stone enclosures, and in them intrapped large numbers. To capture and skin thirty goats was considered no more than a good day's labor for each man. Thus our pile of skins towered higher each day, and promised us a little fortune when we should dispose of them on the continent.

"While enjoying this success, a distant sail was distinguished one afternoon by Pedro, who ran out of his domicile to inform us of the welcome fact. The following day our hut was honored by the presence of one of South America's best and greatest children, the patriotic and learned Don Domingo F. Sarmiento, who, having been sent abroad, by the government of Chili, to visit different portions of the world, to gain information of superior customs, with the intention of introducing such as were practicable to that republic on his return, had first called at this island, which belongs to that government.

"Though sent upon such a commission, Sarmiento was not a Chileno by birth, but had resided in Chili some years, having been exiled from his native country, the Argentine Republic, by the tyrannical Rosas, who was ever uneasy when a philanthropist or scholar was within the land over which he stretched his arm of iron and bathed his hands in the blood of her people. It is unnecessary for me to give you an account of the stay of this great man upon the island; suffice it to say, we became very intimate, he sleeping nine successive nights upon my bed of goat-skins; and when I visited him in Chili, after his return from Europe and North America, he presented me with a copy of his travels, '*Viages de Sarmiento*,' in which you will find the particulars of the visit. Before General Rosas was driven out of office and country, Sarmiento himself had crossed the Cordillera and Pampas, and was fighting against the army of the tyrant; and while on a visit to him, he said, handing me a trusty sword, 'Don Guillermo, your ingenuity is remarkable. I have not been able to clean this instrument. Will you oblige me by removing from it all traces of rust?' He then reached his hand above an *escritorio*, and as he held out another weapon, a smile playing upon his noble features, he said, 'My friend, this sword you need not clean; I shall keep it as a memorial; for upon its surface are blood-stains from the heart of a tyrant, who would have been like Rosas, had not I, while in the engagement, sought him out and thrust my trusty steel through his heart. Now I can go back to the Argentine Republic and to freedom, for the tyrant and his *Masorca** have been driven from their stronghold, and their dread influence is at an end.'

"After remaining some few months on Juan Fernandez and the neighboring Masafuero, a whaler arrived and took off our company with their property. Before the ship left the island, according to a promise I had made to Sarmiento, I cut his name deep in a ledge of rock, where it can be seen at the present day.

"Welcome was the first sight of the main land after months spent upon a small island. When we reached Valparaiso, to our dismay the price of goat-skins and furs had fallen, and in place of receiving the expected several thousand dollars in return for my goods, I quietly pocketed six hundred dollars, and swallowed my disappointment. The goat-skins

* The Masorca was a club of three hundred men, organized by Rosas to cut the throats of his political foes and defenceless citizens, who would not succumb to his tyrannical sway.

brought one real ($12\frac{1}{2}$ cents), and in some cases two reals each, while the seals commanded from three to six reals.

"Not caring to follow a roving life any longer, I proceeded to the capital of Chili, the beautiful Santiago, and for a time found entertainment in pursuing various trades. About this time I made the acquaintance of a young artist from North America. Troubles had driven him, like myself, from a good home, and, being often together, our attachment became such that it was spoken of by every one. One evening, as we walked arm in arm along the Tauamar, and near Fort Santa Lucia, he pointed in the direction of a nunnery, and said, 'Within those walls is a young lady that I would have married long ago, but her parents, despising one they were pleased to call a *gringo*, placed her in that building, fearing that she might elope with her lover to some other part of the country. Once or twice I have received letters from her, and, like myself, she does not care to live longer, and unless we can be united soon, nothing but the death of the suicide is left to me.' I was greatly affected at this disclosure, which only served to bind our friendship still stronger. I was not the only friend from whom the young artist could draw sympathy. A daring North American, armed with a Colt's revolver and a fine key-hole saw, repaired one dark night to the nunnery, scaled its walls, and tearing off the tiles, cut a hole through the porous wood-roof, and took from the praying-room the young betrothed, who had made a vow to her conjuror to resort to that place each night to pray until her prayers were answered, but in a very different manner than the priest would have wished, had he known the blessing asked for.

"The next day the lovers were united, and bade me farewell forever. Before the *vigilantes* were summoned to retake the couple or arrest the perpetrator of the deed, against whom injured Catholicism raised a loud cry, the bride and bridegroom, mounted on fleet horses, were on their way to Bolivia, where they are now probably residing.

"It was proved that, at the time of the rescue, our countryman, the artist, was in some other place; and being his friend, and known to be ingenious, I was pointed out as the culprit. People became excited, and while the *vigilantes* were about, a trusty friend brought me two horses, and volunteering to become my travelling companion, we set out for the Argentine Republic, that lay on the eastern side of the Andes. The Uspallata and Portillo passes were watched, and nothing remained but to follow down the valley of Tupungato to the Planchon Pass. Without sustenance for our animals, and but a small supply of food, we commenced a journey that the old *arrieros* themselves would have turned back from. The lofty sides of the mountains hemmed us in, and we followed on, day after day, until our horses died, and we were on the point of starvation. At last we reached the Planchon, which is close upon Patagonia, and crossing this flat mountain, which is composed of light gravel, resembling snuff in color and fineness of grain, we came upon a little fort, from which a few soldiers ran on seeing us, shouting, 'The Indians! the Indians!' We left them after quieting their fears and receiving a little food

"The next day two Indians approached, and uttered repeatedly the word '*amite*' (friend). They kindly undertook to guide us to Mendoza, a town that lay one hundred and eighty leagues to the north. These two savages captured with their *boliadores* several ostriches and one or two guanacos, upon the flesh of which we feasted. When within two days of the town, our guides pointed out the true direction for us to follow, and, shaking hands with them, we parted.

"Upon arriving in Mendoza I found employment for a while, but, not liking the place, went north to San Juan, while my friend returned to Chili. And here I have lived for nine years, having been married for the last six or seven to the daughter of Don ———, an old soldier, who has fought in the battles of the revolutions which spring up every few years in this province."

After returning to North America, I wrote many letters of inquiry for the benefit of Don Guillermo. Several of these letters were answered. Others, probably, never reached the destinations for which they were intended.

I found that a portion of my friend's family were still living, and their heartfelt letters to me amply repaid the exertions I had made to discover their residences. The history of Don Guillermo has a touch of romance about it. One person wrote as follows: "F. D——g (the father of Don G.) was a younger son of the high chamberlain to the King of Saxony, and as his elder brother took the office and title of his father, he, F., took to the army, as is usual in that country, and, just before the close of our revolutionary war, came to New York as major of a regiment of Hessians. After peace was declared, he remained, and married a wealthy lady," &c., &c.

Thus much regarding his parentage. The cause that drove him from the land that he even now adores, remains a secret with the few in whose breasts it will be sure of a safe keeping.

From another quarter I received the following lines, which were written by the cooper of the Henry Astor, who took charge of the ship on her homeward passage: "In looking over my journal of notes of that voyage, I have not mentioned the coming on board of the young man (Don Guillermo) at Galápagos Islands; but on the 7th of October, 1842, I have merely mentioned that we lost, by desertion, while at Dominica (one of the Marquesas Islands), a boy. The particulars of which I recorded in the ship's log book.

"The particulars of his coming on board, or of his leaving, have passed from me, and I could wish that many other occurrences of that eventful voyage might. H. C."

Letters from Nantucket inform me that the log-book of the Henry Astor was lost in the great fire of 1846. The captain's private journal, brought home by Mr. C., the cooper of the ship, contains the information desired. "A Scotch boy, by the name of James Walker (assumed name), deserted the ship at the Isle of Dominica, one of the Marquesas, on the 8th day of October, 1842; and they had good reason to believe that he was enticed away from the ship."

Not having seen the captain's journal, I cannot learn

anything relative to the men who accompanied Don Guillermo when he left the vessel. I have added these few facts, thinking that they might be interesting to the relatives of Don Guillermo, who are now able to carry on a correspondence with him.

CHAPTER XVIII.

CROSSING THE ANDES.

WHILE the fig, the olive, and the orange trees were clothed in green, and vast herds of cattle from the great pampas were arriving, to be fattened in the clover-fields, the mountains still remained covered with snow, and impassable, save to the trained courier. Still I had seen all that rendered San Juan attractive, and a longing to return to my own country came so strongly upon me, that I determined to risk a passage to Chili at the earliest possible moment.

It was only when my intentions became known that I was made aware of the numbers and kindly feelings of my San Juan friends; for so many were interested in my welfare, and warned me so earnestly of the danger of the journey, and attempted to receive from me the promise that I would remain with them, at least until the snow had disappeared, that I could not but feel I had indeed fallen in with some of the truly hospitable and generous peoples that here and there are scattered over the world, making it, as do the oases in the desert, not all a dreariness.

I learned from these friends that the northern passes that led to Copiapo and Coquimbo were buried in the snow, and that, on the first-named road, a party of eight *arrieros*, while lately attempting to cross into Chili, had been frozen to death. The Coquimbo road was said to be equally as bad, for there eleven experienced guides had just fallen victims to a fierce snow storm in the valleys of the Andes. The two southern passes of Uspallata and Portillo were more elevated than the two northern ones, but were much shorter. The Portillo could not be passed by man. The mail road of Uspallata was the one fixed upon by me as the most practicable; and though the courier reported the loss of two young Chilenos, who probably had been swept away by the mountain torrent, I believed that, having been reared in a New England climate, whose winters are rigorous, I could bear the hardships of the cold better than the native guides themselves.

While I was contemplating an early start, an old man called, and requested permission to give an account of his sufferings, he having attempted the passage of the Cordilleras a few days before.

"We started," he said, "with every prospect of success. The weather had been settled for several days, and with our mules we left the outer sierra, and penetrated far into the mountains. But good fortune did not remain the same, for suddenly a great *temporal* came flying from the south, and enveloped us for many hours in its terrible folds. The snow fell in *clouds*, and I, of all my party, escaped; my companions are frozen in the drifts, and there they will remain until the melting of the snow. Look at my hands; all of the fingers were frozen, and also my cheeks and nose. *No, señor. Norte Americano, no pasa vd. la Cordillera!*"

The poor old guide was in a pitiful condition; but,

undoubtedly, had he been twenty years younger, he would have fared better. I confess that this news, with the entreaties of my friends, forced me to postpone crossing the mountains until a later date. I consented to remain, and for several weeks tried to content myself; but when four weeks had passed, I became resolved, and packing my notes, and a few specimens of natural history, in my canvas bag, I announced to my friends my firm determination of leaving the country.

Don Guillermo, on seeing that I was in earnest, ordered his peon to lasso my horse, and bring him to the corral, and made every preparation for my comfort in the journey that his inventive skill could suggest.

On Saturday, November 10 (the last spring month of that latitude), I bade adieu to the family, and started on the road to the city. Don Guillermo accompanied me to the river, that was swollen by the floods from the valleys of the Andes, and went roaring along its course with a fearful rapidity. At the banks of the torrent my friend bade me farewell, charging me to be faithful to the promise I had made him, namely, that I would endeavor to find out the residence of his surviving relations, whom he had left sixteen years before in North America, during which time he had not heard one word of their welfare or whereabouts. I promised again, and said farewell, and left him; it was necessary for me to cross the river, and I at once spurred my horse into the torrent, and began to ford; fortunately, the animal was sure-footed and strong, and we landed safely on the opposite shore.

I passed most of the next day at a friend's house,

within the limits of the town, and at dusk rode out to the post-house, and presented a letter of introduction to the proprietor, a garrulous old don, whose good entertainment for man and beast had made his house a favorite resort for travellers. The don read my letter, and declared that I should remain with him for some time, as it was impossible to cross to Chili. The next day, Don Carlos Leon Rodriquez, minister to the province of San Luis, attended by a priest, both of whom were on their way to the town, stopped at the *posta*, and corroborated the statement of the *guardo*. The former gentleman offered to present me with letters to his friends in Mendoza, if I preferred going to that town, and remaining until the passage across the mountains was sure and free from all difficulties. Considering that we had never met before, the kind proposal proved still further to me the hospitable feelings that the educated people of the Argentine Republic bear towards North Americans.

I had intended to continue my journey as a pedestrian across the Andes, but it seemed necessary to take with me some beast to serve as pack-animal, to carry my small collection of specimens, blankets, &c., to the port of Valparaiso. As it might become necessary to abandon the animal along the road, I selected a specimen of horse-flesh which would have afforded a student of anatomy easy facilities for osseous examinations, without removing the hide.

During the forenoon I bade *adios* to my new acquaintances, and with one end of my lasso in my hand, and the other fastened to the bridle of my horse, I led the way, on foot, happy in feeling that I had fairly commenced the last stage of my journey towards the Pacific.

Taking a south-westerly course across the desert, I travelled until three o'clock over the same dreary waste, when a deep fissure was observed in the sierra, which I entered, and soon found myself within the Flecha. Before passing this peculiar gap, a word or two regarding it may prove interesting. For many leagues along its course the sierra presents an impassable barrier to man or beast. The Flecha is a narrow passage from the desert on the east to the valley on the western side. The sides of the Flecha are of solid rock, rising perpendicularly to a great height.

The pass exhibits the action of water upon its sides, for the rock has been worn smooth in past ages, and the bed of the passage is covered with pebbles. Undoubtedly, a long time since, a strong body of water found its way through this place, and may have submerged the plain below; but whether this gap was the bed of a natural stream, or mere vent, through which the melting snow escaped during the spring months, cannot now be well determined. The effect that the lofty sides of the Flecha have upon independent objects is very curious. My horse seemed to dwindle to the size of a Shetland pony when I removed a few yards from him, and two muleteers, who passed through at the same time, looked like pygmies.

Half way up the precipice were holes, said to have been cut by the ancient discoverers of the country, to assist in searching for precious metals, but, proving unprofitable, had been abandoned. I continued along the valley until dusk, when the barking of dogs, and occasional glimpses of a light, guided me to one side of the valley, where a few huts constitute the hamlet of El Durazno. These huts were inhabited by muleteers, who suffered greatly from poverty. Here and there the rough soil had been levelled, so as to be susceptible of irrigation, and a few patches of clover gave a cheering aspect, when contrasted with the barren mountains behind the hamlet. An old woman invited me to enter her house, and pass the night, as it was damp outside, and the heavy clouds that hovered about us looked as if about to descend.

The hut was built of sticks and mud, and adjoining it was the kitchen.

Having turned my horse adrift, I entered, and, as I reclined upon a skin couch, commenced inquiring of the hostess relative to the snow on the main Cordillera. I was unable, however, to obtain any information from that source. Our party was soon increased by the entry of several rude-looking fellows, armed with long knives. The place was so small that we reclined, packed one against the other, men, women, and children, promiscuously. The old woman commenced cooking an *asado* upon the fire; it had hardly begun to splutter and crackle, when the dog that had sat beside the fire caught up the meat in his mouth, and commenced masticating it with great *gusto*. The woman, screaming out, "*O, sus Ave Maria!*" made a clutch at the dog, but was unsuccessful in recovering the prize. One of the men caught the animal by the throat, and choked him until the meat was drawn from his mouth, when, with a hasty "*Ha, perro!*" it was returned to the fire, and cooked for the lookers-on. More men and dogs came in, and, thinking it best to retreat while it remained in my power to do so, I requested my hostess to allow me to retire. Taking a saucer of fat, in which a bit of rag was burning, she led the way into the other shanty, and assisted in spreading my saddle cloths upon a rough sofa, built of boards, which had been placed in the middle of the floor to prevent the approach of the *binchucas* that were secreted in the crevices in the walls.

These uncomfortable disturbers of night dreams are as large as the common May beetle, and are armed with a bill resembling that of a mosquito, which is used with great effect upon the victim. Before fixing upon a person, the body of the *binchuca* is thin and flat; but after his feast is over, he is bloated and disgusting to look upon. As this tormentor is many times larger than the mosquito, so does the irritability caused by its leeching process exceed in like proportion that of the other pest.

When about to withdraw from the room, the woman bade me sleep with the utmost confidence, and not fear any harm. But as the conversation of the men in the kitchen had been about the *plata* that might be in my possession, I was very particular to impress her with the idea that North Americans feared nothing; and at the same time I drew a long knife from under my *poncho*, and placed it beneath the sheep-skin that was to serve for my bed. When she withdrew, I lay down; but as I had a thought of the *binchucas* before I prepared for sleep, I carefully rolled myself in my blankets, Indian fashion, and defied them to do their worst.

Hardly had I begun to doze, when a sensation of something disagreeable, touching me, aroused me to the fact that the vile pests were coming from every quarter of the hovel. I could hear them crawling up the sides of the room and across the ceiling, when with their usual degree of impudence, one after another dropped plump upon my body. But my swathing clothes served as an armor, and they could not enter in to the feast. All the while they clung with considarble tenacity to the coarse blankets, trying to effect an entrance, but they had met their conqueror; for, after waiting until the swarming was over, and the army had fairly camped upon me, I suddenly and carefully rolled over and over upon the sofa, until the life was forced out of nearly all of them, when, being satisfied that a great victory had been achieved, I dropped into a deep slumber.

When morning came, and I passed out of the hut, I found that the valley was filled with mist, and I deferred setting out until the thick clouds had scattered. About nine o'clock a breeze sprang up, which soon cleared the valley of mists, and I resumed my journey. Soon after my leaving El Durazno, the valley expanded into a plain of a desert character. The country between the mountains again became undulating and broken; at three leagues from the last hamlet, El Sequion, a collection of two or three mud houses and several ranchos, appeared.

From one of these ranchos a *China* (half Indian) woman came out, and questioned me as to my motives for travelling alone, on foot, in the desolate valley. When I spoke of crossing the Cordillera, the good creature lifted both her hands, and exclaimed in colloquial Spanish, "*Por Dios*, don't go any farther. A man from Chili stopped here the other day — his mouth and cheeks were like a soft peach with the frost!" Another woman joined us, and declared that I was too young to be so far from home, and questioned me to the effect "if my mother knew that I was out." In their inquiries, however, they exhibited a kindness that to me was very gratifying, and I felt that in case of accident upon the road, I had at least two friends near at hand.

Beyond the Sequion, the valley grew narrower, and in places was so filled with stones and detritus as to lame the old horse. The road now became a mere defile, the steep sides of the sierras towering above it to a great height, their bareness being sometimes relieved by dwarf cacti, that grew in crevices where soil had lodged; these plants were in flower, some white, others of a yellow hue.

The clouds again enveloped the mountains, and while I was groping along over the broken rock, the tinkling of a mule's bell broke the stillness, and a moment later I came upon a circle of pack-saddles and mules' cargoes, lying upon the ground. A deep voice called out, "Come here, friend;" and I was soon acquainted with the capataz and muleteers of Don Fernando de Oro, a rich San Juan merchant, who had sent his troop to Uspallata to await an opportunity to cross to Chili, in advance of the troops of the other merchants. The don was daily expected by the capataz, who had been three or four days on the road already. The capataz urged me to remain with the troop until the next morning, which invitation I accepted, and tying my horse to some resinous bushes, I sat down to a sumptuous meal of boiled corn, dried beef, and pepper, while my jaded animal satisfied himself in cropping the tops of the bushes, and a kind of stunted weed that grew among the rocks. Towards dusk it rained, but my heavy blanket kept me dry. The guides huddled around the dying embers, vainly endeavoring to warm their benumbed limbs; around us the hills seemed to be shaken by the heavy thunders that reverberated along the mountain tops.

Fearing that my horse would give out, as he had lived mostly upon bushes and coarse herbage since leaving San Juan, I arose early, and, guided by the bright starlight, caught my animal, and led him up the valley. A spur of the sierra blocked up the valley, and this steep ascent had to be climbed by the poor animal, he halting every few steps to draw breath. Having reached the summit, he heaved a deep sigh, as if conscious of having finished a hard task.

A magnificient view rewarded me for the exertion of making the ascent. The rocky grandeur filled me with awe, for I was surrounded by a sublime chaos — broken hills, valleys, and barren cliffs of the sierra.

A white cloud passed over the valley, shutting me out from sight of the world below; it was no easy task to follow the rocky path beyond; sometimes it led down abrupt descents into dismal valleys, then again almost to the level of the summit of the mountain range. Along this crooked path but one mule can pass at a time, and there are places where it requires but a single unsteady movement to send the loaded animal into the abyss below. For nearly a mile the sierra on the left side was formed of red freestone, and was, in many places, as regular as a castle wall. In this lonely place the least sound would catch my ear.

The sierra that I had crossed is called the Paramilla, or "bleak place;" in the warmest day a cold wind from the snow peaks of the Andes blows drearily across it. Leaving the broken mass of rock, the path descended abruptly into a little valley, which contained a stone hut, and a corral for goats. This desolate spot was enlivened by the presence of one of the prettiest señoras that I ever met. She informed me that her husband, who was then hunting guanacos, supported himself principally by keeping goats that browsed upon the sides of the mountains. When he wished to butcher any of the guanacos, he, with the assistance of a pack of trained curs, drove them into natural rock-walled corrals among the mountains, where, hemmed in, the animals were easily despatched with the *boliadores* and knife.

Leaving the valley, I ascended to a high plain that seemed to be on a level with the summits of the neighboring range of the Cordilleras, and as the sun was about sinking below the western horizon, I perceived that this was to be my camping-place for the night. Laying the saddle upon the ground for a pillow, and carefully spreading the blankets, I lay down to rest, having first tied my horse to a stunted bush, which he vainly tried to eat.

I dropped into a restless slumber; but an hour later, a wild, desolate cry caused me to spring from my blankets, and prepare for defence. I had been told many stories of the cruelty of the puma, or American lion, and at this moment feared that one of these animals was on the plain. It was along this part of the road that guides had seen their tracks, and hunters had run them down with dogs a few miles from the plain upon which I had encamped.

Another wild cry, and the animal passed along the plain without heeding either my horse or me, and, glad to be left in peace, I sank into a sound sleep, that continued unbroken until the rising sun gilded the snowy crests of the lofty Cordillera.

It was a beautiful scene that lay before me. Across the plain floated white clouds of mist, like airy spirits, while before me lay a narrow valley, through which the road led to Uspallata. Upon one side of the plain rose several low hills, green with coarse herbage, upon which a small herd of llamas were feeding, as if unconscious of the presence of man.

I soon was ready to start; but my old horse seemed incapable of moving. I rubbed his stiff limbs until I had worked myself into a perspiration; he was so far recovered as to be able to move slowly. I seized the lasso, and led him on as before.

The road descended to the ravine just referred to, and for an hour or so my journey led through the surrounding cliffs; but at length we again emerged upon a flat plain, covered with low bushes, and over this I led the way until afternoon, when a green spot at the foot of a high range of mountains, and the hut of a farmer, caught my eye, and soon after I drew up before the last house in the Argentine Republic — the Guarde of Uspallata.

Before I could fairly disencumber my horse of his burden, he bolted for the clover-field behind the house, and commenced devouring the fodder with an avidity that told too well of his famished condition.

The person in charge of the house informed me that the passing was very difficult, and advised me to remain a few days; but, knowing too well that delays are dangerous, I made preparations for leaving on the next day. I was to leave the horse in the clover-pasture, and strap my blankets and other articles to my back, and in this way cross the main range of the Andes. From this I had no alternative; and so, after arranging everything for an early start, I lay down under the porch to take a *siesta.*

I was soon awakened by the tinkling of a mule-bell, and upon rising saw three persons before the guarde, accompanied by several mules. Two of these men were dressed in the gaucho fashion, but the other had the garb and manners of a merchant, which he proved to be; for, as I approached him, he offered me his hand, and, with a polite "*para servir vd.*," introduced himself as Don Fernando de Oro, a merchant of San Juan. He informed me that the postmaster near San Juan, with whom I passed a day and two nights, had requested him to keep a sharp lookout for a young *gringo* that was on the road, and to take him safely under his protecting arm to the American consul in Valparaiso. I felt much flattered by this acknowledgment, and at once accepted Don Fernando as my guardian and protector.

The don remarked that his troop of mules, which I had passed two days before, would arrive on that night, and remain in the clover-field until a passage could be effected. The troop came in at a late hour.

The next day was a lovely one; and as the weather gave promise of being settled for a few days, preparations for setting out on the following morning were commenced. The mules for Don Fernando, and two guides, were selected from the troop of ninety, and two extra ones were carefully shod, to answer in case of any emergency. My friend declared that it would be unfair not to allow my horse to accompany us across the Andes, after he had been through so much privation; therefore a heavy pair of shoes were selected from the store mules' pack, and nailed firmly to his feet. "Now," said the don, as he viewed the lank form of the animal with no little merriment, "Art has exhausted herself upon you, and Nature alone must support you on the road to-morrow."

Early on the following morning, Don Fernando, his two guides, and myself, with our animals, crossed the little river that ran past the guard-house, and at sunrise entered a narrow cleft in the sierra, and followed a stony path, until we came in sight of the River Mendoza, which rushed along the bed of the valley, roaring like thunder. The path grew narrower as we progressed, sometimes following the margin of the river, then ascending midway to the tops of the high sierra. It was a scene of great sublimity. The river, which was a deep mud-color, from the alluvial matter brought down from the mountain, was hemmed in by the two parallel sierras, that towered majestically to the height of several thousand feet.

In some places the path wound like a thread along

the bold front of a precipice; then it descended to the water, and followed its course, until it again ascended. As we gazed above, the huge pieces of detached rock seemed ready to fall and crush us.

The melting snow had undermined the soil in some places, and slides of earth and stones had fallen, and covered up the track.

After crossing a little bridge that had been thrown over a stream which flowed into the river of the valley, we came upon several ruined huts, which the don told me once belonged to an ancient tribe of Indians that inhabited the valleys of the Andes, and subsisted principally upon the flesh of the wild llamas.

This was before the country had become independent of Spain; and though many years had passed since their construction by the Indian builders, it was interesting to note that the plaster that held the stones together, and which was nothing but a kind of clay, still remained unbroken, as if the structures had been but recently deserted. These remains of the walls of the Indian dwellings were four feet in height, and were partitioned off into small rooms.

In the corner of one of the dilapidated dwellings was a heap of stones, surmounted by a tiny cross, made of rough twigs. The guides looked serious as we passed it, and in answer to my questioning look, the don told the following story: —

"When a Chileno loves, he loves with a passion so deep and strong that honor, friends, and fortune are secondary in his estimation to her who has thrown around him the network of her affections. A youth not long since came from Chili to visit a relative of the Argentine side of the Cordillera. His stay was protracted, for he had met with a beautiful maiden, far lovelier than those of his native country; and when he left, it was only to receive the permission of his friends to return again, and claim her as his own.

"He crossed these mountains to Chili; but the fierce *temporales* from the south had commenced before he reached the main range on his return, where the risk is greater in effecting a passage at such a season than on any other part of the road.

"He had with him experienced guides, and a favorite mule carried his wedding garments and the presents that he intended to offer his future bride. On the Cumbre pass, at an elevation of twelve thousand feet, a *temporal* struck the party, and one by one the mules became buried in the snow.

"The boy worked like a hero (I was with the company), and during the storm his orders were obeyed by the muleteers with alacrity, for they loved him well.

"But all exertions proved unsuccessful; not an animal escaped; and the weary party descended the Cumbre into the valley, worn out with their tremendous labors. The boy never lived to leave the valley; there he lies," — pointing to the cross, — "buried in his chosen spot. The guides piled stones upon his body, to keep the condors from devouring it. See! there is one now watching the grave."

I looked to the place designated, and saw upon the opposite cliff a huge dark-colored bird, that stood sentinel-like, a solemn watcher above the unfortunate Chileno's grave.

Not far beyond, the path again troubled us by its

extreme narrowness, and a dizziness came over me as I gazed far below into the mountain torrent.

Along this part of the road were piles of the bones of animals that had died upon the road during the past years. Some perished from hunger, and many fell over the precipices, lodging among the rocks, where, after long and painful struggles, they died. It seemed, truly, like going through the Valley of Death, so numerous were the carcasses and bones of cattle in this part of the valley.

Condors were occasionally seen upon the cliffs, sometimes circling high in the heavens. I had often observed these birds with interest when they came in numbers from the Andes, to feed upon carrion around Causete.

The condor is, I believe, the largest of the carrion-feeders; it has a fleshy crest upon the head, with wattle-like appendages beneath the beak; the nostrils extend through the cere, the head and neck are bare of feathers, and the skin of the neck lies in folds; around its base, a little above the shoulders, is a frill of white, downy feathers encircling it. Its flight is graceful, and at times very lofty. The breeding-places of the condors are in hollows of the cliffs, hundreds of feet from their bases; the eggs are laid upon the bare rock.

I have seen these birds in pairs; but in winter months they generally congregate in greater numbers.

While in the air, the condor soars in graceful circles, moving its wings but little: they feed upon carrion, but will kill weak and wounded animals, somewhat resembling the caracara in this respect.

The range of the condor extends along the Andes,

from the Straits of Magellan to 8° north latitude. I have seen specimens kept as pets in the gardens of native gentlemen.

At the Cueste de la Catedral a grand sight awaited us. From the brink of the river there arose a precipice of dark-colored stone, that frowned upon the narrow path which passed along its front. A stream of water fell over the brink of the ledge, and wherever the water struck the rough projections, it was converted into spray, which fell in turn upon other points of the rock, giving to the scene a fairy-like appearance.

Just at dusk we arrived at a point where the valley turned in a new direction, and was particularly distinguished for the desolate appearance of the surrounding rocks, which is, however, somewhat relieved by a bridge of English model, built by the Mendoza government. Across this we hurried, and stood upon La Punta de las Vacas, or Cow Point, where a desolate stone hut had been occupied years before by cow-herds, smugglers, and now sometimes served to shelter the benighted traveller. On the opposite bank of the torrent stood the first *casucha*, or post-hut, built of bricks and plaster. It was very small, and was modelled upon a cheap plan, being without doors, sashes, windows, — a large square hole answering for the first and last conveniences.

During the Spanish reign, these snow huts were liberally supplied with provisions, wines, wood, and bedding; but republican rulers are satisfied to let the four men who compose the mail party carry their own blankets, fuel, and food upon their backs — a miserable rule, that causes much suffering among the post-men, who are often shut up for many days at a time in a cheerless hut, while the snow storms are raging around them.

A league beyond the *casucha*, the guides led the way into a narrow valley, where the animals were turned loose, to graze upon whatever they might find. The don spread a raw hide upon the ground, upon which we laid our blankets, and consigned ourselves to the embraces of the drowsy god.

The long walk had thoroughly jaded me, and it needed no narcotic to insure a sound sleep for the following seven hours.

CHAPTER XIX.

CROSSING THE ANDES—CONTINUED.

WHEN the sun's rays of the next morning had penetrated the valley, we were more than a league from our camping-ground, and had passed the second *casucha*, or snow hut, of the winter courier. This little domicile was built after the model of its distant neighbor at La Punta de las Vacas, and was two leagues farther up the valley. While we were trudging alông, the metallic-sounding whinny of llamas sounded from the sierra, and, looking up, we counted no less than thirty of these graceful creatures gazing curiously upon us. The herd consisted of males, females, and young, the latter of the size of the common goat. As travellers rarely cross the mountains at this season of the year, the llamas instinctively inhabit the valley, where they are free from danger, and find a better living than the rocky cliffs afford.

Again the valley was blocked up by a spur of the sierra, called the Paramilla, the second one crossed since leaving the hamlet of El Durazno. The sides were steep, and Don Fernando cautioned me against walking, observing that riding kept the *puna* (a peculiar effect produced by inhaling rarefied air) at a distance. The summit of the Paramilla was buried in a deep drift of snow, through which we forced our animals at considerable risk; for their exertions to keep a footing almost overtasked their strength. Sometimes falling into concealed holes, they floundered in the great drift until our own services were necessary to rescue them from injury. Finally, a passage was effected, and we wound down the west side to the banks of the torrent in the vicinity of the third snow hut. The color of the water had changed from a muddy hue to dark red, and it seemed to rush along more impetuously than at the entrance of the valley. The many little streams that fell over the precipices along the road were colorless; therefore I judged that either the bed of the torrent, or its source, gave to the water its peculiar color; and it may be of interest to state in this place, that, as far as I could learn, all the rivers that descend into the Argentine Republic, on the east side of the Andes, are of a deep mud color, holding in suspension alluvial mud; while upon the Chili, or west side of the Andes, the waters are clear and colorless.

The coolness of the morning soon gave way to the heat of the sun, and it grew warmer as its rays were reflected upon the snowy sides of the mountains. The sound of a human voice fell upon our ears strangely in this desolate place, as a party of men came into view far up the valley. We soon met, and many were the inquiries made by the members of both parties. The Cordillera had actually been passed, but an hour or two before, by the courier and several persons who had placed themselves under his orders. The courier was a short, square-built man, of very dark complexion; and from the fact of his having performed many daring passages during the past years, we looked upon him with no ordinary interest. He rode on a small mule, the mail bag being slung to his neck by a leather strap, and did not exceed in size a school-boy's satchel. He informed us that the snow was thawing upon the summit of the main ridge, and would not be passable until the cold night air had crusted it over, when we might pass in comparative safety. But Don Fernando was not to be stopped even by the opinion of so experienced a personage as the courier, but ordered us to hurry on with all possible speed.

Soon the main range of the Andes rose before us, blocking up the valley more effectually than either of the previous Paramillas, its rounded top glistening from the reflected light of the sun. The don ordered a halt beside the river, in order to prepare for future action. The animals were allowed to drink a little water, while the don gave us all a dose of starch water and sugar, which we drank. This was a remedy for the *puna*, or at least to cause our stomachs to give off any gases therein contained, to cool the blood and invigorate the system. Don Fernando then bound his face in cotton handkerchiefs, and the guides and myself followed his example. This was to protect our faces from the reflected rays of the sun upon the white, shining drifts that covered the summits of the Cordillera and the neighboring sierras.

The river branched off to the northward, and was lost to view among the mountains. At the base of the Cordillera was the last snow hut of the Argentine Republic: passing it and the river, we commenced our weary ascent. Water had been flowing from the summit for several days previous to our arrival, and there was no appearance of the old path which had been washed away. As the side of this part of the range was composed of gravel and loose stones, it was difficult to obtain a firm footing, and the animals were continually slipping, which obliged us to exercise no little care and labor. The guides dismounted, but the don declared that he had no wish to court the *puna* by exerting himself unnecessarily; therefore he managed to keep upon his mule; but more than once the inclination of the animal's back was such that the rider was only saved by a slide off by the attentions of one of the guides. A direct ascent could not be attempted; our only method was to wind back and forth from side to side, on the face of the Cordillera, thus making the ascent very gradual.

When we were about two thirds of the way up, our anticipated trouble commenced. The baggage mule lost her footing, and rolled over and over down the side of the mountain. Don Fernando shrieked out a hasty *caramba*, the guides a naughty *c—o*, while I stood aghast. But our fears were soon quieted; for the animal struck upon a projecting piece of rock, which stayed her course, without apparently injuring her.

Being the smallest of the party, I was intrusted with the lasso, with which I crawled down to the mule, and fastened it about her neck, when she was pulled upon her feet by the party above. Having been relieved of her cargo, the animal readily commenced ascending, as if nothing had troubled her, and soon she was in the path again with her load upon her back.

After many fallings and backslidings, our party stood

upon the Cumbre, or summit of the Cordillera, at an elevation of twelve thousand feet above the level of the sea. When viewed from the valley below, I was disappointed as to its seeming altitude; but when standing upon the Cumbre, I fully realized the great height upon which our party had halted. The view was confined by the irregular peaks of the surrounding sierras; but a fine scene lay below us on the Chili side, of a peculiar Alpine character. We stood upon the dividing line of the Argentine Republic and Chili, and I inwardly bade farewell to the country that had been my first teacher of travellers' hardships, and had for much suffering given me lessons of usefulness — had impressed upon my heart a truer patriotism, and a more dignified respect for our republic of the north.

As we gazed into the depth below us, a wild scene met our view. The deep valley was filled with snow to a depth of nearly one hundred feet; for as the snow tempests blow along the range of mountains, the fleecy material drifts into the narrow defiles, filling them completely, in some places, to the very tops. This is the case, particularly, farther to the south, where a winter passage is rarely, if ever, attempted. Upon the left side of the descent the first Chilian *casucha* rose out of the snow, differing somewhat in model from those upon the Argentine side, the roof being rounded or oven-shaped, while those on the east side are two inclined planes, like the roof of a New England cottage in the earlier times.

Until now the powerful reflected light had not affected my vision; but I at last began to feel it seriously. I had neglected to bring "goggles," and though a thick cotton handkerchief covered my head, my skin was parched, and tears continually rolled down my face, adding to my torture, from which there was no escape. "Thank Providence that the day is so very clear," ejaculated the don; "for if a *temporal* should pass over, where would we be by nightfall? Either blocked up in that cold snow hut yonder, or buried in the valley below."

The snow had commenced thawing, and the real difficulties of crossing now commenced. The mules floundered in the drifts, often requiring our combined exertions to keep them on a sure footing. Near the *casucha* we came upon hard snow; but the original path lay many feet below, buried in the drift. While the party were pausing to consider the proper course to pursue, I noticed that one of the mules had been caught by Don Fernando, who waded towards the firm snow, leading the little animal by means of a lasso, which had been thrown about her neck. She was the smallest of the animals, and was called the *baqueana*, or guide mule, from the fact that she could follow the hidden path with great accuracy.

Curious to see her operations, I watched her closely as she walked carefully over the drift, with her nose almost touching the snow; and she really seemed to be guided by the sense of smell. The other animals followed, driven by the guides, while the don and myself harnessed ourselves with the lassos, and drew after us the hide upon which had been laid the baggage, saddles, &c.

Beyond the snow hut of the Cumbre, the descent was abrupt, and the line of the narrow path having been lost, we slid down the drifts in a most exhilarating manner. The mules came after, requiring to be well whipped by one of the guides before they would move an inch. Though the guide mule lost the narrow path, after following for some distance correctly, she became valuable to us on this part of the trail. We came to another descent, down which the other mules could not be driven; but when the little *baqueana* sat upon the snow, and gracefully descended without injury, the laggards followed, as one sheep follows another; all but one descended safely; she stuck fast in the drift, and it required our whole number to ascend and rescue her. We found her suffering from the *puna*, and in dubious spirits. Her exertions to free herself in a place where the atmosphere was so rare had almost ruined the poor beast. Blood trickled from her nose, and her breast was swollen like a bladder distended with wind.

At four o'clock Don Fernando ordered a halt upon a pile of loose rocks that protruded from the snow. Here we remained patiently waiting for the snow to crust over, as it had become too soft to allow of safe travelling, Twilight fell upon us in this wild retreat, and found the guides and the don rolled up in their *ponchos*, suffering from the stinging cold. As for myself, I jumped about upon our little territory until the increased circulation of the blood kept me in a warm glow. The guides fortified themselves against the cold air by drinking *aguardiente*; but experience had proved to me that the cold snow water in my flask would give me a firmer step, an easier respiration, and a clearer head than any brandy or *aguardiente* of the San Juaninos.

The moon shone as beautiful as we could have wished, lighting up the valley and its towering walls in a sublime manner. The little cascades of melting snow no longer fell over the cliffs, but froze, coating the dark fronts of the precipices with a shield of sparkling ice, and the sharp "ticking" of the frost sounded strangely, seeming to add to the weirdness of the place.

After remaining for three hours, the guides pronounced the snow sufficiently crusted over to bear us; and, pointing to a sharp angle of the valley, the oldest one desired me to lead my horse in that direction, while the rest of the party attended to the animals.

The River Aconcagua roared along the mountain's sides, and in most places was hidden by the frozen snow. Our course lay along its borders, where many gullies crossed our trail, hidden beneath the frozen crust.

While feeling our way along, old Yellow-skin, my horse, fell through the crust into a torrent that flowed into the river, leaving me standing upon the broken edges of the hole. The guides pulled me from the chasm, and beat the old horse until he became excited to such a degree as to crawl out of his bath with a vigor that satisfied us he would live to reach the open country.

We next crossed a high spur of the mountains, and, descending a precipitous path, came upon the second snow hut of the Chilian government; and after following many windings, and experiencing much danger in crossing the river, the dry, brown earth was reached, and we looked up to the lofty mountains, that shone in the moonlight, with great satisfaction, for our labors were ended. The guides gathered a few sticks together, and succeeded in lighting a fire, by the heat of which a scrap of jerked beef was cooked; but before this had been accomplished, the don and myself, overtasked by the fatigues of our long journey, had rolled ourselves up in the hide, and were sleeping too soundly to be awakened by the peons, who undoubtedly were pleased at the result, for they had all the beef to themselves. When the reader reflects that the preceding stage of the journey had been very long and arduous, we having travelled, with the exception of three hours, from four o'clock of the morning of one day until two o'clock of the next morning, he will acknowledge that our rest was well earned.

CHAPTER XX.

FROM THE ANDES TO THE PACIFIC.

AT daylight we breakfasted on dried beef and *maté* tea, and soon started on our journey, which was now rapidly drawing to a close. The sun was high in the heavens, although we could not for a long time see his face, for the mountains shut us in completely. We continued down the valley, passing near some fine springs of water, which, from the peculiar manner in which they burst forth from the ground, are called "*Los ojos de Agua*," or Eyes of Water.

The first signs of civilization that we reached on the Chili territory was at a place called "*El Guarde Viejo*," the old custom-house of the Chilian government.

This was occupied by a farmer, a new government building having been erected farther down, at the mouth of the valley. Beyond the *Guarde*, at intervals, little huts were seen, the inhabitants of which were garrulous and hospitable.

As we emerged from the valley, and encountered troops of mules and parties of country people, I observed the peculiar characteristics which distinguish the Chilians from the people of the country behind us. The muleteers on the eastern side of the Andes were grave in deportment, and slow in speech and movement.

The Chilians were more energetic and intelligent, — perhaps from more extended intercourse with foreigners. Yet they have the discredit of being less honest than their brethren of the pampa provinces. The men of Chili wore a short poncho, hardly covering the wearer's hips. The Argentinos' poncho is of the longest kind — longer than those of the people of any other South American republic. The Chilian's lasso *hangs* in coils from the saddle behind the rider; the gaucho's is carefully coiled up, and rests on the horse's croup.

The farms now became more frequent as we travelled along; the buildings were neatly roofed with red tiles, and furnished a striking contrast to those of Mendoza and San Juan, which were generally of canes and mud.

As night came on, we reached an irrigating canal, which conveyed water to the town of San Rosa; thrifty little farms were fed by its waters all along the road, and neatness and good order and management were everywhere discernible. The little houses were shaded by groves of fig and orange trees, and the reader can imagine our thoughts and happiness to be travelling through a country bright with blossoming fruit trees, when but a few hours before we had slept near snow-drifts.

Groups of young people were often seen seated beneath the trees, or under the verandas, singing, or playing on the guitar. Before one of the farm-houses we drew up, and, after being welcomed by one of these happy groups, we led our animals from the road, and prepared to remain for the night. An abundant supper was furnished us, and I do not remember a pleasanter night's rest that I ever had, than that.

The next morning I went out to the pasture to bid my old horse *adios*. I found him cropping the rich *alfalfa* on the irrigated field; and as I approached him he seemed rather disinclined to any familiarity, for he had associated me with all the hardships of the journey; and now to leave a land of plenty with me was evidently not to his taste. I lost no time in assuring him that my intentions were pacific, and when I left him he gave a pleasant whisk of his tail and shake of the ears, apparently thanking me for leaving him so literally "in clover."

My pedestrian journey was ended. I would have liked to continue on foot to the sea, which I could easily have reached in a couple of days; but my kind friend Don Fernando would not permit me to leave his troop. I must keep him company.

"You must come with me, my son," he said. "I wish to introduce you to some very nice people. I am a Chilian by birth, and I desire that you shall form a good opinion of my countrymen."

A mule, richly caparisoned, was furnished me by the don, and, mounting our animals, we soon rode into the town of Santa Rosa. Drawing up his mule before the entrance of a large mansion, before which paced a soldier with musket in hand, Don Fernando inquired if Don José Ynfante, the governor of the department of Santa Rosa, was at home.

The soldier replied that that gentleman was at Santiago on official business, but that his son Don Manuel was at home. While a servant went to announce our arrival, I had time to note that the national flag of Chili floated above the stately mansion, while a peep within the yard revealed beds of beautiful flowers and well-kept walks.

In a moment Don Manuel appeared, and, cordially embracing his uncle, exclaimed, "Welcome to Chili, and to Santa Rosa!" The don introduced me to the other gentleman, who greeted me warmly, uttering at the same time many expressions of good feeling for me and my countrymen. We then entered the house, and passed a most pleasant day in social intercourse, to which the agreeable and cultivated manners of the young don added no little charm. Don Manuel, as if to bring our recent hard fare more strongly to our imaginations, feasted us upon strawberries and sherbet; and the reader can form some faint idea how acceptable they were to us. The ice for the sherbet had been brought down from the Cordillera on the backs of mules.

On the following day we mounted our animals, and, bidding *adios* to Don Manuel, resumed our journey for the coast. Leaving Santa Rosa, we passed over an interesting country, and in the afternoon crossed a fine bridge of foreign construction, and entered the town of San Felipé, — which has a population of about twelve thousand inhabitants, — where we passed the night.

The River Aconcagua irrigates the gardens and farms in this district, and the soil is very fertile, yielding abundant crops of grain, potatoes, melons, maize, beans, walnuts, figs, peaches, tobacco, and grapes. The town is about eighty miles from Valparaiso.

Resuming our route on the next morning, and travelling all day, we entered, at dusk, the town of Quillota, which contains about ten thousand souls, and is about thirty-five miles from Valparaiso.

Here we found some large and well-cultivated farms, and the whole country was quite interesting.

On the following morning Don Fernando started in advance of our party, to prepare for our arrival at Valparaiso, this being the last day of the journey.

I remained with the people of the troop, and kept them company during the whole day. No incident occurred worthy of record here; and before the twilight had begun to fall upon the heavens, we were descending the high *cuestas* that overlook Valparaiso, which city lay stretched out below us on the shore of the great Pacific, its white plastered dwellings glistening like silver in the rays of the declining sun.

Winding down the stony path, we entered the city before dark, and were soon ensconced in comfortable quarters.

On the following day I presented my letters of introduction to the United States consul, George Merwin, Esq., who, after giving me a kind reception, and warm congratulations on the success of my long journey, interested himself so much in procuring me a berth in an American vessel, that before twenty-four hours had passed I was comfortably settled on board the fine ship Magellan, Captain Charles King, and I once more entered upon the routine of life before the mast. A few weeks later, and we were scudding down the western coast of Patagonia, and "going around the Horn" on our journey home.

Reader, my story is told. If you have been enabled in these pages to glean a little instruction or amusement for your leisure hours, I shall feel well rewarded;

and if, when in imagination you followed me in my weary journey, you, perhaps, felt some little sympathy for the hardships I sometimes experienced, I shall never regret my pedestrian trip across the "PAMPAS AND THE ANDES."

www.ingramcontent.com/pod-product-compliance
Lightning Source LLC
LaVergne TN
LVHW020219110826
845151LV00003B/763

* 9 7 8 1 4 2 5 5 3 3 0 7 6 *